SOUTHERN HOME LANDSCAPING

by Ken Smith
Landscape Architect ASLA

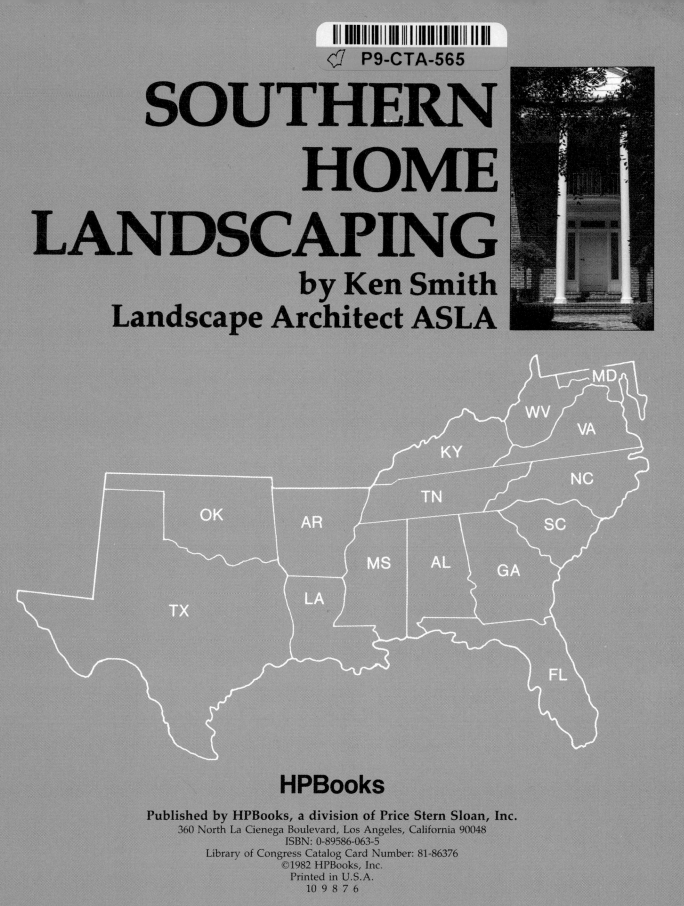

HPBooks

Published by HPBooks, a division of Price Stern Sloan, Inc.
360 North La Cienega Boulevard, Los Angeles, California 90048
ISBN: 0-89586-063-5
Library of Congress Catalog Card Number: 81-86376
©1982 HPBooks, Inc.
Printed in U.S.A.
10 9 8 7 6

COVER PHOTO: E. Alan McGee, Atlanta

Contents

Landscape and You

Bargains are hard to find today, but here's a big one: Imaginative development of outdoor space can make a small house *seem* like a large one. Patios, fences, lawns and trees still cost much less than floors, walls, carpeting and roof. And you don't have to be an expert to install them.

All it takes is common sense, lots of hard work and a little guidance along the way. That's what this book is all about. Garden construction and planting can be fun—when they're done right. Do-it-yourself projects are not only satisfying, they save money.

You can benefit from good landscape ideas even if your estate is limited to a small condominium patio, a tiny mobile-home lot or a miniscule balcony. In fact, the smaller the area, the more important it is to make the most of the limited space.

PURCHASING OR BUILDING A HOME

It takes a great deal of time and effort to select a new home. It is usually the most important purchase made by a family in a lifetime. It can have a profound effect on health and happiness.

Let's assume the house is of sound construction and pleasing design. It should also have ample space and be located in a desirable neighborhood, convenient to shopping, fire and police services, schools, recreation areas and transportation. It should also be within the financial reach of the family, with a little left over for

Raised deck makes good use of this sloping property in Dallas and offers a choice of sun or shade for entertaining and dining. Landscape architect: Lambert's.

outdoor work. After all these, there are still many landscape considerations that can make the purchase a wise or an unsound one.

Visit the site to evaluate existing trees, views, soil conditions and drainage. Talk to local residents to see if there are seasonal or prevailing winds that could be a problem or an asset. Choose an orientation suited to the specific climate. In most areas of the South it is preferable for the major

glass areas to face away from hot, afternoon sun, or be protected by trees or a wide overhang.

Determine what use areas will be needed. Is there room for a patio or screened porch, swimming pool, spa, game court, vegetable garden or whatever else is required? Look for good indoor-outdoor relationships so outdoor living areas will be convenient and the garden will be part of the house.

An inviting patio can help transform an average house and lot into a pleasing and comfortable living environment.

Make a budget allowance for at least some immediate landscape costs such as paving, lawn, fencing and trees as needed.

Check utilities to see if there are sewers, reliable water supplies, unsightly power lines or gas. Find out about easements, deed restrictions or other requirements that might limit development of the property. Verify property lines—there should be surveyor's stakes marking the corners.

Study site plans and zoning maps to determine what may be built on adjacent property. Will the upstairs windows of a neighboring house look down on your back yard? Will there be apartments or a gas station across the street?

Anticipate room additions and future developments, and make sure there is sufficient area and access. If the house is to be built or isn't yet completed, ask the builder to provide high-pressure hose-bibbs for convenient portable watering or a supply line for permanent sprinklers. Install electrical stub-outs with indoor switches for garden lighting and for a pool or spa. Protect paving from damage during construction or install after all work has been completed. Erect temporary fences around existing trees and other plants to avoid damage from trucks and workmen. Remove and stockpile existing topsoil from the construction area so it can be used for lawn and other planting later on. Plaster, wood, concrete and other trash should be thoroughly cleaned up and removed from the site—not buried.

If landscaping is included in the cost of the home, ask the builder in advance for an itemized breakdown of what is included. After all, you're paying for it. Frankly, it is usually not very well done. It is better to get a credit for the work than to end up doing it over.

Investigate the workmanship of tract sub-contractors before having them do any paving, walls, lighting, grading or other work. The price may be right, but they may not be set up for custom work.

Try to picture the completed living environment of house and garden.

This back yard is truly an outdoor room. A carpet of dark blue water contrasts with a floor of brick. The walls are covered with lush foliage. There's room for lounging under the handsome shade structure or for sun-bathing on the brick decking.

Front yards can be both beautiful and functional. A gracious walkway leads to an entry court defined by elegant wrought-iron fencing in this Miami garden.

Sound, basic planning lasts a long time. A lot of changes have been made in this yard, but the major elements of my original design for Dr. and Mrs. Jerry Sievers remain intact after 18 years.

Can it be "just what you want" or will it always be an unsatisfactory compromise?

Maybe you'll have to settle for a little bit less than your ideal. Obviously, no property is perfect. Some small items you can easily live with or handle yourself. But try not to overlook any major problems. Years ago, the Federal Government had a complex rating system for land suitable for housing. Using this system, one site was rated far above others in a sample, somewhere around 96 percent. Years later it was discovered what the missing 4 percent represented—the land was subject to periodic flooding.

It is easy to panic when you find yourself surrounded by a barren yard with only weeds and dust or mud to look at. The temptation is to call a "concrete man" to pour a patio, or a landscape company to put in a lawn. Stay away from the phone and resist the urge to rush outside to start planting.

There is a logical order that a landscape professional normally follows when a complete garden is to be installed at one time. This is shown in the accompanying box. Actually, there is considerable overlapping and coordination, but the general order prevails.

Budget restrictions, site conditions and special priorities may modify this sequence. You may want to install fencing or a hedge as soon as you move in. A pool or screened porch can be a future addition if the budget won't stand the strain right away.

When you have to modify this sequence, it is important to allow for work that you plan to do later. Install pipes or sleeves that must go under paving. Include footings for posts in a patio. Keep plants and piping clear of future construction. Leave room for equipment access. A little foresight now can save a great deal of time, effort and money later.

TOLERANCES

You will likely notice that I use *most, many, probably, often, generally, could, sometime, such as, if, but, however, approximately, usually* and other qualifying words thoughout this book.

Sometimes you inherit an existing garden. Landscape contractor Dave Geller expanded an old flagstone patio, built a wood seat in the shade of a large Southern magnolia and added latticework on top of a concrete block wall for extra privacy.

Logical Order of Installation

1 Design
2 Rough Grading and Retaining Walls
3 Spas and Swimming Pools
4 Paving
5 Finish Grading and Drainage
6 Fencing
7 Sprinkler Systems
8 Lighting and Electrical Work
9 Shade Trellises and Patio Roofs
10 Miscellaneous Construction
11 Soil Preparation and Weed Killers
12 Planting
13 Lawns
14 Furniture and Finishing Touches

Do you have a problem with a narrow side yard? Landscape contractor Jim Keener of Landscape Associates turned this previously unusable space into a pleasant sitting area.

The logical order of installation here is to build walls and fences first to keep pets and children in or out. Wide side yards present easy access for patio and other future construction.

Installing your own landscaping is easier and more fun when the entire family participates. Jason isn't old enough to sweep or mix mortar, but he's good with a hose.

It is not that I don't know what I'm talking about. It's because there are many variables, especially regarding personal preferences and requirements of living plants.

We may live in the age of the computer, but rigid formulas are as difficult to apply to the landscape as they are to people. It would be nice to have a chart that would say, "Apply 3.2 quarts of water every 36-1/2 hours and 16.2 pounds of 6-10-4 commercial fertilizer every 44 days." Or, "Install 378 square feet of concrete paving and 12-2/3 cubic yards of topsoil." It just doesn't work that way. Consider the alternatives, assess the possibilities and make a decision best suited to the specific situation that is constantly changing. If there is any rule at all, it is that *generalizations are no good.*

Tolerance is a closely related subject. Don't try to apply the fine standards of the furniture or aircraft industries to the landscape. You'll only be frustrated. It is impossible to impose a hundredth-of-an-inch tolerance to bricks or planks when they themselves may vary a quarter of an inch. Overall straightness, level, plumb (verticality) and pattern are *usually* more important than precision of the individual parts. When installing any landscape work, stand back occasionally to see if it looks "right." This is often a better test than the tape measure or level.

A FIRST STEP

A garden is very complex and has many interrelated parts. Make a list of your specific requirements and what you want your garden to be. Take a drive to observe what appeals to you and what leaves you cold. Go through garden magazines and clip out photos of what you like. Study the descriptions of the various garden styles and decide what overall feeling you want to achieve.

Restrain yourself a little longer. It is time to start designing—no digging yet.

STYLES

Despite the wide geographical distribution, varying climates and diversity of cultural influences, the South does have a certain continuity of landscape style. There are many plants that flourish throughout most of the South, many of which don't do as well or won't even survive in other states. Azalea, dogwood, Southern live oak, hollies, English boxwood, Asiatic jasmine, ternstroemia (cleyera), slash pine, Southern magnolia, liriope, tulip tree and crape myrtle reach their peak here. And, there is often a kind of restrained elegance that lends serenity and dignity to the landscape.

Spacious lawns, masses of azaleas and fine, old trees characterize what could be termed *Southern* style.

A large-scale driveway and specimen Southern live oak trees impart a distinct *Southern* feeling to the home of Mr. and Mrs. Gary Beach. Landscape architect: Lambert's.

Even without the definitive Japanese stone lantern, this delightful garden has an *Oriental* flavor.

There is also considerable variety. Some gardens borrow from other times, achieving a flavor of what is admired from the past. There's nothing wrong with this, as long as it is adapted to the specific site, architecture, climate and way of life. The following descriptions of various styles or motifs are intended to serve as general guides, not specific historical formulas. Most successful present-day gardens combine elements from more than one style. When these elements are skillfully blended, a new style evolves that is often more practical and appropriate—and just as beautiful as its predecessors.

Colonial—Straight lines, angles, rectangles, balanced and restrained precision. Brick paving and walls, white picket fences, clipped hedges, topiary, espaliers, crushed rock paths, sundials and arbors. English boxwood, hollies, crape myrtle, ivy, dwarf periwinkle, roses, dwarf tobira, privet, tulip tree, muscadine, bulbs, flowers, vegetables, herbs and fruit trees.

Southern—Sweeping curves, terraces, large scale and grandiose. Stone, brick, wrought iron, rolling lawns, rail fences, large driveways and gazebos. Southern live oak, azalea, rhododendron, pachysandra, Confederate jasmine, Carolina jessamine,

An outstanding example of classic *Colonial* style in historic Williamsburg.

This *Natural* stream bed is actually in a small front yard. Lush dichondra ground cover is left unmowed. Design and installation by the owner, Kirk Aiken.

The *Formal* style of the Louvre is appropriate for its setting, but I doubt that you'd want to keep *your* yard this way.

The Governor's Palace in San Antonio is built around a *Spanish-Mediterranean* courtyard featuring a central fountain, vine-covered arches and hand-set pebble paving.

clematis, English boxwood, camellia, hosta, Southern magnolia, dogwood, viburnum and perennials.

Spanish-Mediterranean — Informal, antique, simple. Adobe, slumpstone, plastered walls, wrought iron and tile. Pergolas, fountains, clay pots and decomposed granite. Yuccas, aloes, lantana, geranium, Texas sage, century plant, pampas grass, barrel cactus, oleander, prickly pear, loquat, Jerusalem thorn, Texas umbrella tree and fan palms.

Oriental — Serene, natural, but neat and orderly. Ponds, pebbles and boulders. Stone lanterns, bridges and bamboo tubs. Korean grass, mondo grass, liriope, Japanese black pine and other pines, junipers, cycad, aucuba, camellia, nandina, bamboos, Japanese yew, dwarf azalea, wisteria, redleaf maple, ginkgo and flowering cherry.

Sophisticated materials and forms were used in this pool garden. I didn't have a specific style in mind when I designed it, but if it has to have a name, I'd call it *Modern* or *Combination.*

This is a "real" Japanese garden designed by famed professor Nakane of Osaka University. But it is in Singapore and the plants, such as the striking yellow flame tree, are tropical. It shows that you can adapt any style to almost any locality and still have a successful design.

Unless you live in a no-frost area, you won't have much luck trying to duplicate a *Tropical* scene like this one. However, you can achieve similar results in a protected patio or atrium by using big-leafed plants, colorful foliage and flowers adapted to your climate.

Tropical—Cool, exotic, lush, overgrown. Logs, mounds, volcanic rocks. Waterfalls, lagoons and aviaries. Philodendron, hibiscus, bamboo, aralia, ferns, bougainvillea, ixora, Algerian ivy, wedelia, palms, croton, cajeput trees, dichondra and royal poinciana.

Natural—Rambling, rough textures, relaxed, flowing lines, contours. Streams, boulders, split rail and grape-stake fences, stone walls. Railroad ties, flagstone, pebble concrete, redwood tubs and barrels. Junipers, sycamore, periwinkle.

Formal—Symmetrical, axial, geometrical and refined. Slate, brick, tile, crushed rock, cut stone. Central fountain, sundial, sculpture, large pots, arches, borders and clipped hedges. English and Japanese boxwood, waxleaf privet, roses, Italian cypress, beds of bulbs and annuals, yew pine, Southern magnolia, Deodar cedar, Asiatic jasmine, Hahn's ivy, pachysandra, camellia and manicured lawns.

First Comes the Design 2

Every garden is designed by someone. Complex projects call for the services of a professional, but the average yard can often be designed successfully by anyone—with proper guidance. If you decide to design your own garden, first sift through the free advice offered by friends, relatives, neighbors and everyone who has ever laid a brick, built a fence or planted a plant. Some of their suggestions can be helpful, others disastrous.

This book should answer most of your questions. See page 188 for other books and places to get assistance. If you still get stuck, consult a professional.

PLANNING

Regardless of who is doing the designing, there is a general procedure that everyone should follow.

First, prepare an accurate plan of your land at a scale of either 1/8 or 1/4 inch equal to one foot. Graph paper makes it easier to convert the measurements to the plan. Show existing conditions such as the house, property lines, easements, underground and overhead utility lines, paving, walls, fences, trees and slopes. Include doors, windows and overhangs. Also mark down the direction of the prevailing wind, good and bad views, north arrow, drainage flow and similar items.

Lay a piece of tracing paper over the plan. Now is the time to explore, experiment, dream, reject, erase—all the while trying to picture the completed garden. Think in terms of the style you've selected as described in Chapter 1.

A diagrammatic layout of use areas,

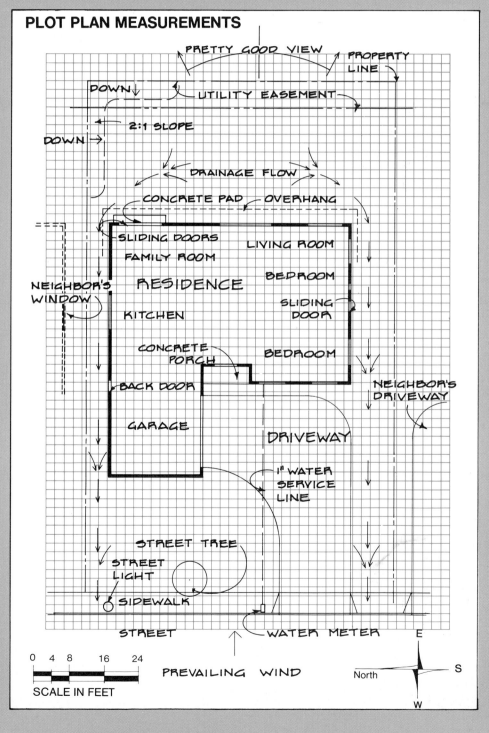

PLOT PLAN MEASUREMENTS

Beautiful design compositions require a skillful blending of form, color and texture, along with a knowledge of construction and plants. Landscape architect: Lee Sharfman.

as shown here, is a good way to begin. Carefully integrate circulation, privacy, wind, noise, views, drainage and sun/shade patterns with the overall organization.

As your ideas begin to crystallize, you can draw in the paving and other structures such as walls, fences and shade trellises. Next, decide what uses the plants are to serve, where they should go and how big they should get. Shade, privacy, noise reduction, windbreak and erosion control are a few of the important uses for plants. Then make tentative selections based on the plant lists in Chapters 6 and 14.

BEAUTY

Sadly enough, a garden can function quite well and still not be pleasant to look at or be in. Try to apply basic art principles to your designs. Proportion, color, texture, unity and rhythm are just as important to a garden as they are to a painting. Think of your garden as three-dimensional—even four-dimensional—when movement through time and the ever-changing nature of living plants is considered. Coupled with all the practical factors, this makes a garden infinitely more difficult to create than other art forms. But don't be overwhelmed. Here are a few suggestions:

● Limit the number of construction materials and repeat those that are used in the house wherever possible. Likewise, stick with the house colors.

● Don't try to use every plant in the nursery. Think in terms of areas, groups and masses. One-of-this and one-of-that usually looks terrible.

● Start out with simple and restrained plans. Many plants will eventually provide a bonus of seasonal displays that may not be evident when they're first planted. You can add accents later if you still feel something is lacking.

● Concentrate on the overall concept and avoid fussy details and gaudy gimmicks. Be bold. If in doubt, make it larger, not smaller.

CHECKING YOUR PLAN

This is a good time to give a critical eye to what you've come up with so far. If you have trouble picturing it, it might be helpful to go outside and make a "mock-up" with stakes and

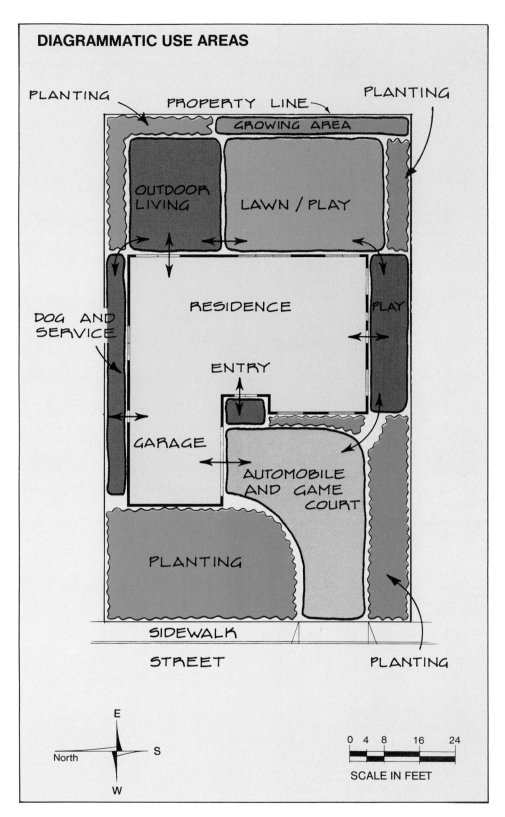

DIAGRAMMATIC USE AREAS

Famous "Sand Garden" in Kyoto, Japan, is for meditating, not family entertaining or touch football. Decide what functions your garden must accommodate before you design.

Front entrance was laid out first with stakes and string to get a feeling of size. Footing was then dug for railroad tie wall.

strings. Pretend you're having friends over for a barbecue, or you're one of the children. Does the proposed plan serve everyone well? Does it accomplish all your desired uses?

Involve the entire family. If the plan passes the test at this stage, you're on the right track. Make sure the plan meets local building codes and deed restrictions, and doesn't violate any setback or easement requirements. Technical plans for structures, sprinklers, lighting and drains don't have to be completed until you are ready to install them, but they should be roughed out at this time. This will allow you to include sleeves, stub-outs and footings where they will be needed. Don't forget to consider possible future additions such as a swimming pool, spa, playhouse or extra bedroom.

Before making final decisions on materials, size of plants and the extent of paved areas, you'd better make an overall cost estimate. If you intend to have all or part of the work done by others, call in several reputable contractors and ask for competitive bids. If the prices come in much higher than you can or want to invest, this is a good time to consider substitutions.

Maybe the patio will have to be made of concrete instead of brick. Or all the plants will have to be smaller to start with, or the lawn will have to be planted from seed instead of being sodded. Rather than cutting the basic quality, some items can be set aside as future phases and installed when finances allow. One of the advantages of a good plan is that everything will fit together, even if it is not all installed at one time.

HOW MUCH WILL IT COST?

There's not much you can do about house payments and property taxes. Furniture, carpeting and drapes are usually essential. With the outdoors you have more choice. It would be nice to have a completed landscape the day you move in. More often it is a matter of setting priorities, doing the most important items first and waiting for the remaining elements until your budget recovers from the shock of moving.

Once you have a plan worked out, you can come up with a reasonable estimate of cost. It will undoubtedly differ from the chart below, but the basic items and general costs will be similar. The chart is based on the *aver-*

Landscape Costs	
Type of Work	**Typical Cost Range in $**
Design	500 to 1000
Rough Grading	200 to 300
Paving	1500 to 2500
Finish Grading & Drainage	300 to 500
Fencing (Assumes cost split with neighbors)	500 to 2000
Sprinkler System	500 to 1500
Lighting	200 to 500
Miscellaneous Construction	300 to 500
Soil Preparation	300 to 500
Planting	800 to 3000
Lawn	300 to 1000
Furniture & Finishing Touches	500 to 1000
Total	$5900 to $14300

It takes considerable skill to construct a 6-foot masonry wall. There are many other landscape projects better suited to doing-it-yourself.

age builder-constructed house in the $75,000 to $125,000 price range on a level 7,500-square-foot lot. All materials and labor are provided by a landscape contractor. Do-it-yourself items normally save approximately 50 percent of the contracted figure.

Few homeowners have the time, capability or desire to do everything. Unless you've had previous experience or can get experienced help, it is best to leave certain items to the experts. Concrete paving, masonry walls, chain-link fences, 110-volt electrical work, gas lines, spas and swimming pools, and planting large specimen trees should be attempted only after careful consideration. You should be able to handle brick-on-sand paving, wood fences, sprinkler systems, minor construction, simple trellises, low-voltage lighting and most planting. Getting the family involved is not only fun, but can really speed up a project and be a rewarding experience for children.

Ten to fifteen percent of the cost of the house and property is considered a reasonable investment for landscaping by most realtors. The cost of a spa, swimming pool, patio roof and other major construction would be additional.

Financing is readily available for construction work, but is sometimes more difficult to arrange for planting. The best way is to have landscape costs included in the first mortgage—

when possible. Interest on a personal loan could be 18 percent or more on the total amount for each year of the loan—a very expensive way to go if the payments are stretched out over several years. In most cases, the interest is pre-charged so you don't save anything by paying it off ahead of time.

When you need $3,000 or more, and if you have a reasonable amount of equity in your home, it is better to use the property as collateral and benefit from simple interest on the declining balance, the same as on a first mortgage. A second mortgage or home equity loan that permits you to use the money for any purpose has an interest rate around 15 percent. Normally, you can borrow up to 80 percent of your equity.

A similar loan that requires proof of improvement of the property carries a lower percentage rate and you can get 100 percent of your equity. Usually you can pay off either one of these loans early without a penalty charge.

Shop around at different banks or lenders for specific information.

CAPITALIZE ON YOUR CLIMATE

Indigenous architecture usually takes advantage of the best characteristics of a site and helps overcome some of the disadvantages. The prairie sod house, the arctic igloo and the thatched hut of tropical climes are well suited to their location. They are also oriented to benefit from desirable sun and breezes, and to exclude unwanted elements.

Unfortunately, we usually have less luck with climate. The typical mass-produced house is plopped indiscriminately down on the lot with no regard for exposure. The sliding glass doors are likely to face the hot sun and the wide overhang often occurs on the north side where it is least beneficial. Insulation is needed to help correct mistakes and forced-air heating or air-conditioning must be run most of the year to make the place tolerable.

Screened porch in Orlando provides shade and protection from rain and insects. Open-air balcony captures welcome breezes.

Few people have the opportunity to start from scratch and design a house to truly fit the site and climate. But most of us *can* do something with the landscape, such as locate the major patio area in the most desirable exposure. For hot climates this usually means the east or north side of the house. Along the ocean where cool breezes are an almost daily occurrence, the south or west side may be more comfortable.

Sometimes a small, secondary sitting area can be a sun-trap for winter warmth, or it can be a shaded area you can use to escape from summer heat. Shade trellises can break the sun on patios and house walls. A removable covering such as the shade cloth used by nurseries can be changed with the season. If winds are a problem, even narrow windbreaks can filter strong winds and reduce their intensity.

In our desire for year-round effect, we often overlook the advantage of deciduous trees. They can shade the house during the hot months and then conveniently drop their leaves to allow the welcome sun to enter during the winter. Indoor temperatures can be lowered as much as 10 to 20 degrees when the roof is heavily shaded. High-branching trees on the east and south sides, and low-branching ones

This house in Borneo works *with* the climate. The high-peaked, thatched roof permits hot air to escape and provides protection from torrential rains. Stilt construction allows cool air and high water to flow under the house, and discourages cobras from entering—not something everyone has to worry about.

on the west are most effective. You can also use shrubs to shade walls and windows.

Lawn and ground covers can reduce glare and radiation, significantly affecting the temperature of the surrounding area. Not only is the general comfort increased by using garden structures and plants as climate modifiers, but there are significant savings in heating and cooling costs.

LEGAL CONSIDERATIONS

In a society as complex as ours, even landscaping is subject to restrictions, codes and laws. As in all business transactions, it is advisable to deal only with properly licensed and insured companies. Secure signed contracts that clearly define the work, and receive labor and material releases before making final payment.

Be sure to verify property lines before starting any work. Check for easements or right-of-way that might limit use of the property. Locate septic tanks and cesspools if you have no sewer service. Find out about any deed restrictions and if there is an architectural committee that has to approve the plans. Cooperation with neighbors on fencing, planting and views may not be required legally, but it is almost always beneficial.

Fran Harris enjoys her new front yard patio. The old one in the back yard is larger and more convenient to the kitchen, but is usually too chilly in the cool coastal area where she lives.

Two fruitless mulberries shade the front of this house and part of the roof during hot summer months. Being deciduous, they admit the winter sun when the warmth is desirable.

BUILDING CODES

Most cities and counties have building codes and may require permits for landscape work. *Check with the agency having jurisdiction in your area.* Here is a list of common restrictions.

Grading—Cuts exceeding 5 feet, fills exceeding 3 feet, or movement of more than 50 cubic yards of material require permits. Most lots must drain into the street or storm drain, not over banks or onto neighboring property.

Banks—Approved erosion control, ground cover, shrubs and trees are required. Hazardous brush must be removed and replaced with fire-resistant plants in fire danger areas.

Spas and Swimming Pools— Engineering and installation require permits. Power lines may not cross over. Pumps or other equipment may have to be located in a *mandatory* side yard.

Fences—There is usually a 42-inch height limitation within a front yard setback, 72 inches for side and rear yards. Pool fences must be 54 to 60 inches high with self-closing gates and lockable latches.

Retaining Walls—Normally, no permit is required for walls less than 48 inches high, including footing, without a slope behind. Still, retaining walls should be well constructed.

Sprinklers—Supply lines must be of approved size and material. Heavy plastic pipe is accepted by most agencies if buried 18 inches deep. Anti-siphon devices to prevent backflow of possibly contaminated water into potable supply are often required for sprinkler heads at ground level.

Lighting and Electrical—Permits are required for all work except low-voltage types. Conduit must be buried 12 inches deep or protected under paving. Direct burial cable is now accepted by some departments.

Parkways—Property lines normally begin 6 inches back from the sidewalk, leaving from 3 to 10 feet of parkway owned by the city or county, but maintained by the property owner. Paving and planting are usually restricted within this area. For example, street trees cannot be removed or changed without permission. Where the sidewalk is adjacent to the street, the prop-

Why can't you cut down a street tree or plant one you like better? Because it is really not on your property. But, in most cities, you have to take care of it. The ginkgo tree is an excellent choice for this narrow parkway.

erty line or an easement is located in the yard to allow for street trees.

Patio Roofs and Screened Porches—Design and installation need approval. Aluminum and canvas awnings, and detached pergolas of 400 square feet or less, are usually exempted. No power lines can pass over.

Gas—All piping, valves and equipment must be approved. Some uses are prohibited entirely.

Wood Decks—Footings, spans and railings must conform to building codes for raised decks and those extending out over a slope.

CONTRACTOR'S RESPONSIBILITY

Poor drainage, concrete cracks and plant guarantees sometimes become legal problems. Some small amounts of standing water are virtually unavoidable, especially after a heavy rainstorm. However, large areas that don't drain and paving or planting areas that obviously slope toward the house usually indicate the need for correction by the contractor. He may also be liable for water damage if the area drained properly before the work was performed.

Building departments are usually strict about hillside decks because they have a way of slipping and collapsing if not built properly. Landscape architects Lang and Wood designed this one to last.

Hairline cracks in concrete are inevitable and do not indicate defective work. Some shifting and cracking may occur in expansive soils even if proper precautions are taken. Large cracks caused by too thin a pour, laying over dry adobe soil with no precautions and lack of required expansion joints are usually considered the responsibility of the contractor.

Maintenance is almost always assumed by the homeowner as soon as planting is completed. Still, the question often arises as to who killed the plant—the contractor when planting it or the owner by improper care. Normally, the contractor gives a 30- or 60-day guarantee and allows for the replacement of a few plants, regardless of the cause.

If the garden is bone dry or extremely wet and many plants die, the responsibility may lie with the owner, especially if watering needs were properly explained. Failure of seed to germinate is usually due to improper watering. Weeds are hardly ever brought in with the seed or fertilizer.

THE LANDSCAPE INDUSTRY

Few people know what the differences are between the several divisions of the landscape industry. Various roles used to be played by one person—now it takes an entire cast. To further complicate matters, there is considerable overlapping of the parts. The following should help you to know whom to call for what.

Landscape Architect—This type of architect is required to be licensed in most states and is the planning expert best qualified to design outdoor areas. Training is comparable to that of an architect or engineer. He usually holds a degree from an accredited university and often has additional experience in other phases of the industry. The initials *ASLA* (American Society of Landscape Architects) signify membership in a professional group similar to the *AMA* (American Medical Association) in the medical profession.

The landscape architect does not sell a specific plant or product, but wants only to create the best living environment possible for the client. He receives payment through professional fees rather than through discounts

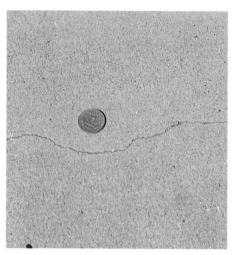

No need for concern if a few hairline cracks appear in your concrete—they really don't hurt anything. In the past we used a dime to indicate scale, but it's up to a quarter now.

or profits. He considers total site development including structural elements, along with planting and sprinklers. When possible, he should be called in while a tract house is still under construction. On custom houses he should collaborate with the architect when the house is being designed.

Landscape Contractor—Also licensed by most states, the landscape contractor is the person who installs the garden based on the plans of the landscape architect. Not only does he handle planting, he will usually install the paving, sprinklers and outdoor structures as well. Sometimes his own crew will do all the work. At other times he will function as a general contractor, seeing that various subcontractors perform their work properly. Most landscape contractors belong to an association such as the *ALCA* (Associated Landscape Con-

tractors of America) or a state organization, through which they keep abreast of latest developments and methods.

Nurseryman—The nurseryman is charged with the important job of supplying plant material for a garden. Most of the time he grows at least some of the plants himself, ordering the rest from wholesale growers. He does his utmost to keep a stock of healthy, well-grown plants of suitable size.

He will not substitute plants that may be difficult to find, but will advise the owner to ask the landscape architect if a substitute is in order. He is usually qualified to offer general planting and maintenance advice, and often is an expert on local climatic conditions.

In some states, a nurseryman may have *certification,* which means he has satisfied requirements of competency and experience. Many of the nurserymen you'll be dealing with belong to the *SNA* (Southern Nurseryman's Association), the *AAN* (American Association of Nurserymen) and various horticultural societies.

Gardener—The highly complex art of gardening requires many years of training and experience. Unfortunately, there is no state registration act that assures the homeowner that a gardener is qualified. City licenses are for tax purposes only. Frankly, most of the really good gardeners are in such fields as golf course, park, cemetery, commercial and estate maintenance.

The homeowner must carefully assess the ability of the individual gardener, keep close watch on the work, and be prepared to pay a fair price for his time. Clarify if watering is to be the gardener's responsibility, or if you will do it yourself. Partial services for cutting and edging lawns, and general clean-up and weeding are more common than complete care.

When a gardener is to be completely in charge of a garden, he receives the finished product from the landscape contractor and guides it to its ultimate form. He must be receptive to the intent of the landscape architect and owner, yet he will have to make many interpretations of his own as the years go by. If you are thinking of a casual, natural effect and your gardener is of the old school and shears everything into a sphere or cube, there's bound to be trouble. It is wise to explain what your personal preferences are before hiring someone. One day with the hedge clippers can destroy years of growth.

Landscape Designer—This title is often used by those engaged in landscape design but *unlicensed* as landscape architects. Some are well-qualified, some are not. The public has no way of knowing from the name alone. A landscape designer may be in business for himself or work through a contractor or nursery. Some are deeply involved and give considerable personal attention to their work. Those with commercial ties are more apt to function as salespeople.

Multiple Roles—Much confusion is caused by overlapping services. Some nurserymen and gardeners design and install gardens, some landscape contractors offer planning services, and some landscape architects are also landscape contractors. With proper licensing, this is not illegal and there is much to be said in favor of the efficiency possible under such multiple businesses. Natural gardens are often better created during installation. Small towns may not be able to support a design specialist. However, commercial interests can limit design, and the spreading of talent and energy over several fields can result in lower quality services.

LANDSCAPE DESIGN SERVICES AND FEES

There seem to be three main reasons why more homeowners don't hire a landscape architect to design their property. First, they think it will be too expensive. Second, they're afraid their own ideas will be disregarded. Third, many landscape architects are totally involved in large projects and are not available for residential design.

Expense—Fees vary considerably with the job and the individual landscape architect. Most have a consultation fee of $50 to $100 to visit the site and to offer ideas and advice. This is a relatively inexpensive way to get a professional's input without being obligated any further. If additional consultation or a plan is desired, many landscape architects charge for all services on an hourly basis, usually with an estimated range of time for specific work. Others charge a percentage of construction cost or a lump-sum fee.

Typical basic plan cost for an average residence is between $600 and $1,000. Cost depends on the complexity of the site, amount of structure, overall budget and client/designer relationship. This basic plan service normally includes an initial meeting on the site; one preliminary plan, cost estimate and site review; and construction drawings based on the approved preliminary plan. Preparation of the basic plot, major revisions or changes in the scope of the work, securing of bids, and supervision are usually additional.

For a small property, a portion of a garden or a very simple development, some landscape architects will provide a one-trip service by drawing a plan on the site. Drafting and details are completed at the office and final prints are delivered by mail. This method eliminates a considerable amount of drafting and travel time, while still providing the essential design concept. This very efficient way of working ranges in cost from $200 to $500.

A landscape architect can also provide valuable services other than drawing plans for a new garden. Among them are: property selection, siting of house and collaboration with the building architect on the basic house design, selection of a house already built, general consultation, addition of a patio roof, shade trellis, swimming pool or spa, design of part of a garden, remodeling an existing garden and maintenance advice.

There seems to be no obvious reason for butchering these wax-leaf privets. It not only looks bad but wastes gardening time that could be put to better use.

Your Wishes—Most landscape architects encourage as much client participation as possible. Having a list and portfolio of clippings beforehand is very helpful.

Availability—This is quite often a problem. Spring and fall are usually the busiest seasons, so it is sometimes easier to find one during summer or winter. When a registered landscape architect isn't available, it is possible to get the help you need from a landscape designer. Fees are usually lower than for a landscape architect. In many cases, charges and methods of operation are quite similar.

INTRODUCTION TO MASTER LANDSCAPE PLANS

My mathematically minded son tells me that if I took the following four basic lot types, with four basic styles, four basic climates and four different orientations to the sun, the total would equal 256 possible master plans. If I added the factors of family composition, budget and maintenance preference, the figure would be astronomical.

What I'm trying to illustrate is how the overall feeling of a certain style and the needs of a family determine the garden uses, and how climate and orientation also influence design—especially plant selection. Note that the climate zone mentioned at the bottom of each plan refers to the map on page 87.

The sample plans in this book are intended to enable you to choose the ideas and solutions that apply best to your specific situation. They may appear complicated and confusing at first, but after looking them over several times they should become clearer. If you're lucky, you might discover that you're one of those people who can project the plan into three dimensions in your mind.

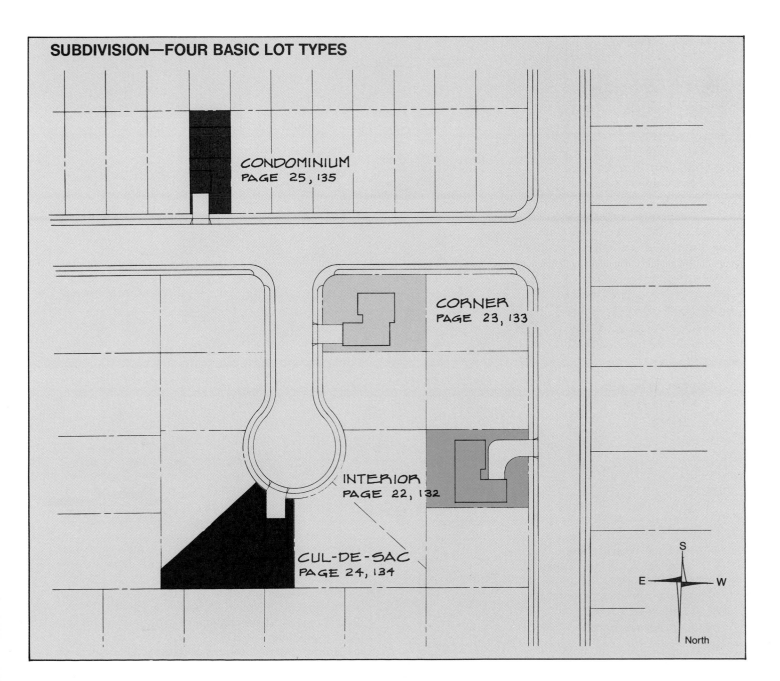

SUBDIVISION—FOUR BASIC LOT TYPES

CONDOMINIUM
PAGE 25, 135

CORNER
PAGE 23, 133

INTERIOR
PAGE 22, 132

CUL-DE-SAC
PAGE 24, 134

MASTER PLAN—Interior Lot

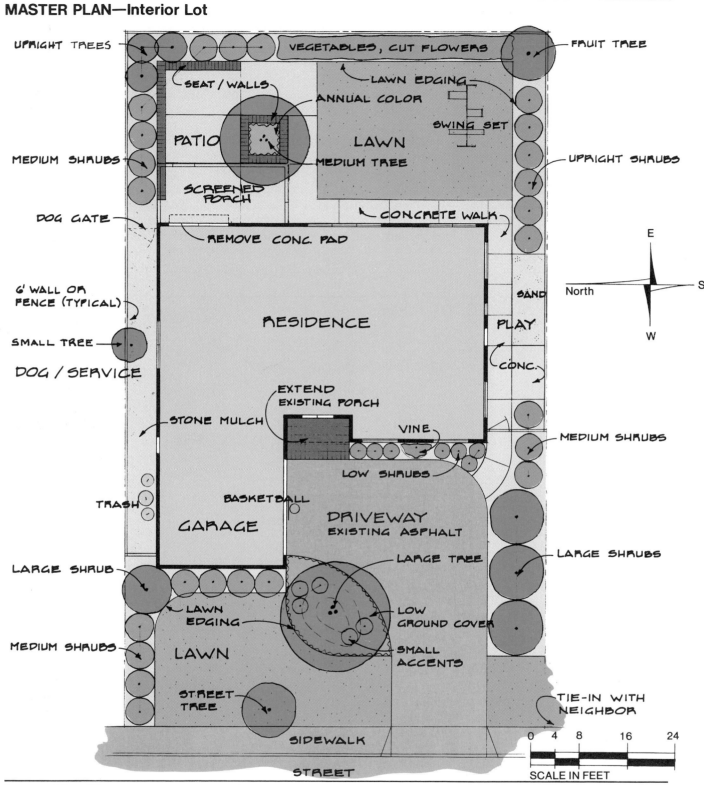

- UPRIGHT TREES
- VEGETABLES, CUT FLOWERS
- FRUIT TREE
- SEAT / WALLS
- LAWN EDGING
- ANNUAL COLOR
- PATIO
- SWING SET
- LAWN
- MEDIUM SHRUBS
- MEDIUM TREE
- UPRIGHT SHRUBS
- SCREENED PORCH
- DOG GATE
- CONCRETE WALK
- REMOVE CONC. PAD
- 6' WALL OR FENCE (TYPICAL)
- RESIDENCE
- SAND
- PLAY
- SMALL TREE
- CONC.
- DOG / SERVICE
- EXTEND EXISTING PORCH
- STONE MULCH
- VINE
- MEDIUM SHRUBS
- LOW SHRUBS
- TRASH
- BASKETBALL
- DRIVEWAY EXISTING ASPHALT
- GARAGE
- LARGE TREE
- LARGE SHRUBS
- LARGE SHRUB
- LAWN EDGING
- LOW GROUND COVER
- MEDIUM SHRUBS
- SMALL ACCENTS
- LAWN
- STREET TREE
- TIE-IN WITH NEIGHBOR
- SIDEWALK
- STREET

North · E · S · W

0 4 8 16 24
SCALE IN FEET

Assumed Conditions

- Zone 10—Tropical climate.
- Young family with small children.
- Modest budget.
- Medium to low maintenance.
- *Combination* style.

Design Considerations

- No particular style is emphasized. Overall effect is neat, simple and organized.

- Children have ample play area in side and back yards, with front basketball area and separate side entrance for when they get older.
- Screened porch provides rain and insect protection for outdoor dining; patio is shaded by tree.
- Ample paving, stone mulch and restrained planting is easy to maintain.

See Planting Plan for Interior Lot, page 132.

MASTER PLAN—Corner Lot

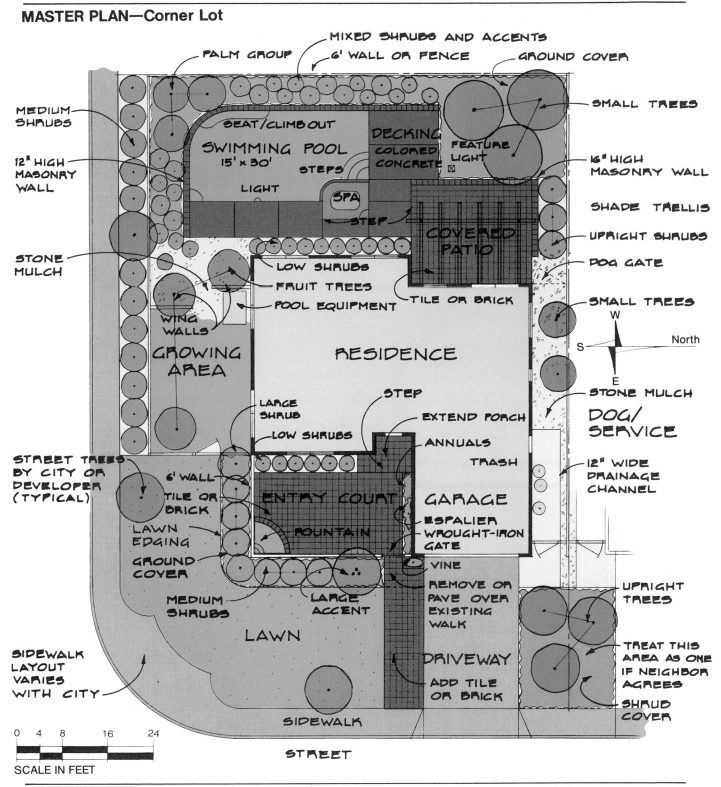

PALM GROUP

MIXED SHRUBS AND ACCENTS

6' WALL OR FENCE

GROUND COVER

MEDIUM SHRUBS

SMALL TREES

12" HIGH MASONRY WALL

SEAT/CLIMBOUT

SWIMMING POOL 15' x 30'

DECKING

COLORED CONCRETE

FEATURE LIGHT

16" HIGH MASONRY WALL

STEPS

SHADE TRELLIS

LIGHT

SPA

STEP

COVERED PATIO

UPRIGHT SHRUBS

DOG GATE

STONE MULCH

LOW SHRUBS

FRUIT TREES

POOL EQUIPMENT

TILE OR BRICK

SMALL TREES

WING WALLS

GROWING AREA

RESIDENCE

STONE MULCH

STREET TREES BY CITY OR DEVELOPER (TYPICAL)

LARGE SHRUB

LOW SHRUBS

STEP

EXTEND PORCH

ANNUALS

TRASH

DOG/ SERVICE

6' WALL

TILE OR BRICK

LAWN EDGING

GROUND COVER

ENTRY COURT

FOUNTAIN

GARAGE

ESPALIER

WROUGHT-IRON GATE

12" WIDE DRAINAGE CHANNEL

MEDIUM SHRUBS

LARGE ACCENT

VINE

REMOVE OR PAVE OVER EXISTING WALK

UPRIGHT TREES

LAWN

DRIVEWAY

ADD TILE OR BRICK

TREAT THIS AREA AS ONE IF NEIGHBOR AGREES

SIDEWALK LAYOUT VARIES WITH CITY

SHRUB COVER

SIDEWALK

STREET

0 4 8 16 24

SCALE IN FEET

(compass) W / North / S / E

Assumed Conditions

- Zone 9—Sub-tropical climate
- Active couple with no children. Frequent parties and entertaining.
- Ample budget.
- Medium to high maintenance.
- *Spanish-Mediterranean* style.

See Planting Plan for Corner Lot, page 133.

Design Considerations

- Plaster walls, wrought iron, tile or brick paving, and a classic Spanish fountain carry out the theme.
- Covered patio and small swimming pool with built-in spa are ideal for entertaining.
- Paving added to driveway allows room for both cars and people. Enclosed entry court is comfortable for evening sitting.
- Growing area makes use of large, sunny side yard.

MASTER PLAN—Cul-de-sac Lot

Assumed Conditions

- Zone 8—Moderate climate.
- Family with teen-age children, lots of relatives.
- Average budget.
- Medium maintenance.
- *Natural* style.

Design Considerations

- Contours, boulders, stone walls and paving, wood path lights, stone mulch and free-flowing lines contribute to natural effect.
- Extra parking is included for RV and teen-agers' cars.
- Multi-use game court and open lawn are ideal for family games.
- Patio has choice of sun or shade. Fire pit extends use into evening.

See Planting Plan for Cul-de-sac Lot, page 134.

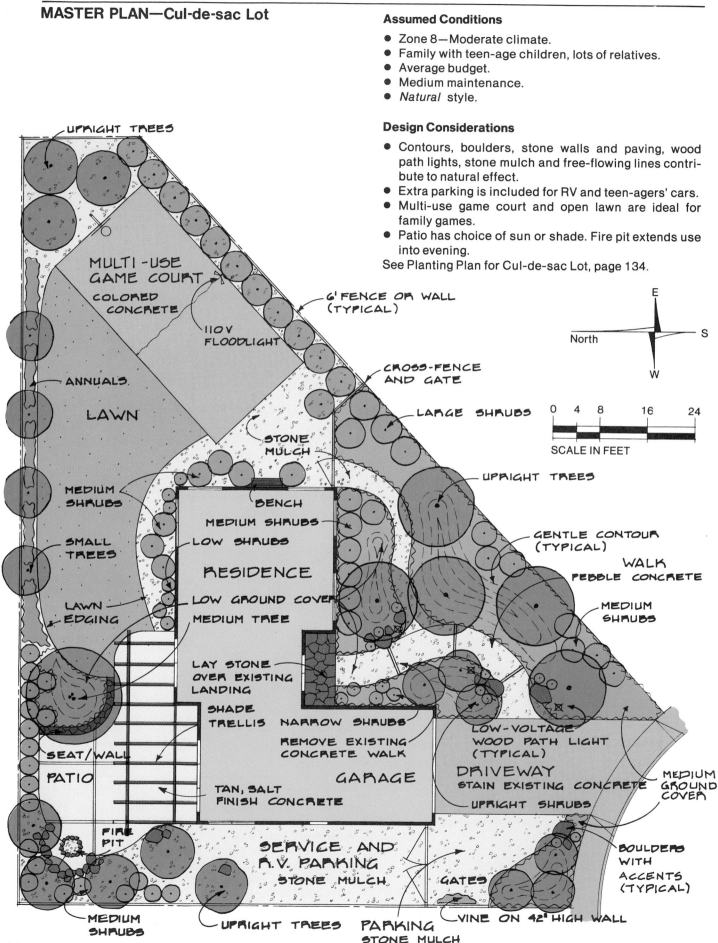

MASTER PLAN—Condo Lot

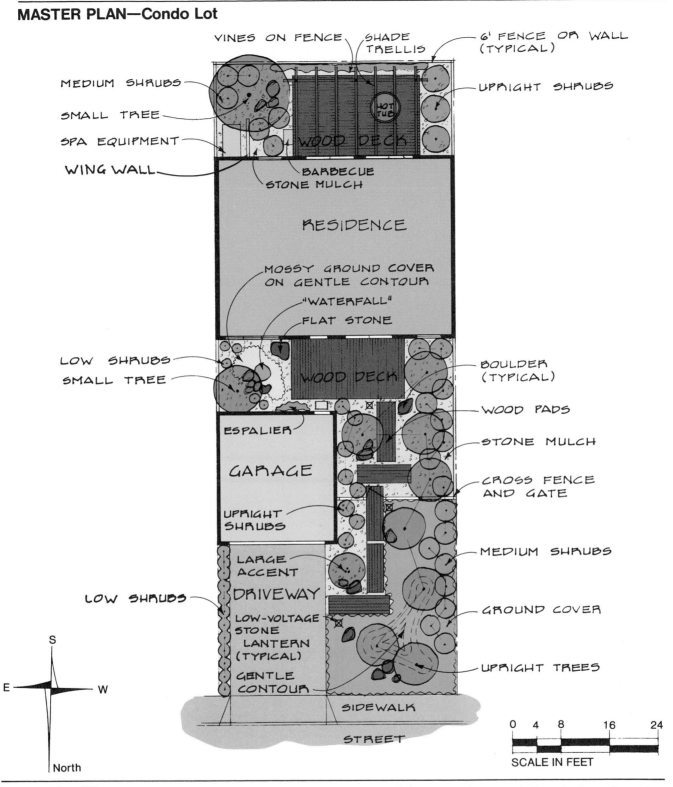

VINES ON FENCE   SHADE TRELLIS   6' FENCE OR WALL (TYPICAL)

MEDIUM SHRUBS

SMALL TREE

SPA EQUIPMENT

WING WALL

UPRIGHT SHRUBS

HOT TUB

WOOD DECK

BARBECUE

STONE MULCH

RESIDENCE

MOSSY GROUND COVER ON GENTLE CONTOUR

"WATERFALL"

FLAT STONE

LOW SHRUBS

SMALL TREE

WOOD DECK

BOULDER (TYPICAL)

WOOD PADS

STONE MULCH

ESPALIER

GARAGE

CROSS FENCE AND GATE

UPRIGHT SHRUBS

MEDIUM SHRUBS

LARGE ACCENT

LOW SHRUBS

DRIVEWAY

GROUND COVER

LOW-VOLTAGE STONE LANTERN (TYPICAL)

GENTLE CONTOUR

UPRIGHT TREES

SIDEWALK

STREET

S / E / W / North

0 4 8 16 24

SCALE IN FEET

Assumed Conditions

- Zone 7—Severe climate.
- Retired or working couple, no children.
- Ample budget.
- Low maintenance.
- *Oriental* style.

Design Considerations

- Wood decks, boulders and stone mulch, natural water feature, contours and stone lanterns impart an Oriental feeling.
- Front wood walk and deck provide a gracious entry and sitting area.
- Water feature can be viewed from both inside and outside.
- Back deck with hot tub and barbecue is protected by shade trellis. Fences, shrubs and vines are used for privacy.

See Planting Plan for Condo Lot, page 135.

Relaxing & Entertaining 3

Travel is expensive. Beaches, campgrounds, parks and other vacation spots are crowded. Home recreation is convenient, inexpensive and often more restful than harried trips.

Think of your yard as an outdoor room that needs a floor, walls and a roof. Incorporate some of your family's favorite activities. Allow for cooking and gracious entertaining. Now you have a garden that not only looks good, but truly serves your living and recreational needs.

Begin with the entrance. Because most arrivals will be by automobile, make sure there is adequate parking and unloading space. Standard driveways can be widened to allow for easier walking and extra parking. If you have a boat, trailer or camper, perhaps it can be accommodated unobtrusively alongside the garage.

Guests will appreciate a landing strip next to the curbing. A wide, gracious walk is an inviting approach to the front door. When you inherit a typical 3-foot-wide walk, consider adding to it so it is more in scale with the house and property. Even a brick strip along each side will help considerably. If the only way from the street to the front door is via the driveway, it may be wise to build a separate walkway.

A generous landing or porch with a convenient bench is good for saying hello as well as goodbye to departing friends. Here again, you'll probably have to expand what's already there to improve the scale and usability.

So guests don't have to walk up the driveway, landscape architect Roy Seifert designed this separate entrance.

Brick strips make an attractive and inviting curbside landing.

Sweeping brick driveway makes an impressive approach to this San Antonio residence.

Brick stairs are well lighted at night for safety. They impart a warm, welcome feeling to visitors.

A gracious entry walk in Richmond welcomes guests to the front door.

Appropriate furniture is important. This white wrought-iron set seems perfect for this secluded patio.

Rocking chairs and carefully placed plantings can turn a covered porch into a bonus sitting area. Landscape architect: Steve Coenen, New Orleans.

PATIOS AND TERRACES

The terms are used interchangeably. So for convenience, let's just call them patios. First, they should be pleasing to look at, but they are primarily for people to use. As discussed in the last chapter, they should be located to make the most of your specific climate and orientation. Or you may need more than one to give a choice between warm-and-protected or cool-and-breezy.

A successful patio must be large enough for entertaining guests, but should have an intimate feeling for family use. An 8x10' space may hold a table and chairs, but would obviously be cramped. Approximately 15x25' could be considered a minimum size. This allows for furniture, a barbecue and some storage, with room to move about without stubbing a toe. Privacy, wind protection and the relationship to the kitchen or family room should also be considered. If a patio is too far from the house, placed in the prevailing wind or within view of the neighbors, it probably won't get much use.

A properly located patio may be comfortable without any additional shade. However, in most southern climates, a shade tree or roof of some sort is usually essential. A shade trellis of open lathwork filters the sun without excluding light from adjacent rooms. A solid roof costs considerably more, but provides protection from

The Don Thompsons asked me to design an outdoor room that would be comfortable for everyday use, but still accommodate an occasional large group. The secret is the built-in seating and spaciousness broken up by the fire pit and circular tree well.

rain. Screening can be added in areas where mosquitoes and other insect pests abound.

PATIO ROOFS, TRELLISES AND SCREENED PORCHES

Many general building contractors find this type of job too small—they'd rather build houses. Many landscape contractors consider them a nuisance, and try to avoid getting involved. Most homeowners are overwhelmed with the thought of building one themselves. Try to find a company specializing in patio construction. If you can't, one solution is to work along with a carpenter, contributing as much time and experience as you can.

The basic framing is the same

These shade trellis posts are set on top of retaining wall. The built-in wood bench eliminates the need for space-consuming furniture.

By repeating materials and colors from the house, a screened porch can look like an integral part of the original house.

Vinyl-treated canvas lasts about 5 years and requires only a simple pipe frame.

whether the roof is solid or open. Lumber costs are approximately $300 for an overhead area of 200 square feet. Add $100 for 2x2s, or $200 for 1x6 sheathing and mineral-coated roll roofing. A good price from a contractor doing all the work would be $5 per square foot for a shade trellis and $8 per square foot for a solid roof, including footings. The patio floor and staining or painting will be additional. Shingle and tile roofs require a steeper pitch and cost considerably more than roll-type roofing.

Even if you hire experienced helpers, most of them are strong on construction and weak on design. If you know of an example that you like, have them take a look at it before giving a bid.

By using one wall of the house for support, it is a simple task to attach a patio roof or trellis. A screened porch is similar, but a little more like an actual room. The trick is to make the addition look like part of the original construction and not an unrelated afterthought. Repeating existing house materials and colors will make it more harmonious.

Oversize rafters, beams and posts are more in scale with the outdoors than minimum dimensions. Use 3x6 or 4x6 rafters rather than 2x6s. Standard 4x4 posts and 4x8 beams can be enhanced with *plant-ons* of 1x2 or larger strips for a built-up effect. Most building departments have span charts indicating minimum lumber sizes and can offer over-the-counter advice. A building permit is required by most agencies, and footings must be inspected before pouring any concrete. Setback distances from property lines must also be complied with.

Rafters alone are seldom enough to provide sufficient shade. Usually a covering made of 2x2s or lath is added on top at right angles to the rafters. The spacing determines the amount of shade—the closer together, the less sunlight gets through. Grapestakes, 2x3s, 1x2s, bamboo poles, netting and various types of shade cloth can also be used.

Removable panels allow for more sun during the cool months, but are a nuisance to take off and store. The best way to determine how much shade you want is to finish the framework first. Then lay whatever material you've selected on top, without nailing, for a trial run.

CONSTRUCTING A SHADE TRELLIS

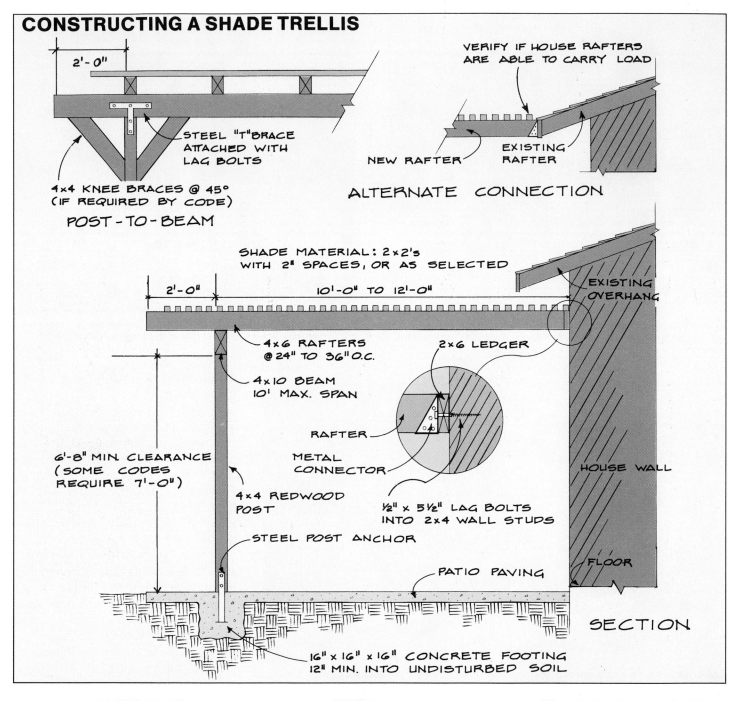

2'-0"

STEEL "T" BRACE
ATTACHED WITH
LAG BOLTS

4x4 KNEE BRACES @ 45°
(IF REQUIRED BY CODE)

POST-TO-BEAM

VERIFY IF HOUSE RAFTERS
ARE ABLE TO CARRY LOAD

NEW RAFTER

EXISTING
RAFTER

ALTERNATE CONNECTION

SHADE MATERIAL: 2x2's
WITH 2" SPACES, OR AS SELECTED

2'-0"   10'-0" TO 12'-0"

EXISTING
OVERHANG

4x6 RAFTERS
@ 24" TO 36" O.C.

2x6 LEDGER

4x10 BEAM
10' MAX. SPAN

RAFTER

METAL
CONNECTOR

6'-8" MIN. CLEARANCE
(SOME CODES
REQUIRE 7'-0")

4x4 REDWOOD
POST

STEEL POST ANCHOR

½" x 5½" LAG BOLTS
INTO 2x4 WALL STUDS

HOUSE WALL

FLOOR

PATIO PAVING

SECTION

16" x 16" x 16" CONCRETE FOOTING
12" MIN. INTO UNDISTURBED SOIL

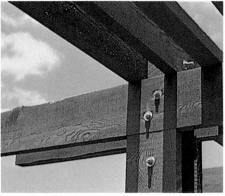

This built-up post is made using two 2x8s with a 4x4 inside.

Another way to build up a post is to nail 1x2s on all four sides of the 4x4.

***Knee braces* can be turned into a design feature with a little fancy sawing.**

HIGHLIGHTS OF CONSTRUCTION

Post anchor was set in concrete patio with footing below. Bolts will be put through the post to prevent shifting. If you must leave a post anchor unused for any period, cover it with an overturned plastic container to avoid accidents.

Connect rafters to the house with steel fasteners lag-bolted directly to a ledger plate. This is stronger and usually preferable to attaching to an existing roof overhang. Existing fascia is notched to receive the rafters.

Steel fasteners are also used for post-to-beam and rafter-to-beam connections. They are stronger than toenailing. Bolts are stronger than nails for anchoring fasteners.

The 2x3s are shifted to test desired shade density before nailing permanently.

This is a *knee brace* required by most building departments to eliminate side sway or *shear.* The steel "T" brace is too small to do the job alone.

Effectiveness of 2x3s is shown by the shade pattern on the previously sun-drenched wall.

Lath strips make an attractive and relatively inexpensive shade covering.

Sometimes an open framework is all that is needed if there's a tree to help out.

An obvious disadvantage of using a shade tree to cool a patio is growing time. Even fast growers such as fruitless mulberry, evergreen elm and sycamore take four or five years to do the job when starting with a 5' to 6' size.

Where there is access, a large specimen tree can be planted for about the same cost as a shade trellis as shown in Chapter 9. This way you can sit under its spreading branches the day it is planted. Shade trees don't have to be evergreen. Deciduous trees permit the sun to enter during the winter just when you need it most.

Other structural considerations are footings, size of posts, connection to house, shear bracing and sheathing. A 16-inch-cube concrete footing with a steel post-strap to receive the post is adequate for most situations. If there is a possibility that the patio may be enclosed as a room some day, a continuous footing should be included at the future wall line.

Size of posts is seldom an engineering problem. A redwood 4x4 or a 2-1/2-inch steel pipe column is more than adequate to support most patio roofs. You may want to use 6x6 posts if you're looking for a heavy timber effect. Pipe columns look better if encased in brick or concrete block. Decorative wrought-iron supports give an airy effect.

Ferns thrive under this shade cloth stretched over 4x6 rafters. Landscape contractor: Bill Peterson.

This leafy arbor is really a neat place to sit and relax on a hot, summer day.

It is poor practice to attach anything other than a light shade structure to an existing overhang. The best procedure is to bolt a 2x6 *ledger* to the house wall directly underneath the existing overhang. Attach the rafters to the ledger with metal connectors.

Shear bracing is needed to keep the roof from moving sideways, parallel to the house wall. This can be accomplished by *knee braces* at the posts.

They do the job but look terrible. A better way is to bolt steel *"T" braces* to the post and beam if your local building department will allow it. Steel pipe columns set 36 inches deep in concrete provide shear support and eliminate the need for braces.

Sheathing is especially important for patio roofs because it is seen from below. Tongue-and-groove 1x6s are a standard size and easy to install.

PERGOLAS AND GAZEBOS

Pergolas and gazebos are another way to provide immediate shade. A pergola is a freestanding structure, usually consisting of simple posts, beams and rafters of heavy timber. Grape, wisteria, banksia rose and coral vine are frequently planted at each post for additional shade.

Gazebos are also freestanding, but they are lighter weight and semi-enclosed. Hexagon shapes are most popular, although squares are easier to build. Lath is a common gazebo covering, either in a right angle or diamond pattern, for a somewhat Victorian look. Pre-cut kits, ready to assemble, can simplify the job considerably.

You can still have fun and save part of the cost by putting it together yourself.

Change the materials and design to fit in with your chosen garden style. You can create an Oriental teahouse, an old-world iron cage or a modern geodesic dome. They all serve the same general purpose of providing an inviting, shady sitting area.

If you can master the center connection, you can build almost any gazebo.

What a place to sip a long, cool drink and enjoy the view of a sparkling beach in the Bahamas.

Lath gazebo nestles nicely in the corner of this back yard. You don't have to be a skilled carpenter to build a simple structure—just take your time.

This old-world gazebo of iron grillwork and stone columns is more of a sculpture than a place to sit.

A solid roof is well worth considering if you want rain protection for outdoor dining.

BARBECUES AND FIRE PITS

Cooking outdoors is a natural for mild climates. Pre-fabricated gas barbecues consume no more fuel than indoor cooking, or you can use charcoal instead. Portable barbecues have the advantage of being movable out of the wind and stored out of sight when not in use. Built-in counters and storage spaces save repeated trips indoors. Fire pits extend comfort into the chill evening hours. It is great to gather around a friendly fire after a session in a pool or spa.

Now that natural gas has become a precious resource, the old wood campfire is a logical substitute. Be sure to check if there are restrictions concerning open wood fires in your area.

This fire pit uses radiant heat from volcanic rock to make the most of a natural gas fire.

Built-in gas barbecue is efficient and unobtrusive.

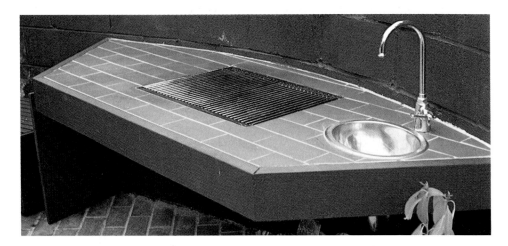

This combination cooking grill, tile counter and sink was designed for George and Myrna Weiss by landscape architect Jack Smith, ASLA.

PLAY AREAS

Play and game areas can serve all members of the family along with providing fun activities to share with guests. The main problem is to avoid creating an expensive and unattractive "white elephant" that takes up space and is seldom used.

Family interests vary throughout the years. Children will outgrow sandboxes and swing sets. Teen-agers may play a certain game for months on end and then turn to some other pastime away from home. Grown-ups are just as fickle in their preferences. It all adds up to the fact that temporary, expendable, convertible and multi-use areas are often better than unchangeable, permanent installations.

Pre-schoolers may accept being fenced in for a while, with mother watching from the kitchen window. In a year or so they outgrow the enclosure and are happier if allowed to roam the entire yard rather than one small area. Along with older children,

Swing sets have almost universal appeal. This one is actually in far-off Malacca.

they also seem to go out of their way to snub elaborately contrived apparatus. They often end up digging a hole in the dirt or building a house out of boxes and scrap lumber. Imagination and creativity are more important than a sophisticated structure that pleases the parents. However, don't overlook swing sets. They are universally popular and, when placed on a lawn, require no garden remodeling after removal. A sandbox or, better yet, a pile of sand, is always a favorite with young children and easily disposable when obsolete.

Standard-size playing courts for badminton or volleyball take much more space than is generally realized, especially when proper clearance is allowed for safety and to avoid damage to nearby plants. The chart on this page shows the space required for a specific activity. Make a cut-out the same scale as your plan and see where it fits best.

You'll probably find that you just don't have the space required. Don't despair. Most playing courts can be scaled down considerably and still be fun. Even as small an area as 20x40' can work reasonably well as a multi-use badminton, volleyball, tetherball and half-court basketball court.

If it is a choice between having a lawn or paving the entire back yard, remember that badminton, volleyball and croquet are perfectly at home on a tough grass such as hybrid bermuda, tall fescue or St. Augustine. Grass is also usable for mini-games of baseball and football.

If you have a wide enough driveway or a motor court, perhaps it can serve double-duty for games such as basketball and tetherball. Of course, it has to be fairly level and safe from street traffic. If you live in a classy neighborhood, you may want to use removable poles and a fold-down basketball backboard so you don't offend the neighbors.

Ping-pong is enjoyed by all ages. The table is easy to move around or store if interest wanes temporarily. It can be played on a lawn, but paving is better. The garage is fine for the average game. Outside, it should be located out of the wind and with some shade for daytime games.

A 30x60' game court turned this back yard into a popular recreation area for family and friends. Construction by Sport Court.

Dancing, archery, catch and similar activities that require no special or elaborate installation are no problem. You just do them. A horseshoe court can be installed at relatively small cost, to be used or abandoned with no great loss. Shuffleboard can be marked off on any long and relatively smooth concrete area. A full-size, specially constructed court is seldom worth the cost unless it is going to be played quite often.

Tennis courts are major investments and space-takers. They should be built only after very careful investigation. A possible alternative is paddle tennis. It requires about one-half the space and is a challenging game in its own right.

Give swimming pools just as much thought before rushing into building one. Pools, spas and hot tubs are discussed in Chapter 4.

A shaded place where spectators can sit—be it a low wall, steps or bench—is a welcome addition to a recreation area. To save wear and tear on the kitchen and mother's nerves, a drinking fountain is also a good idea. Adequate lighting should be provided for evening use, but avoid glare on neighboring property.

Space Requirements for Outdoor Activities

Activity	Actual Size in Feet	Total Space Required
Badminton	20 x 44	30 x 60
Basketball	50 x 94	60 x 100
Croquet	30 x 60	40 x 75
Horseshoes	8 x 50	12 x 60
Paddle Tennis	20 x 44	35 x 70
Ping-Pong	5 x 9	12 x 20
Shuffleboard	6 x 52	10 x 60
Spa or Hot Tub	6 (diameter)	14 (diameter)
Swimming Pool	16 x 36	28 x 52
Swing Set	6 x 12	16 x 20
Tennis	36 x 78	60 x 120
Tetherball	6 (diameter)	20 x 20
Volleyball	30 x 60	45 x 80

PAVING

By now it is apparent that a large part of a garden is often covered with a solid surface. Function should dictate the form and size the paved area will take. Don't skimp on size. Generous areas of well-designed paving not only increase the usability of a garden and reduce maintenance, but can also be attractive.

Use also determines which materials are most suitable. Appropriateness to site and personal preference narrow the choice down a little further. Finally, cost rears its ugly head once again and influences the final decision. Cost can be reduced considerably if you do some of the labor.

Once you've recorded the shape and extent of the various paved areas on the plan, you can concentrate on making your selection of the type of paving. The following descriptions and the paving materials chart on page 51 will help you wade through the bewildering number of options.

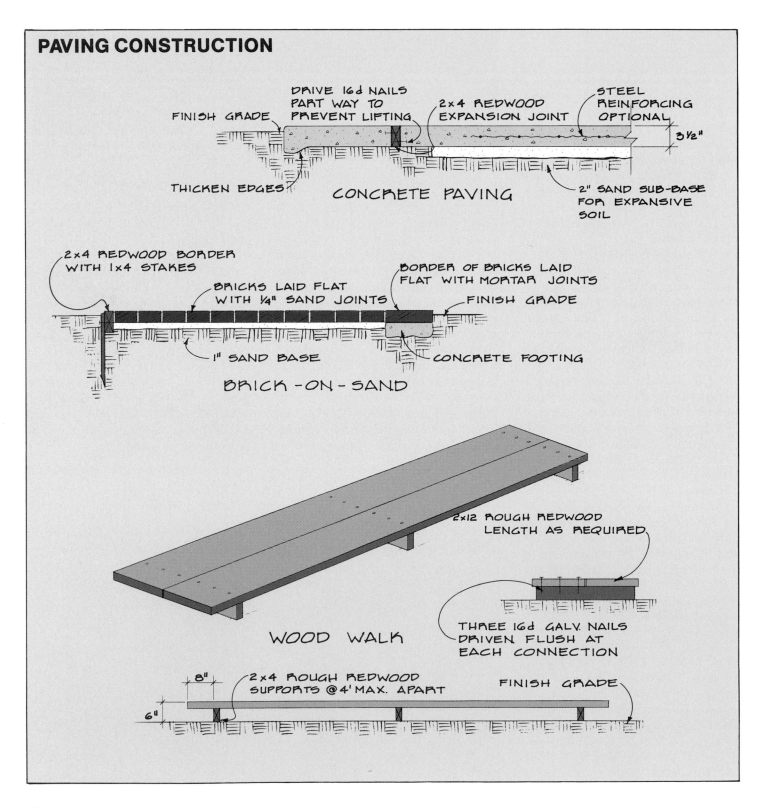

PAVING CONSTRUCTION

FINISH GRADE
DRIVE 16d NAILS PART WAY TO PREVENT LIFTING
2×4 REDWOOD EXPANSION JOINT
STEEL REINFORCING OPTIONAL
3½"
THICKEN EDGES
2" SAND SUB-BASE FOR EXPANSIVE SOIL

CONCRETE PAVING

2×4 REDWOOD BORDER WITH 1×4 STAKES
BRICKS LAID FLAT WITH ¼" SAND JOINTS
BORDER OF BRICKS LAID FLAT WITH MORTAR JOINTS
FINISH GRADE
1" SAND BASE
CONCRETE FOOTING

BRICK-ON-SAND

2×12 ROUGH REDWOOD LENGTH AS REQUIRED
THREE 16d GALV. NAILS DRIVEN FLUSH AT EACH CONNECTION

WOOD WALK

8"
6"
2×4 ROUGH REDWOOD SUPPORTS @ 4' MAX. APART
FINISH GRADE

LAYING CONCRETE

Forms made with 2x4s are easy to work with and strong enough to hold the fluid concrete in place. A 2-inch base of rock dust, decomposed granite or similar material helps prevent cracking on any soil, but is essential on clay soils.

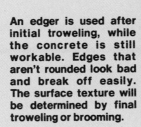

Concrete is struck off or *screeded* with a straight 2x4. Low spots are filled in along the way.

Using a *bull-float* takes a delicate touch. A float with no handle, called a *darby*, is used for walks and small areas.

An edger is used after initial troweling, while the concrete is still workable. Edges that aren't rounded look bad and break off easily. The surface texture will be determined by final troweling or brooming.

CONCRETE

Concrete is the most widely used garden paving material. It is practical, durable, relatively inexpensive and available in a variety of types and treatments. The surface should be non-skid, colored or textured to break glare. It should also be divided for design interest and to prevent cracking. Place expansion joints at corners and stress points, and through areas larger than 200 square feet. Redwood 2x4s, vinyl dividers and deep-driven joints are better looking than commonly used fiber strips. Shallow scribe lines are of little or no value in preventing cracks.

In clay soils that expand when wet, the sub-soil should be soaked before laying the concrete to avoid raising and cracking. A 2- to 4-inch deep base, such as sand, crushed rock or decomposed granite, should be used on this type of soil. Also use a sub-base where winter frosts are severe enough to cause heaving. Wire mesh or steel bar reinforcing is an added safeguard against major cracks. Hairline cracks are almost unavoidable and are not cause for concern.

Concrete requires 1/8- to 3/16-inch pitch per foot for good drainage. Allow a little bit more, 3/16 to 1/4 inch, for pebble and patterned finishes. Pouring concrete, especially large areas, is not a job for an amateur. A good procedure for the homeowner who wants to do part of the job himself is to do the grading, lay the forms and then assist an experienced finisher.

One cubic yard of ready-mix will cover about 80 square feet, 3-1/2 inches thick. But order a little extra so you don't run short. Another approach is to use redwood or other dividers to cut the job into small units that don't have to be done all at one time. Ready-mix comes in minimum loads of 3 to 6 cubic yards. Mix it yourself in a wheelbarrow or rent a mixer when doing only a few square feet at one time.

TIP—A good Concrete Mix:
- 1 part cement.
- 2-1/2 parts washed sand.
- 2-1/2 parts 3/4-inch crushed rock aggregate.
- 5 gallons of water per sack of cement.

VARIATIONS WITH CONCRETE

Rock salt is sprinkled on wet concrete at a rate of 5 to 10 pounds per 100 square feet and tamped in with a wood float. It is dissolved with water after the concrete hardens. Post anchor is for 4x4 post.

Tan, salt-finish concrete with a deep-driven joint.

Concrete is a fluid material. Its shape is determined by the forms. This entrance walk has a stone-like quality. Landscape architect: Roy Seifert for Dr. and Mrs. George Zucconi.

Plain concrete, exposed pebble concrete and railroad ties are combined in these handsome steps by landscape contractor Bill Peterson. Note louvered step lights recessed into railroad ties.

Troweled-on topping is cool to the feet. It is an excellent surface for pool decking in hot areas.

Owner John Mrak did a neat acid-staining job to give this concrete walk a flagstone appearance.

Colored concrete is impressed with a patented steel form to impart an antique-block paving effect.

38

LAYING COBBLESTONE

Cobblestone paving is a good do-it-yourself item. First, large round stones are tapped into a 2-inch bed of sand until level.

Mortar is used to fill in between the stones and tooled until firm.

Surface is cleaned with a brush and water so that stones are visible.

Finished paving fits perfectly with railroad ties and looks a hundred years old. Landscape architect: Jack Smith, ASLA.

Pebble concrete with a redwood 2x4 divider. The crushed rock was part of the concrete mix. It was rough troweled and exposed with a fine spray of water.

Hand-set stone paving is fun to do yourself. The contracted cost is quite high because of the time involved.

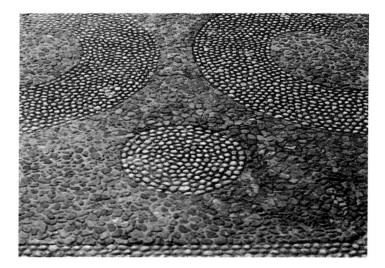

Brick-on-sand is set on a 2-inch sand base. A 2x4, notched the thickness of a brick, levels the sand to the proper depth.

Fine sand is swept into the joints to make a firm surface. No mortar is needed.

BRICK

Because of its various sizes, colors and patterns, brick is an outstanding garden paving. Common red bricks are of medium hardness and texture, approximately 4x8 inches and a little more than 2 inches thick. Allow five bricks per square foot, which includes some breakage.

You can also get bricks that are smoother or harder, thinner or thicker or wider or longer. They come in other colors such as light red, dark red, yellow, buff, brown and splotchy "used." You can lay them flat, on-edge, side-by-side, diagonally, overlapping and many other ways. They can be laid on sand or concrete, the joints swept with sand, filled with mortar or ground cover. In addition, brick paving is cool, glare-free and not slippery.

Perhaps the only drawback is that installed cost is significantly more than concrete. However, about half of that cost is for materials. Do it yourself and save the difference. Unlike concrete, you don't have to finish it immediately once you've started. Lay as many bricks as you want at one time and come back to it whenever it is convenient. Another way to cut cost is to lay bricks over existing concrete. This way you don't even have to tear out and haul away the old paving.

Square the pattern every 3 or 4 feet. Otherwise you may get an unpleasant surprise when you stop to admire the completed project.

BRICK PAVING PATTERNS

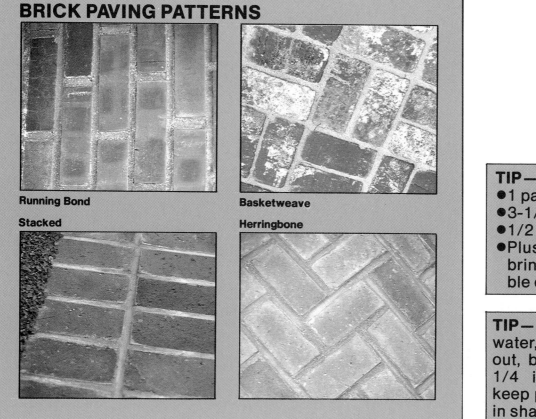

Running Bond

Stacked

Basketweave

Herringbone

TIP—A good Mortar Mix:
- 1 part cement.
- 3-1/2 parts washed sand.
- 1/2 part lime or fire-clay.
- Plus enough water to bring to a plastic, workable consistency.

TIP—Brick paving absorbs water, which helps it dry out, but a pitch of 3/16 to 1/4 inch per foot helps keep paving dry, especially in shaded areas.

If you're mixing a lot of mortar, better use a full-size *contractor's wheelbarrow.* It is also handy for mixing concrete and for hauling soil and materials.

A professional brick mason brought this brick water-saw to the job. Some supply yards will saw bricks, tile, stone and pre-cast concrete for 10 to 25 cents per cut.

These bricks are laid over an old concrete patio, tapped into level position on a 1/2-inch mortar setting bed. Mortar joints will be filled later, all at one time.

SETTING BRICKS WITH MORTAR JOINTS

A homemade grout bag is filled with mortar made from pre-mixed mortar.

Grout bag is used to squeeze mortar into joints like cake frosting. Used bricks with rustic joints require less precision than new bricks.

Professionals carefully line up brick courses with strings, and constantly check level.

Mortar is scrubbed into joints with a piece of burlap. Surface is immediately cleaned with a wet sponge, before mortar dries out.

ASPHALT

Asphalt should not be ruled out as a valid paving for certain garden uses. If you've tried to keep grease spots off a concrete driveway, you'll agree that asphalt is more practical where cars are involved. It is also quite satisfactory for game courts and service yards. Softness and heat accumulation during summer and an uninspiring appearance make it unsuitable for uses such as patios and entrances.

The main advantage of using asphalt is to save money. Even with the tremendous increase in the cost of petroleum, asphalt still costs much less than its nearest rival, concrete. This is true *if* there is a clear access for the large trucks and rolling equipment, and *if* the area is large and open.

Asphaltic concrete, as it is correctly called, is laid 2 inches thick over a 2-inch rolled base for most residential uses. A soil sterilant keeps bermudagrass and other weeds from breaking through. Edges should be bordered with sturdy, decay-resistant 2x4s securely staked and laminated for curves. Concrete, brick or steel borders can also be used—at added cost. Pitch should be at least 1/4 inch per foot. Any depressions or *dishes* in the surface should be corrected before the final bill is paid.

This is not a do-it-yourself item unless you happen to own a big, dirty dump truck and a 10-ton roller.

FLAGSTONE

Flagstone is a beautiful paving—if it just didn't cost so much. If you live near a quarry, it *might* come out about the same as brick. With transportation costs, it is often prohibitive.

Colors range from almost white through tans, pinks and browns in sandstone, to grays and blues for granite and slate. Thickness is from 1/2 to 4 inches and sizes of individual pieces go up to several feet across. Wide variety and natural appearance make flagstone easy to fit into any garden. A concrete base with mortar joints is usually best for patio-type uses. For informal areas, flagstone can be laid in sand or just dug into the ground with grass or creeping plants growing in the cracks.

This asphalt driveway was widened with brick to make a more convenient and better-appearing entry.

A 3-inch-thick flagstone makes a sturdy and good looking step.

Dark gray slate is set on a sand base with open joints for a natural effect.

Multi-colored sandstone-type flagstone cantilevers are used over pool edge.

Flagstone is not the easiest paving to lay. It is hard to get the feel of it. Amateurish jobs look just awful. If you want to tackle it yourself, look at some good examples to see how the joints were fitted and how the mortar was installed. Plan to lay out the stones ahead of time, allowing 1/4 inch per foot of slope for drainage unless water can soak into the sand or soil base.

TILE

Tile comes in as many colors and even more shapes and sizes than brick. Textured and casual finishes are more at home in most gardens than slick and precise types. The effect has a Spanish or Mediterranean feel and fits in well with rough plaster, wrought iron and tile roofs. Cost and installation methods are similar to brick. Tolerances are a little tighter, but if you can lay brick, you can lay tile.

PRE-CAST CONCRETE

This is a good way to let the manufacturer take the worry out of trying to finish concrete. Of course, you pay for the advantage. There is an amazing range of shapes, sizes, colors and finishes on the market. Look them over and you might find some preferable to brick or tile. Installation is similar to brick and tile. Design so you can use full-size pieces or you'll have to cut them with a masonry saw.

WOODEN GARDEN FLOORS

Wood is a great garden paving material and can give many years of service when used properly. Here are some suggestions:

● Use pressure-treated wood or a decay-resistant species such as heart redwood, cypress or cedar, when wood will be in contact with the ground or footings. Preservatives applied without pressure are usually of little value.

● Thin boards tend to warp when subjected to outdoor conditions. Two inches thick is minimum. Boards should be securely nailed in place.

● Rough surfaces are less apt to be slippery when wet and don't show marks and defects as readily as

Swirling pattern of brown tile is emphasized by the white mortar joints. Layouts like this take lots of cutting.

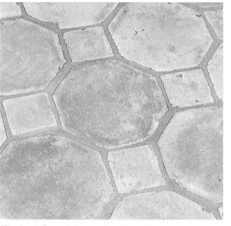

Typical Spanish-style tile using square and octagonal shapes.

Thin-set mix is easy to use for laying tile and brick. It can be spread less than 1/4-inch thick.

Interlocking pre-cast concrete paving units fit together like a jigsaw puzzle. They can be installed on a 1-inch sand base with sand joints.

Redwood 2x4s hold the edges in place and define the planting areas. Designed and installed by landscape contractor Jim Keener.

smooth finishes. Slivers are not as big a problem as generally anticipated. Go over the edges with a wood rasp and sand the surface lightly with coarse sandpaper to make it a little more comfortable for bare feet.

● Paints and shiny finishes deteriorate rapidly. It is better to apply a stain or just let the wood weather naturally.

● Nails should be galvanized, aluminum or stainless steel. Drive them flush in a pleasing pattern rather than trying to hide them by setting.

● Lay railroad ties, 2x4s on edge, cut logs, six-inch-long end pieces cut from 4x4s, and similar boards directly in the ground. It is simple and effective, and fun to do. A sand base or sandy soil helps in the leveling. Where excessive moisture and termites are a severe problem, avoid direct contact with the ground by building a raised deck.

Lumber is expensive—material alone will be a dollar a square foot or more. If you can find a cheap source of scrap lumber, it will help keep the cost down. But remember that the wood must be pressure treated or decay resistant.

DUCK BOARDS AND DECKS

Duck boards and low-level decks are other ways to use wood as garden paving. They are just as easy to build as laying the wood in the ground. In fact, there is usually less digging to do. Pressure-treated or decay-resistant 2x4 or 4x4 *stringers* are laid directly on the ground or on concrete or brick supports for termite and moisture protection. The planking is nailed to the stringers and the weight holds it in place. Space the stringers to suit the planking. Flat 2x4s will span two feet with a little flexing. Placed on edge and nailed together, they'll reach 6 feet. Boards 2x6 and wider are acceptable for 3-foot spans.

As the deck gets higher, construction becomes trickier and requires a permit. You'll need a railing and steps for any height above 18 inches. Work with a carpenter unless you have experience and confidence. Standard *pier and girder* support is satisfactory for most situations. For normal deck loading, 4x6 girders spaced 3 feet apart will span 6 feet between piers.

A 16d galvanized nail is used as a spacer while two nails are driven flush with the surface of each 2x4.

Here is an easy way to build a curbside or any wood walkway. Two redwood 2x4s laid on edge support 2x4 planks.

Finished result is neat and simple. The low-voltage wood path light was designed to tie in with the angles of the 2x4s. Landscape architect: Ken Smith, ASLA.

Hillside decks are another story. Most agencies require a structural engineer to calculate the spans and footings. Contractor's costs are high and it is an overwhelming project for most homeowners. If you have enough level space on solid land that will serve the need, it is almost always better to avoid the complication and expense of a deck precariously cantilevered over a hillside. If your usable space is limited and you have a sensational view, by all means consider a dramatic deck to gain full use of your property.

SEMI-PAVINGS

What do you do with an area that doesn't require a solid paving, yet is unsatisfactory for lawn, ground cover or bare dirt? For example, take the side yard where you want to keep some firewood and walk occasionally. Or a path to the back corner that isn't worth doing in concrete or brick.

What you need is a material that drains rapidly, is easy to install, low in cost, can be walked on, is reasonably free of mud and dust, fairly stable, low maintenance and pleasant appearing. Believe it or not, there are quite a few common granular, stone and bark materials that fill the bill rather well.

Landscape contractor Dave Geller designed and installed this walk of redwood 4x6s. Note the piece tapered to fit the subtle bend in the walk. The shrub cover at top is Confederate jasmine.

A walk made of log cuts with sand in between gives a pleasant rustic effect.

What could be simpler? Two rough redwood 2x12s were nailed to 2x4 supports to create a fun walkway that took only a few minutes to build.

Wood deck adds valuable outdoor living space on a steep hillside lot and provides a gorgeous view of the James River.

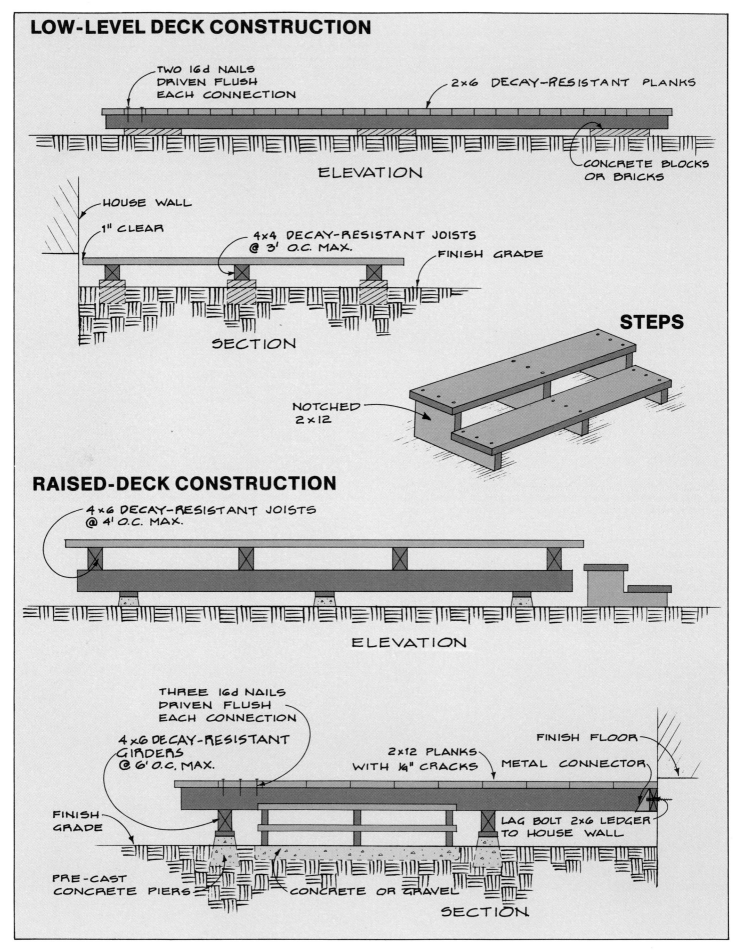

LOW-LEVEL DECK CONSTRUCTION

TWO 16d NAILS
DRIVEN FLUSH
EACH CONNECTION

2×6 DECAY-RESISTANT PLANKS

ELEVATION

CONCRETE BLOCKS
OR BRICKS

HOUSE WALL

1" CLEAR

4×4 DECAY-RESISTANT JOISTS
@ 3' O.C. MAX.

FINISH GRADE

SECTION

STEPS

NOTCHED
2×12

RAISED-DECK CONSTRUCTION

4×6 DECAY-RESISTANT JOISTS
@ 4' O.C. MAX.

ELEVATION

THREE 16d NAILS
DRIVEN FLUSH
EACH CONNECTION

4×6 DECAY-RESISTANT
GIRDERS
@ 6' O.C. MAX.

FINISH FLOOR

2×12 PLANKS
WITH ⅛" CRACKS

METAL CONNECTOR

FINISH
GRADE

LAG BOLT 2×6 LEDGER
TO HOUSE WALL

PRE-CAST
CONCRETE PIERS

CONCRETE OR GRAVEL

SECTION

46

BUILDING A DECK

Jane and Billy join in as Bill Becher digs holes for pre-cast concrete piers. The piers must be carefully leveled or the whole deck will be crooked.

Rough redwood 2x4 stringers are nailed to the piers and finished redwood 2x6 planks are laid across them. Planks are extended over the old concrete step, instead of tearing it out. Leave a 1-inch space between the wood and the house to protect against termites.

String indicates to nailer where the 2x4 is underneath.

Chalk-line is snapped to mark a straight edge.

A portable rotary saw is used to trim off excess wood. Edges are smoothed with a rasp or a former.

Not bad for a day's work. They deserve a rest before doing the planting.

You can grow shrubs and trees directly in them. When conserving water is crucial, some of these materials can also be used as lawn and ground cover substitutes.

They do need borders such as curbings or edgings to help keep them in place. They should be limited to reasonably level ground to prevent erosion. It is unnecessary to put plastic underneath. This impedes water penetration and always seems to become exposed to view. Weeds can be pulled by hand or controlled by sprays as shown in Chapter 13. All it takes to install semi-pavings is a little common sense and a strong back.

Sacked products are convenient, but expensive for all but small areas. Most of these materials are sold in bulk, by the cubic yard, ton or skip load at a much lower cost. You can haul them yourself in a pick-up or trailer, or arrange for large deliveries with a dump truck. Cost varies considerably with quantity, availability and distance of haul.

It takes a mathematician to calculate how much of which to cover what. The safest way is to measure how many square feet you have to cover. Convert that number to cubic feet by dividing by 6 for a 2-inch thickness. Then, divide by 27 to get cubic yards. Ask the supply yard to give you the equivalent amount—plus a 10 percent safety margin—no matter how it is sold.

Granular Materials—Common semi-pavings include decomposed (disintegrated) granite, rock dust, select natural base and brick dust. Laid 2 or 3 inches deep, they pack solidly and take to raking very well. They're good for walks, parking areas and even game courts. Color range is gray, tan, brown and red. They'll scratch floors, so it is best to keep them away from entrances to the house.

Stones and Gravels—These start at pea size, about 1/4-inch diameter, and go up to 2 inches and larger. Heavy, 3/4-inch mixed gravel stays in place the best and is easiest to walk on. Earth colors are most pleasing and don't show leaves and debris as much as light colors and white. Lay at least 2

An occasional raking keeps decomposed granite looking neat.

Path of tan gravel helps create a woodsy feeling. Landscape architect: Eldon Russell, Houston.

A layer of 3/4-inch mixed stone is walkable with shoes on. These rich colors are found in *Rusty* types that contain iron.

Grayish tones are easier to find. Here they blend well with concrete pads in Polly Martin's garden.

inches deep for foot traffic and 4 to 6 inches deep for driveways. Keep slightly below the border or adjacent paving to prevent scattering. Loose stones can be a nuisance in parkways or along public sidewalks. Avoid lightweight volcanic types unless well confined.

Bark Products—Not only can these be walked on, they make excellent mulches for plants when placed at least 2 inches deep. Large chunks look good, but can float or wash away and should be kept away from moving water. Smaller sizes can be mixed in with the soil so they stay in place a little better. Shredded bark placed 6 inches deep is safe under swing sets and slides.

Volcanic rock is neat looking, but tends to displace more easily than heavier types. (I ran out of quarters.)

All types of bark decompose and need replenishing at least once a year. Pecan and walnut shells serve a similar purpose and are longer lasting, but have sharp edges that are hard on bare feet. Pine needles are a good natural-appearing covering. They're free or sold as inexpensive pine straw. Avoid using pine needles where they'll dry out and be a fire hazard.

In some areas bark products may be a problem, particularly if you have pets. Ticks and other undesirable insects will sometimes take up residence there and become pests.

COSTS

The chart on page 51 gives estimated costs of various paving materials. In general, you can assume that flagstone will cost three or four times as much as gray concrete and that asphalt is usually the cheapest of the solid types. Actual cost often depends on how busy contractors happen to be and how much competition there is. Small areas—less than 500 square feet—are almost always more expensive per foot than large areas.

If you have hard soil, difficult access and need extra grading, footings and complex forming, you're obviously going to have to pay more. If a contractor's bid seems too high, get a comparison bid. If you plan to do it yourself, you can figure that materials alone will be approximately one-half the installed cost.

GRADING

After you've made a choice as to what kind of pavings you'll be using, you're almost ready to start with the installation. But first you have to prepare the ground.

Rough grading of most lots is performed by the builder. The typical lot is graded to drain away from the house to the street. A building department inspector is usually needed to approve the work. This existing drainage pattern should be carefully preserved during subsequent grading and construction to protect the house, prevent erosion and avoid damage to neighboring property. Earth *berms,* or low dikes at the top of banks, can usually be made less obvious by flattening

Shredded bark is walkable and useful under play equipment.

Newly planted shrub areas look good right away when mulched with bark chunks.

Walnut and pecan shells make good paths. They're also good for mulches in planting areas and can even be rototilled into the soil as an amendment.

Gravel driveways can be beautiful. They also cost less than solid paving.

them out a little, but their function of keeping water from flowing over the bank must not be impaired.

If paving patterns, terracing, contouring or other features that might affect grading can be anticipated, a few passes with the tractor can save much hand work later on. Be sure to reroute drainage flow if the old route is blocked by added paving. Side yards are frequently a problem. A good way is to leave an open channel at least a foot wide along the property line. Lawn and planting areas should be approximately 2 inches below adjacent paving rather than flush, to allow for soil from planting holes and the addition of soil amendments.

Don't do any planting until you're sure that your entire property drains properly. Approximately 1/4 inch per foot slope is advisable for lawn and planting areas. This means 2-1/2 inches of slope for every ten feet, or at least 2 feet in 100 feet. Testing the drainage first by observing the flow of rain or applied water and correcting low areas is much easier before planting.

Stockpiling of topsoil to be replaced in planting areas is highly desirable. This is possible only if the house is constructed singly rather than in a tract. Do not bury concrete, plaster, lumber and other debris. Boulders and rock outcroppings should be looked upon as potential features. They can often be incorporated into the design rather than hauled away at considerable expense.

Grading permits are usually required for any cut exceeding 5 feet or any fill exceeding 3 feet, or if more than 50 cubic yards of material are involved. When large portions of a garden are paved, soaking in of rainwater is eliminated. Water coming from a paved area often reaches such volume and velocity that erosion and flooding result, unless drainage to the street or storm drain is provided.

If roof water must drain to the street, unsightly surface gutters of asphalt or concrete should be avoided. Walks and driveways can often serve as drainage channels, but underground lines are often advisable. When there are existing drain lines, it is easy to tie into them at relatively little expense.

Sloping and hillside lots require careful grading design. Strict ordinances must be followed. In most instances, some retaining walls are necessary to fully use the site. Ideally, the house architect should consider grading as an integral part of his design. Collaboration with the landscape architect at this stage is quite rewarding.

LAYING PAVING

Here are some basic tips that are useful for laying any paving:
● Stake out the proposed area on the ground and make last-minute modifications if necessary.
● Decide the final elevation for the top of the paving. Sometimes you can raise or lower it a little and save lots of digging or filling.
● Grade for the slope and thickness required by the specific paving. Allow extra depth for sub-base, if used. Include footings and post anchors and arrange for any required inspections.
● Build forms and mark where dividers and expansion joints will be.
● Install reinforcing and piping, conduits and sleeves that need to go under paving.
● Soak the ground thoroughly to minimize expansion of clay soils.
● Lay the paving of your choice, referring to the description, detail sketches and photos. Watching a professional for a few minutes on a job similar to your own is the next best thing to hiring him.

Painters, plasterers and other workmen raise havoc with paving that is installed too soon during construction of a house. If possible, obtain an allowance from the builder and have it installed after other work is completed. This will also give you time to consider the design more carefully. If loan requirements necessitate earlier installation, insist that it be protected against damage.

NEXT THE WALLS

We've talked about the garden floor and roof in this chapter. Without the garden walls, most people will feel exposed and uncomfortable. This brings us to the use of walls, fences and screens to make your garden a private retreat. These are described in the next chapter.

Consider putting excess soil to use before paying to have it hauled away. This earth *berm* gives privacy and reduces noise from adjacent road. Planting with a colorful ground cover will add beauty and protect against erosion.

PAVINGS: COSTS AND COMPARISONS

Paving	Installed Cost per Square Foot
CONCRETE	
Basic Gray—Can be monotonous and will glare in sunlight. Broom, sweat and swirl finishes are safer and more interesting than smooth, steel-troweled surfaces that tend to be slippery.	$2.00 to $3.00
Colored—It's easier to order color mixed in with the concrete direct from the ready-mix company, rather than dusting it on the poured surface. Select colors from samples, not just names. Colors will fade unless sealed or waxed.	$2.25 to $3.25
Salt-Finish—Very popular because it's fairly easy to do. Just press rock salt into the troweled surface while it's still soft. The pitted effect adds interest and fits into most garden scenes. Often used with colored concrete.	$2.25 to $3.25
Pebble or Exposed Aggregate—Workmanship and types vary considerably. Be sure to look at samples before giving the go-ahead. The unevenness can be a problem for furniture and is difficult to keep clean.	$3.00 to $4.00
Patterned—A steel form is used to impress soft concrete to give a brick, cobblestone or tile-like effect. Installation is by franchised contractors only.	$3.50 to $4.50
BRICK	
Sand Base—Quite stable when the sand is 1 to 2 inches deep and well-compacted. Best when held in place with a redwood 2x4 or other type of permanent border. One of the few materials you can practice with or start over if you don't like the results.	$3.00 to $5.00
Concrete Base—Usually laid with mortar joints. This makes it easier to sweep clean than a sand base. Install on new or over existing concrete. This saves the cost of a new base. Used bricks are best laid this way to allow for irregularities. Cost of old bricks is even higher than new bricks in most areas due to limited supply.	$5.00 to $7.00
ASPHALT	
The larger the area, the better the price per foot. Redwood edging, weed killer and 2-inch base are included.	$.75 to $1.50
FLAGSTONE	
Sand or Earth Base—Grow lawn or a walkable ground cover in the joints for a natural effect. Easy to change.	$3.00 to $4.50
Concrete Base—Mortar joints make it more practical for furniture and general use.	$5.00 to $7.00
TILE	
Sand Base—Weak tile will crack unless firmly bedded. Sand joints are not as satisfactory as with brick.	$1.50 to $2.50

Paving	Installed Cost per Square Foot
Concrete Base—Excellent for laying over existing concrete because of the thinness of tile. This saves the cost of a new base.	$5.00 to $7.00
PRE-CAST CONCRETE	
Sand or Earth Base—Avoid thin types that will crack.	$1.50 to $3.00
Concrete Base—Same advantages as tile.	$3.00 to $5.00
WOOD PAVING	
Railroad Ties—Laid directly in the ground with 8-inch side up. Not a smooth surface. Can be spaced to include lawn or walkable ground cover between.	$3.00 to $5.00
Log Cuts—Odd shapes between cuts are a problem. Concrete looks bad, stone or bark moves around. Lawn or a low ground cover works best and keeps logs moist, which helps prevent cracking.	$1.50 to $3.00
End Pieces—Lots of labor involved, but very attractive.	$4.00 to $6.00
Laminated 2x4s—Parallel lines give it a sophisticated quality.	$2.50 to $5.00
DUCK BOARDS AND DECKS	
Duck Boards—Pallet-like modules fit together for walks and patios. Easily moved about.	$2.00 to $4.00
Low-Level Decks—Perfect way to eliminate the common 6-inch step down from a sliding door.	$2.50 to $5.00
Medium-Height Decks—Cost doesn't include steps or railings.	$3.00 to $6.00
Hillside Decks—Costs may double if you have to include engineering, permits, footings and railings.	$10.00 and up
SEMI-PAVINGS	
Decomposed Granite—The best-looking is tan or brown with a uniform texture about the same as coarse sand.	$.40 to $.60
Rock Dust—Mixed gravel with *fine mineral deposits* often used as a base under concrete or asphalt. Usually a neutral gray and not especially decorative.	$.25 to $.50
Select Natural Base—Fine mineral deposits dug directly out of the ground. Looks like tannish gray dirt but packs like concrete and isn't too muddy. More utilitarian than pretty.	$.20 to $.30
Brick Dust—Red color goes well with tile roofs and brick work.	$.25 to $.50
Bark—Brownish red chunks available in 1/2-inch to 2-inch sizes. Use shredded bark where softness is important.	$.40 to $.60
Common Stones and Gravels—Whatever you can find at the local building materials yard. Look for brownish tones and non-garish colors.	$.25 to $.50

Make A Private Retreat 4

As affordable lots continue to get smaller, privacy becomes more and more important. There was little need for a solid wall or fence in the old days when a neighbor was several hundred feet away behind a grove of trees. It is a different situation now when there is often only 10 feet between houses. Anyway, you don't have to be anti-social to enjoy freedom from the prying eyes of your neighbors. It is nice to be able to relax in your own little world and do your own thing.

In most cases, privacy is desirable for everyone involved. This means a solid structure or heavy planting—if you're willing to wait at least a year for it to fill in. A masonry wall or a well-constructed wood fence is often the best solution. Hardly anyone wants to wait for plants to grow.

Even with a 6-foot solid enclosure, plants are still often necessary to achieve total privacy. Shrubs that grow above a wall or fence not only add to privacy but help block wind and noise as well. They also soften the harsh lines of the structure. Where width is limited, choose upright plants that can be kept narrow without constant trimming. Well-placed trees can screen a neighbor's second-floor window that looks down on your patio. Where the situation is uncomfortable, consider putting in good-size trees rather than having to wait years for results.

Hillside lots are more of a problem, especially if you happen to be on the downhill side. It is best to talk it over with your neighbors before planting a forest that will block their panoramic view. With cooperation and careful plant selection, you can both be satisfied. Sometimes a shade trellis can be used as a horizontal screen to cut off a

Sometimes extra height is needed to achieve total privacy. The height of this wall is doubled by colorful oleanders.

This fence is almost 8 feet high, but it looks lower because of the stone wall base.

disturbing line of sight into your windows.

Walls and fences normally look better if their tops are level. It is preferable to jog or definitely slope the top of a fence to adjust to a change in grade, rather than make it slightly slanted. However, informal rail fences, rustic stakes and see-through fences can usually follow the land.

Before you decide what kind to build, there are several other benefits

to consider in addition to your privacy.

First, a wall or fence is usually needed to provide protection for children and pets, and to deter intruders. Walls can also help break the wind. Surprisingly, a fence that filters the breeze works better than a solid wall that the wind may go up and over. Finally, sound from neighbors, highways, playgrounds and other sources can be reduced by solid fences and walls.

Allen Fong designed this elegant restyling of a plain back yard. It accommodates large groups, yet provides an intimate retreat for the family. Photo: Leyland Y. Lee.

A horizontal screen and lots of container plants are used here to restrict the view from the higher lot into this bedroom. Landscape contractor: Howard Olsen for Mr. and Mrs. Jack Howard.

Change in grade is turned into a design feature by jogging fence sections rather than precisely following the slope of the land.

Ornamental wrought-iron panel relieves closed-in feeling of a solid wall. Planting provides privacy.

Plantings can soften the bare expanse of a block wall.

This 4-foot-high block wall afforded no privacy at all. A 2x4 sill was bolted to the wall to support the added wood section.

Many gardens have a nice view in one direction but need privacy in another. By installing a section of see-through fencing, it is possible to have both a view and privacy. In a small yard, see-through panels give a feeling of openness.

BEFORE YOU BUILD

Be sure to verify property lines before building *any* wall or fence. The maximum allowable front-yard height is normally 42 inches. Back-yard height is usually limited to 72 inches. There are places where a 72-inch fence isn't quite high enough. If you and your neighbor both agree, you shouldn't have any problem building one a little higher, or adding on to an existing one. Masonry walls over 72 inches high should have extra reinforcing, so it is easier to use wood.

Some cities require permits for all walls and fences, and may frown upon *any* type over 72 inches high. Check before you build. Incidentally, if there's any chance you might add a swimming pool, hot tub or spa, you might as well plan all fences to meet applicable ordinances.

You'll get a lower bid for several hundred lineal feet—or better yet, for several neighboring yards done at one time. Good access can also lower cost, especially for concrete block. Material-to-labor ratio is close to 50-50 for most types. Cost doesn't include

Concrete block walls enclosing condominium patios are plastered to match buildings.

Wrought-iron fencing and gates are the logical choice for this old New Orleans mansion.

painting or staining. Add $50 to $75 for each 36-inch-wide gate.

CHOOSING A STYLE

Unless you've been through it before, it is hard to believe the hassles that can develop over fencing. Try picturing three adjacent neighbors who want three different types of fencing—all different from the kind you prefer. Assuming you want to split the cost, it is worth considerable effort to come to a mutually agreeable choice.

Often the style is set by what's already existing in the neighborhood. Hopefully, it will be compatible with the houses. For example, grapestakes look fine with shingle roofs and wood siding; brick walls are an obvious choice for a brick house; and picket fences are appropriate with Colonial architecture. The following descriptions of various types of walls and fences and the cost chart on page 64 should help you make a choice.

MASONRY WALLS

They are sturdy, permanent, practically maintenance-free and have the additional advantage of cutting out a lot of sound. Although brick, stone, adobe and poured concrete are sometimes used, concrete blocks, especially lightweight cinder and slump types, are by far the most common types of garden masonry walls.

These blocks come in a wide range of sizes, colors and textures, or they can be plastered to match the house.

Blocks 6 or 8 inches wide, 8 inches high and 16 inches long are standard. Blocks 4 inches wide are economical, but require pilasters every 16 feet and additional steel for extra support.

The main drawbacks of block walls are their relatively high cost and their tendency to create a closed-in feeling, especially in a small yard. Panels of grille blocks or wrought iron will relieve the prison effect and allow welcome breezes to enter. Generally, it is better to have block walls installed by an experienced contractor unless you have lots of time, muscle and experience. If you're undaunted by this warning, then follow this construction procedure.

BUILDING MASONRY WALLS

Always locate property corners and set string lines *before* digging the foundation. For normal soils, a 12-inch by 12-inch concrete footing with one 1/2-inch horizontal steel reinforcing bar is sufficient. Soft edges of fill slopes offer poor support for heavy walls. Extend the footing at least 12 inches into undisturbed soil and below the frost line to avoid settling and cracking. In soggy, unstable soil, it is often better to avoid masonry walls altogether and use wood.

The base row, called a *course,* is either set into the wet footing or added with a layer of mortar later. I recommend using vertical reinforcing bars centered 24 inches apart and another horizontal bar in the top course. The vertical bars are embedded in the footing and connected to the horizontal bars with tie-wire. Fill all cells containing steel solidly with

The base course is embedded in concrete footing. The pilaster contains steel bars and will be completely filled with grout. Note step-up pyramid for holding string line.

It is important to get the base course level. This one is especially tricky because of the step down.

concrete grouting. When mixing grout by hand, use one part cement, two parts sand and two parts pea gravel, and pour in the cells. Some building departments require permits for all masonry walls and can usually give advice and free plans to follow. Retaining walls should always be con-structed according to an engineered plan.

Build the corners first like step-up pyramids. This gives a handy ledge to stretch a guide line for filling in the blocks in between. Move it up as you complete each horizontal course.

Joints are approximately 1/2 inch wide. By adjusting each one a little bit, the blocks can be fitted with a mini-mum of cutting. Usually the joints are left open in the bottom course to allow water to flow through. Mix just enough mortar to last you half an hour or so using the mix on page 40. *Butter* the lower block and the edge of the block to be set with mortar. Tap the block gently with the trowel handle until it is in line and level in both directions. It takes a while to get the hang of it. Low planter walls are good practice before attempting the 72-inch-high variety.

Finish the joints with a joint tool or piece of 3/4-inch pipe as soon as the mortar is firm but still workable. Or you can cut the joints deep, called *raking,* for a shadow effect.

Fill the top cells for a flush or rounded concrete cap. Or use a solid block for the top course, or a matching concrete brick or decorative brick. Another alternative is to attach a 2-inch-thick wood plank with bolts set into the top cells. Concrete glue brushed on or mixed in the mortar helps prevent dislodging of the cap course.

BRICK WALLS

Structural bricks with hollow cells are just as easy to lay as concrete blocks. They cost approximately 50 cents each for a 4x8x12-inch brick or about twice as much as a concrete block of comparable size. This is still much more economical than building a solid brick wall or applying solid bricks as a veneer. In addition, bricks are an excellent covering for an exist-ing wall that needs improving.

The reason that walls of solid brick are more difficult to build is that bricks are smaller than blocks and there are no convenient cells for the steel reinforcing and concrete grout. The most common method is to lay two separate walls about 4 inches

A curving brick wall is stronger than a straight one. Thomas Jefferson designed one like this for the University of Virginia.

Low planter walls are a good use of brick and well within the capabilities of an owner/builder.

apart and use the space between for reinforcing. The top can be finished brick with solid grouting, or a 12-inch-long brick can be laid cross-wise as a cap course.

Mortar is handled similarly to hollow block work, except it is laid out on top of each brick and *furrowed*

Hollow structural brick is made like a concrete block.

Well-laid, cut-stone wall is neat and sophisticated.

When it is important for the ends and the backs to look good, use structural bricks that are textured on all four sides. Steel and solid grout add strength.

Stones of various sizes and textures are skillfully blended. This is not an easy task, even for an expert.

Laying a veneer of flagstone over concrete block doesn't take nearly as much stone as building a solid wall.

with the trowel point to form a setting bed. Because of the high cost, fewer brick walls are being built than before. A good way to introduce brick into the garden is to use it for seat-high planters. Use less expensive materials at the property lines.

STONE WALLS

Stone is another story. The most common method is to treat it as a facing veneer over a concrete wall. This is something you might want to tackle, especially if the wall is low. Adding concrete glue to the mortar won't help during construction but once it is dry, the wall will be practically indestructable. Solid stone walls require a great quantity of material and soil. In fact, it is almost a lost art. If you have a lot of free stone that you don't want to haul away, then it might be worth your while. Otherwise, forget it.

CONCRETE WALLS

Properly laid broken concrete can give a stone-like appearance at much less cost. It is heavy enough to be used for low terracing walls without mortar, which gives a pleasing casual effect. Laid in mortar with regular courses, it can be surprisingly attractive.

Poured concrete is fine for curbings, seat walls and low retaining walls. But, by the time you build sturdy enough forms, you could have built it from block. The main justification is if you want to create some far-out free-form shape or you want a pebble-finish surface.

WOOD FENCES

Wood is softer appearing and generally less expensive than masonry. Wood fences are available in an almost infinite variety and can fit any situation. You don't have to be a cabinet-maker to build simple wood fences, which makes such projects great for the non-professional. When allowed to weather naturally, they require little maintenance. Redwood, cedar and rough textures are best. If color is desired, staining is preferable to painting.

Posts must be *pressure-treated* or made from *decay-resistant* wood. Even then, they are subject to deterioration, but no one seems to worry too much about it. They'll usually last for quite a few years without falling over. Steel pipes can be used if permanency is extremely important, but at additional cost.

Once you decide on the basic frame, you can select from the many choices of materials and patterns. Or you can modify the framing for non-wood materials described under miscellaneous fences.

BUILDING WOOD FENCES

Start by lining up the fence with a string-line. Be sure not to encroach on

Steel pipe posts are advisable where soggy soils cause rapid deterioration of wood posts.

property lines. Locate the 4x4 posts *inside* the line at a maximum of 8 feet apart. The boards laid across the space between posts are *stringers*. They'll sag if they're any farther apart. Unless your lot line happens to be an exact multiple of 8, divide the length into equal spaces not to exceed 8 feet, rather than ending up with an odd panel at the end. If you are working with pre-cut stringers, the posts have to be set carefully or the pieces won't fit properly.

A hand auger or clam-shell digger is fine for a few holes or for soft soil. Use a power auger if many holes are involved and if digging is tough. The idea is to end up with a hole not much larger than 6 inches in diameter—so don't use a shovel. A hole 24 inches deep will leave 6 feet above ground if you start with an 8-foot post. Or you

The look of this dry-laid, broken-concrete wall is softened by creeping thyme. Design by Jack Smith, landscape architect, ASLA.

can use 7-foot posts and let the boards extend 12 inches above the top stringer for a 6-foot height. You can pack crushed rock around the posts, but concrete will hold them more securely. A little extra depth and additional concrete is advisable for gate posts and at the top of slopes. Some building codes require banking the cement against the posts to form a mound above ground level.

Set the corner posts first. Brace them securely and run a *taut* string to line up and determine the top of the posts in between. Be sure the string doesn't sag. For long runs, it is better to set the posts extra high and cut off the excess later.

Let the concrete cure for a day or longer before nailing on the stringers. Running the bottom 2x4 stringer on edge adds vertical strength. Using the

A 2-man power auger is considerably faster than the clam-shell post-hole digger in the background.

WOOD FENCE CONSTRUCTION

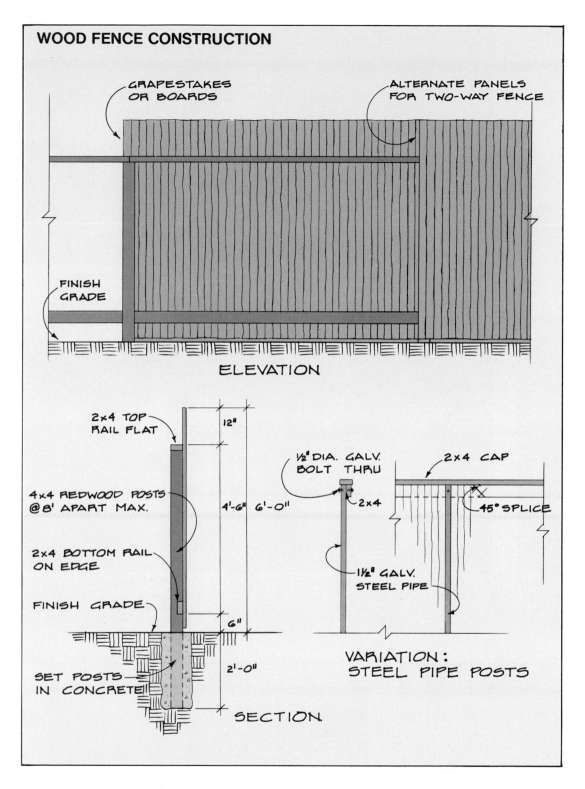

GRAPESTAKES OR BOARDS

ALTERNATE PANELS FOR TWO-WAY FENCE

FINISH GRADE

ELEVATION

2×4 TOP RAIL FLAT

12"

4×4 REDWOOD POSTS @ 8' APART MAX.

2×4 BOTTOM RAIL ON EDGE

FINISH GRADE

SET POSTS IN CONCRETE

4'-6" 6'-0"

6"

2'-0"

SECTION

½" DIA. GALV. BOLT THRU

2×4

2×4 CAP

45° SPLICE

1½" GALV. STEEL PIPE

VARIATION: STEEL PIPE POSTS

The ends of the bottom stringer are cut-in and toe-nailed to the posts. The top stringer is nailed flat.

Boards are nailed vertically. Note how these extend above the top stringer for full 6-foot height.

top 2x4 flat helps keep the fence in line. Nailing the top stringer to the posts with two 16d nails is easy. The bottom one is harder because it is cut to fit between the posts and *toenailed* in place with two or three 8d nails. If you don't have a helper to hold the stringer while you nail, a temporary block to rest it on saves frustration.

Applying the boards, grapestakes, panels or whatever is a snap. Decide what size nails are needed and how far apart they'll be. Two 6d nails are normally used at the top and bottom for 1x6 boards. One 8d nail at each connection point is common for grapestakes. To avoid rust streaks, use stainless steel or aluminum nails.

Most boards or other fencing materials are applied vertically. Check frequently with a level to avoid tilting. Add a middle stringer for thin boards and fences more than 6 feet high. A 2x4 or 2x6 cap gives a clean top line. To do this, you will need 9-foot or taller posts so they extend full height for nailing.

WOOD FENCE VARIATIONS

Board-and-board allows air circulation and looks the same from both sides. Gray stain soaks in and does not require restaining.

Board-on-board makes a solid fence. Panels must be alternated to avoid one-sided effect. Redwood can be stained or allowed to weather.

Picket fences keep intruders out without blocking the view.

Rustic rail fence defines yard boundary without looking heavy or unfriendly.

This grapestake fence has alternating panels. Watermarks are sometimes a problem on unstained wood fences where sprinklers continually hit the same area.

Handsome fence of overlapping, horizontal boards is stained a weathered gray.

WROUGHT IRON

This is preferable to chain link for an open fence when close-up viewing is important. Hollow bars are commonly used—at a much lower cost than the old solid type. Even with that, cost is still approximately *double* that of chain link. Metal primer and high-quality paint should be used to minimize the need for repainting. Wrought iron isn't well-adapted to the do-it-yourselfer. Some welding is usually necessary at the site. However, there are pre-fabricated panels available that can be used without any welding if you measure very carefully.

CHAIN LINK

This is a perfectly good solution where immediate solid enclosure is unnecessary or undesirable. Chain link also costs considerably less than masonry or wood. To make it less obtrusive, leave off the top rail and use black vinyl-coated mesh. Where semi-privacy is desired, wood strips can be inserted. It is also an ideal support for vines and shrubs. Eventually the framework will be totally hidden by foliage.

Chain link isn't difficult to install with the proper tools, but it is not much fun. Prices are fairly low anyway, so there's little to save by doing it yourself. Call on a good professional and get the job done right.

Chain-link fences make an excellent support for vines and supple shrubs that can be woven into the wire. An existing chain-link fence can be made higher by slipping pipes into the existing posts and running horizontal wires 6 inches apart along the top of the fence. Hall's honeysuckle, Algerian ivy and other rapid growers will quickly cover the added portion and create a solid green wall. The chart on the following page lists some of the best plants to use with chain link. Plant lists in Chapter 6 give some additional information.

Climbing roses add color without closing the view through wrought-iron fence. Concrete block columns appear very substantial.

Owner Curt Reedy built this brick wall and added ornamental wrought iron according to my plan.

Black vinyl-coated chain link is less obtrusive than standard galvanized type.

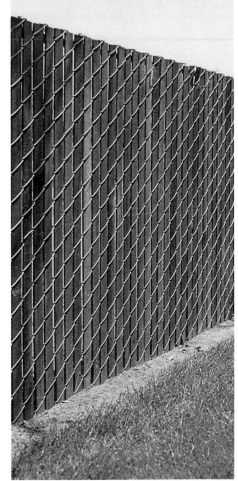
Redwood lath strips are slipped into chain link mesh for added privacy. Privacy isn't total, but the effect is quite pleasing.

PLANTS FOR CHAIN-LINK FENCES
Listed in order of hardiness to cold.

Common Name *Scientific Name*	Degree of Privacy	Remarks & Spacing
Climbing Rose *Rosa* species	Open	Deciduous. Thorns add security. Space 4' to 6' apart.
Hall's Honeysuckle *Lonicera japonica* *'Halliana'*	Solid	Rapid growth, needs cutting back. Space 3' to 5' apart.
English Ivy *Hedera helix*	Solid	Slow growth, easy to control. Space 2' to 4' apart.
Pyracantha *Pyracantha coccinea*	Open	Thorns add security. Space 4' to 6' apart.
Carolina Jessamine *Gelsemium sempervirens*	Open	Gets top-heavy. Space 3' to 5' apart.
Fraser Photinia *Photinia fraseri*	Partial	Easy to control. Space 4' to 6' apart.
Sasanqua Camellia *Camellia sasanqua*	Partial	Slow growth, but choice. Space 4' to 6' apart.
Coral Vine *Antigonon leptopus*	Solid	Deciduous in cold. Rapid. Space 3' to 4' apart.
Algerian Ivy *Hedera canariensis*	Solid	Rapid growth, needs cutting back. Space 3' to 5' apart.
Confederate/Star Jasmine *Trachelospermum* *jasminioides*	Partial	Slow growth to start. Space 3' to 4' apart.
Bougainvillea *Bougainvillea* species	Partial	Rapid and rampaging growth. Thorns add security. Space 6' to 8' apart.

CHAIN-LINK COVERS

English Ivy, see page 108.

Bougainvillea, see page 118.

Carolina Jessamine, see page 112.

Coral Vine, see page 112.

OTHER MATERIALS

In special situations, materials such as glass, plastic, shingles, bamboo, plywood, canvas, expanded metal and precast panels may be a good answer to a fencing problem. The limiting factor is usually cost. These custom-type fences are best used to enclose or divide a small area adjacent to the house rather than an entire lot. Usually you can use a wood frame similar to that described under wood fences. Just make sure the spans fit the size of the material that you've selected and the frame is strong enough to support the weight.

Cozy alcove is shielded by colorful canvas wind screen. Landscape architect Roy Seifert designed the panels for easy replacement every five years or so.

Railroad ties combine with pecky cypress 1x12 planks for a country effect.

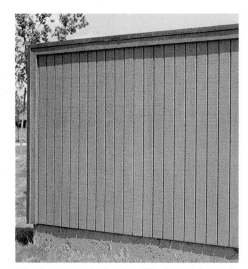

Handsome and simple, this fence is made of exterior siding plywood that comes in 4x8' panels in various grooved patterns and textures.

Custom fence of 1x12 and 1x2 boards allows air circulation without loss of privacy.

Rather than introduce a new material, the house shingles were extended as a fence. It is a good do-it-yourself project if you're willing to take the time.

Lath is an easy-to-use screening material. This one was custom made on the site, but you can adapt pre-fabricated panels to most situations.

FENCES: COSTS AND COMPARISONS

	Installed cost per linear foot for 6-foot height			Installed cost per linear foot for 6-foot height
WOOD FENCES			**Standard Brick**—Best for low retaining walls and low seats.	$8.00 to $10.00 (3 feet high)
Boards—1x8 roughsawn redwood or cedar are quite common but boards come in various widths and many patterns.	$6.00 to $8.00		**Stone**—First you build a concrete block wall—then you apply stone veneer.	$5.00 to $10.00 (3 feet high)
Woven Boards—Interlaced, flexible boards. Pre-cut packages are easy to install.	$5.00 to $7.00		**Poured Cement**—For retaining walls and low seats.	$5.00 to $10.00 (3 feet high)
Grapestakes—One of the most popular wood fences. Casual appearance. Rough texture requires no stain, ages well. Add 50¢ per linear foot for 2x4 cap.	$6.00 to $8.00		**CHAIN-LINK FENCES**	
			Standard—Looks commercial and offers no privacy. Secure and maintenance-free. Vines and shrubs can be added.	$5.00 to $7.00
1x1s, 1x2s, Combed Stakes—More sophisticated than grapestakes, but not as strong. 2x2s are sturdier, but cost more.	$6.00 to $8.00		**Standard with Wood Inserts**—Looks surprisingly good. Privacy isn't total. Filters wind.	$7.00 to $9.00
Woven Palings—Sturdy poles woven with wire.	$8.00 to $10.00		**Colored Link**—Black vinyl is almost invisible when the posts are painted black.	$6.00 to $8.00
Plywood—Use *textural exterior* types only. Neat, strong and easy to nail. Back is blank; not for situations where both sides will be seen.	$8.00 to $10.00		**WROUGHT-IRON FENCES**	
Louvers—Greatly overrated. Difficult to build; warp easily. For special uses only.	$10.00 and up		**Standard**—The best answer for pool fencing. Especially appropriate with Mediterranean-style house. Embellishments are okay for gates, but simple uprights are usually preferable.	$8.00 to $12.00
Lath—Pre-fab panels and wired rolls save labor and are stronger than individual pieces. Good way to add height to an existing wall or fence.	$5.00 to $8.00		**Pre-fabricated**—Drop-in panels can be used if the spacing is correct.	$6.00 to $8.00
Shingles—Great choice when the house has shingle walls. Can be applied over an existing wood fence.	$10.00 and up		**MISCELLANEOUS FENCES**	
Rail—Obviously not for privacy or security. You can set the posts in gravel or directly in the ground. Looks good with ranch houses and shake roofs.	$3.00 to $5.00 (3 feet high)		**Glass**—For view and wind protection. Safety requires 1/4-inch-thick tempered plate glass. Plexiglass is somewhat cheaper but scratches.	$15.00 and up
Picket—Better for keeping out animals and people than a rail fence. Looks best painted to coordinate with house.	$4.00 to $8.00 (3 feet high)		**Plastic**—Corrugated fiberglass isn't very classy. Some flat panels are quite handsome, but hard to obtain in exterior grades. Lets light through for small garden enclosures.	$10.00 and up
Custom—Tends to be gimmicky unless done tastefully. Have fun, but don't get carried away.	$10.00 and up		**Bamboo**—Quite a chore to install individual canes. Sometimes available in wire-woven rolls. Woven reed is inexpensive but temporary.	$10.00 and up
MASONRY WALLS			**Wire Mesh**—Inexpensive see-through fence, easy to install. Needs frame on all sides or will wobble.	$5.00 to $7.00
Concrete Block—Plain, colored, slump, grille and textured. Avoid fancy patterns.	$9.00 to $14.00		**Expanded Metal**—Can look commercial. Needs rust-proofing.	$10.00 and up
Plaster over Concrete Block—Good way to tie in with a plastered house or to upgrade an old wall. The problem is to find a plasterer.	$10.00 to $15.00		**Canvas**—New vinyl coatings last for about five years. Nice colors available.	$10.00 and up
			Various Panels—Asbestos cement, pebble surfaces, pressed fibers and others. Good possibilities when well-designed.	$10.00 and up
Structural Brick—Available in several colors. Makes a handsome wall. Strong and costs less than solid bricks.	$12.00 to $15.00		**Railroad Ties and Poles**—Striking when set vertically in the ground. Can be used as low retaining walls. Repeat clusters as accents.	$10.00 and up

This simple wood gate has no exposed latch.

Z-brace resists downward pressure and keeps the gate from sagging.

Wood gates don't have to be solid and heavy. However, intricate designs like this one are not for a beginning carpenter.

Wrought iron is ideal for wide driveway gates. These are electrically controlled for convenience.

This elegant wrought-iron gate enhances the entrance and provides security.

GATES

These go along with walls and fences. No matter how solidly a wooden gate is built, it always seems to sag or bind. Use lightweight dry wood along with heavy-duty hinges and adequate bracing. Allow an extra 1/4 inch for swelling when the wood gets wet. Avoid wooden gates more than 4 feet wide.

If you must have a solid driveway gate, build it on a steel frame and in-stall a running wheel to relieve the strain. Chain-link gates work fine, but aren't pretty and afford no privacy. Wrought-iron gates are desirable for workability and appearance when seeing through doesn't matter.

PLANT SCREENS
AND HEDGES

Plants can be used for both privacy and protection. A tall hedge will not only keep people and animals out of a yard, it will also absorb noise and soften wind. Hedges and screens are also better looking than many types of fencing.

There are two major drawbacks. First, you must wait the year or more it will take for a hedge or screen to grow and fill in. This is a long time to wait for privacy. Second, plants require maintenance to keep them alive and to maintain their appearance.

Maintenance can be reduced if you select a plant that will naturally stay the height and width you want with minimal clipping. This will not only save a lot of unnecessary labor, but will also look more natural and usually more pleasing. If you want a screen or hedge at least 8 feet tall, but you only have an allowable space 4 feet wide, Japanese privet, golden bamboo or yew pine are good choices.

The plant list on the facing page suggests some of the best screens or hedges and their approximate sizes. The lists in Chapter 6 give additional information such as best exposure, climate and a description of each plant.

Panels of Japanese privet are framed by brick curbing and pilasters.

Naturally a little sprawly, Fraser photinia takes a bit of training to encourage upright form. New red growth is a distinctive feature.

Try spirea where you want a flowering hedge with a casual feeling, and where winter bareness is not a problem.

It takes a lot of clipping, but Australian pine makes a great hedge with a distinctive texture.

Yew pine is my first choice for a well-behaved narrow hedge.

PLANT SCREENS AND HEDGES

Listed in order of height. Indicated size assumes some pruning or clipping.

Common Name *Scientific Name*	Height x Width	Remarks & Spacing	Climate Zones
Wintergreen Holly *Berberis julianae*	5x3'	Spiny barrier. Space 3' to 4' apart.	Zones 6-10
Rose *Rosa rugosa*	5x4'	Deciduous; thorny. Space 2' to 4' apart.	Zones 3-9
Variegated Chinese Privet *Ligustrum sinense* *'Variegata'*	5x4'	Clip to renew foliage. Space 3' to 4' apart.	Zones 7-10
Sandankwa Viburnum *Viburnum suspensum*	5x4'	Needs clipping to keep narrow. Space 4' to 5' apart.	Zones 8-10
English Boxwood *Buxus sempervirens*	6x4'	Can be kept smaller by clipping. Space 3' to 4' apart.	Zones 5-9
Spirea *Spirea vanhouttei*	6x4'	Deciduous; arching habit. Space 3' to 4' apart.	Zones 4-9
Fraser Photinia *Photinia fraseri*	6x4'	Needs clipping to keep narrow. Space 4' to 5' apart.	Zones 7-10
Yew Pine/Japanese Yew *Podocarpus macrophyllus*	8x4'	Naturally narrow; slow. Space 3' to 4' apart.	Zones 7-10
Compact Carolina Cherry Laurel *Prunus caroliniana var.*	8x5'	Clipped or natural. Space 4' to 5' apart.	Zones 7-10
Japanese Privet *Ligustrum japonicum*	8x4'	Clipped or natural. Space 4' to 5' apart.	Zones 8-10
Chinese Holly *Ilex cornuta*	8x6'	Good barrier. Space 4' to 5' apart.	Zones 6-10
Golden Bamboo *Phyllostachys aurea*	10x4'	Rapid, upright growth. Space 5' to 6' apart.	Zones 7-10
Oleander *Nerium oleander*	10x8'	Best as natural screen. Space 5' to 6' apart.	Zones 8-10
Glossy Privet *Ligustrum lucidum*	12x6'	Clipped or semi-natural. Rapid. Space 3' to 5' apart.	Zones 8-10
American Holly *Ilex opaca*	12x6'	Can be kept fairly narrow. Space 6' to 8' apart.	Zones 5-10
Arborvitae *Thuja orientalis*	15x10'	Size and width according to variety. Space 4' to 8' apart.	Zones 6-10
Australian Pine *Casuarina* species	20x6'	Rapid growth; requires frequent clipping. Space 4' to 6' apart.	Zones 9-10

Sandankwa viburnum can be kept 3 feet tall or allowed to reach its full height of 5 feet or more.

Arborvitae are often plagued with red spider mites and tend to look unhealthy. But it is hard to find fault with an attractive planting such as this.

HOT TUBS AND SPAS

It is strange how most of us are comfortable at a crowded pool or at the beach with thousands of people, but dislike swimming or sun-bathing in our own yard without total privacy. Full-size swimming pools are difficult to screen from every angle. Small pools, hot tubs and spas are easy to tuck into a secluded corner beyond the view of nosy neighbors. They also take less space, are comparatively inexpensive, don't require as much energy to heat or water to fill, are less of a chore to keep clean and don't add as much to your tax bill.

For sociable soaking and tension relief, nothing can beat a hot tub or spa. They're actually miniature swimming pools with aerated bubbles. Water is heated to 100F (38C) but because they use less than 1,000 gallons, gas and electric cost is only $10 to $20 per month with average use.

Redwood hot tub blends beautifully with wood deck, railroad tie wall and barrel planters. Removable lid keeps water clean and conserves heat.

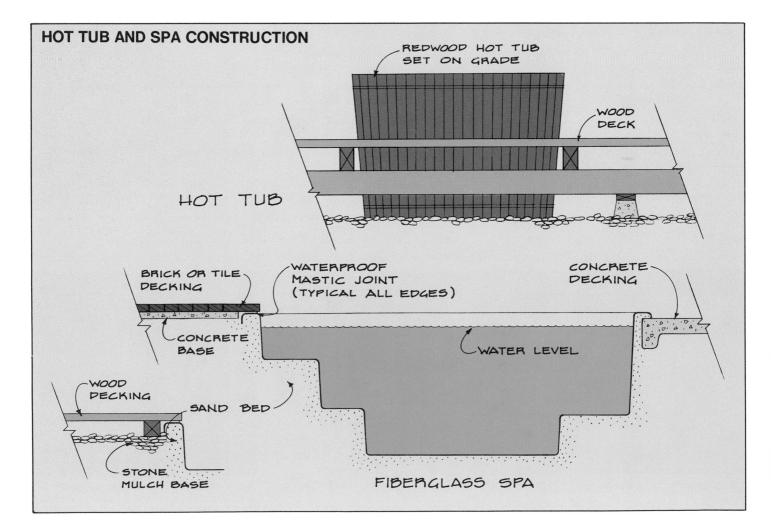

HOT TUB AND SPA CONSTRUCTION

REDWOOD HOT TUB SET ON GRADE

WOOD DECK

HOT TUB

BRICK OR TILE DECKING

WATERPROOF MASTIC JOINT (TYPICAL ALL EDGES)

CONCRETE DECKING

CONCRETE BASE

WATER LEVEL

WOOD DECKING

SAND BED

STONE MULCH BASE

FIBERGLASS SPA

Complete kit prices including wood tub or fiberglass spa, heater, pump filter and hardware range between $1,000 and $2,000 for most models. You can double the kit price to get a pretty good estimate of how much the total hook-up and installation package will be. Access, distance to gas and electricity and other site conditions will affect the cost.

If you've been doing some mental calculations and figure you can start soaking for as little as $3,000, you're only partially correct. Even if you already have an existing garden in which to place a tub or spa, better

allow at least another $1,000 for decking and additional planting. The big wallet-breaker could be whether or not you already have adequate protective fencing and if your building department has a pool fencing ordinance. Check it out before signing up.

Gunite spas made of sprayed-on reinforced concrete are only economical when constructed along with a swimming pool. Otherwise, the cost of a Gunite spa is approximately twice as much as a comparable size fiberglass type.

Both hot tubs and fiberglass spas can be installed by a homeowner.

Building departments require permits and inspections. It may be a good idea to hire licensed contractors for the electrical and plumbing work if your experience is lacking in these areas.

A good way of achieving privacy for tubs and spas is to place them under a shade trellis or in a gazebo. The shade is welcome on hot days and the protection from wind and prying eyes is appreciated during evening use. Add some lush plants that will thrive in the warmth and humidity and you've created a cozy, intimate spot all your own. See pages 28 to 33 for more on building trellises and gazebos.

Plan ahead and you can make your hot tub really work. This one is completely private, yet has a beautiful view to enjoy while the owner soaks. Photo courtesy of California Cooperage.

Tile coping and interior trim gives this fiberglass spa an elegant built-in look. A shade trellis provides privacy.

Interior designer Fran Elson wanted me to incorporate a work of art with a spa. We recessed a mural in a niche in the wall and selected brown fiberglass with tile trim to coordinate the colors.

Blue-gray plaster and tile lend enchantment to this small pool. The angular shape was carefully contrived to make it look larger. Designers: Michael and Nina Foch Dewell; Ken Smith.

Stone wall built at the pool edge allows pindo palms to arch gracefully over the water. Note underwater seat in corner for resting and safety.

SWIMMING POOLS

Don't rush into installing a full-size swimming pool without carefully weighing all advantages and disadvantages. Probably no other garden element presents as many problems. Practical considerations such as noise, glare, drainage and safety impose rigid limitations.

Added to these is the problem of budget. The cost of the pool itself is only the beginning. If enough money isn't allowed for decking, fencing, planting, lighting, furniture, interest on the loan, taxes, operating costs and maintenance, the project is apt to be a financial burden. The average pool costs closer to $12,000 than the tempting $6,995 "girl-in-the-bikini" ad in the Sunday supplement.

The simplest solution is a plastic pool sitting on the back lawn. It is not very glamorous, but for a mere $500 or $600 including the filter system, you can have a spot of water for you and the kids to paddle around and cool off on hot days. Sink it into the ground and add some decking and it becomes fairly presentable.

If you have ample space, *if* the budget will stand the strain and *if* you're convinced that a full-size permanent pool will really be enjoyed, then go ahead. But do it right. You can trade in a lemon car—you're stuck with a pool forever.

In terms of water conservation, it takes a lot of gallons to fill a pool—approximately 24,000 gallons for a 16x36' size. With good maintenance, a pool will rarely need draining and refilling. It will require the addition of water to replace losses due to evaporation, but that loss is no greater than for a lawn of similar size.

Spa is separated from main pool by stone bridge. Dark blue plaster gives a mountain-lake effect.

Landscape architect Eldon Russell and owner Marvey Finger carefully tucked this pool into the wooded setting to disturb as few trees as possible.

Mr. and Mrs. Frank Rotolante of Miami decided to put their pool in the front yard out of the prevailing wind, then added a screened cover for safety, cleanliness and protection from insects.

The pool should be located for maximum sun and privacy, and shielded from prevailing winds. Either keep it far enough away from the house so it doesn't dominate the view, or design it as part of the view. There should be ample space for lounging, sun-bathing and entertaining, with easy access to dressing rooms and bathrooms.

Sprayed concrete construction methods allow flexibility of shape, but be careful. Choosing a shape in relation to the setting is much more important than choosing one for its own sake. A rectangular pool carefully placed within a rectangular area might be more pleasing than some jazzy, unrelated form selected from a pool catalog.

Most activity takes place in the shallow area, even in families with expert swimmers, so this should be the greatest percentage of the pool space. Large, offset steps add interest and leave the main swimming area unobstructed so that even a 16x35' size with parallel ends is large enough for serious swimming

An even smaller pool is sufficient for most families. It is better to try one on for size at a friend's house than build your own larger than necessary.

The widest decking should occur in relation to the shallow area and steps. In some cases it is even possible to eliminate the walk area at the back side entirely. Underwater seat/climbouts can replace ladders and serve as convenient resting places. A spa will often induce non-swimmers to use the pool. One can be added for $2,000 to $3,000, much less than when it is built separately.

Diving is great fun and can be included in some form in almost every pool. A professional, 16-foot-long, one-meter board requires a 9-foot depth and a 20x40' pool. A 30-inch-high, 10-foot-long board is adequate for most divers and easier to fit into a smaller pool. Where space is limited, a 6-foot-long jump board or a raised decking area is more challenging than just diving off the edge.

POOL DECKS

Concrete is most frequently used for pool decking because it is practical and economical. The surface should be non-skid and well-drained, with expansion joints placed at frequent intervals. Color and texture such as salt-finish help break glare and add richness. Changes in level and cantilevered decking that eliminates coping are effective design elements.

In expansive soils, precautions must be taken to avoid cracking and shifting of the soil. Mastic or plastic expansion joints and a 2-inch-deep sub-base of rock dust or decomposed granite, along with thorough soaking before pouring, are advisable. Special engineering of the pool structure is also necessary in expansive soils.

Other common decking materials include flagstone and brick. On hillsides, wood decking is frequently used. The main limitation is that they all cost much more than concrete. One solution is to use them in small areas for a welcome contrast to the concrete. For areas with hot summers, a troweled-on cool deck that reduces surface temperature is a sole-saver. It is sold under various names and adds about 50 cents per square foot to the basic concrete cost.

FILTERS

Filtering equipment should be placed as near as possible to the deep end of the pool for economy and maximum efficiency. By increasing the size of the piping, it can be moved to a less obtrusive location, at additional cost, of course.

Every pool builder has a favorite manufacturer, but most agree that a filter of 36-square-feet rating with a one-horse-power motor is adequate for a 600-square-foot pool. This equals a 16x36' rectangle with offset steps. A separation tank eliminates the nuisance of backwash water. An overflow pipe will maintain proper water level despite heavy rains.

You can run the filter during the daytime, so noise is not a problem during sleeping hours. A spa aerating motor is another story. It needs to be placed fairly close to the spa and should be enclosed in a sound-proof chamber because it is a lot louder than a pool pump.

Pool maintenance is easier with a good filter system and with the skimmer located to catch debris from summer breezes. Spacing three adjustable return lines for a 600-square-foot pool will improve water circulation and filtering efficiency. An automatic cleaning system will reduce, but not eliminate, pool care at an installed cost of $600 and up.

HEATING AND LIGHTING

Solar heating is rapidly replacing gas for new installations. At approximately $1,500 for installation, the cost is double that of gas—but you save in the long run because you won't be using precious fuel. Use of gas for pool heating is restricted in many areas anyway. You don't have to install the entire solar heating unit right away. Be sure to include piping and stub-outs so solar heating can be added later. Spas and hot tubs require high temperatures and are often used at night, so back-up heating is advisable. However, they're easy to cover when not in use, which conserves heat and reduces maintenance.

Check out solar heating companies carefully. Because these systems are relatively new, few people have much experience with them. Ask to see a completed system in operation, the older the better, and talk with the owner. This is good advice not only for solar heating, but for any work you intend to contract for, whether it is a swimming pool, concrete paving or a sprinkler system.

A 500-watt light under the diving board is usually standard equipment for a pool. If the main view from the house or patio is directly toward the light, it can be shifted to the side of the pool to reduce glare. An ink-blue lens on the light also reduces glare and adds interest. A fuse or breaker box for the light is usually located above grade outside the decking near the light. It should be placed in a shrub bed or hidden. Additional lighting, such as in an attached spa, phone jacks and outlets for appliances should be planned for at this time to avoid installation problems later.

PLANTING, WATER FEATURES AND FENCING

Planting around a pool should be clean and protected from chlorine water by raised beds or deck drains. Some planting near the water that casts a reflection on the surface is dramatic and helps relieve the flat plane of the water and decking. Building a raised planter directly at the pool edge is a good way of handling it. Stone or bark mulches adjacent to the

Bubble plastic pool cover is a good way to keep heat in and dirt out. Material cost is about 50 cents per square foot.

It is fun to swim under the bridge in this elongated pool.

Planting box raised to upper level is protected from chlorinated water. Blue Atlas cedar is pruned in a bonsai fashion.

Poolside waterfall at the Tom Kennedy home is backed by lush foliage and a Mediterranean fan palm.

Reflecting pool gives a tranquil and dignified mood to this gracious Houston garden designed by landscape architect C.C. Pat Fleming.

Balcony with open railing offered no privacy for sun-bathing.

Solid panels were added to block the wind and prying eyes. Plant in corner is *Acmena Smithii*—one of the few named after a Smith.

paving are better than groundcovers. They eliminate mud and dust, require little care and are not damaged by chlorine.

Waterfalls and fountains should be planned with caution. They can be quite effective but must relate to the design of the site and pool. A separate pump that can be turned off without interfering with pool operation is best. Slides are popular with children, but look obtrusive—so take your choice.

Many cities and counties have laws requiring non-climbable fencing 54 to 60 inches high with self-closing gates around any body of water more than 18 inches deep. This is usually interpreted to include spas and tubs. A door at the back of a garage that opens onto the pool area also requires a self-closing device.

When small children are involved, consider placing this fencing around the pool itself rather than at the property lines. This will provide protection for family members as well as the public. Or, an openable or temporary fence can be included within the yard and removed when the children are older.

With a little imagination, the interior safety fence can be turned into an asset rather than an eyesore. Wrought iron, expanded metal or welded wire can be attractive, look-through barriers while still providing protection.

SUN-BATHING

Sun-bathing is another activity that calls for privacy. Because it is often associated with a pool or spa, try to place some of the decking where it gets plenty of sun—without being in view of the neighbors. Of course you don't have to have water to sun-bathe. Walk around the house and try to pick a spot that is out of the wind and will get sun during the time of day you want it. Be sure you won't block the sun when you build high fences or plant trees.

Rooftops and balconies are always potential sunning areas. Sometimes a partial screen is all that's necessary for privacy and wind control. Use a few container plants to dress up the area. Beware of helicopters.

PLAN AHEAD

If a pool is to be constructed at a later date, room should be left for access of heavy equipment. Also, it is best to do as little as possible in the entire area. Unless a very carefully considered master plan is drawn for the complete project, major changes and damage will occur when the pool is finally constructed. Water, electric and gas service lines may have to be stubbed-out to avoid costly breaking through pavement.

CAUTION

Pool contracting is a highly competitive business. Question free services. The ideal way is to have a plan before getting bids from several companies. Then carefully compare before signing any agreement. Clarify exactly what is included in the contract. Unforeseen extras can turn the low bidder into the high bidder.

Many pool companies have gone bankrupt, leaving the homeowner with an unfinished pool or with a new installation that requires repairs or adjustment. To make matters worse, you can be required to pay twice if the pool company doesn't pay its bills! Never pay for more than what has been installed. Secure material and labor releases for all work. A completion bond or payment through a bank gives added protection.

There's plenty of decking for sun-bathing around this desert pool designed by landscape architect Warren Jones. Cool-to-the-feet topping was used over concrete to minimize the desert heat.

It is almost time to furnish your outdoor room with plants, but first you must plan how to keep those plants healthy and alive. If you live in an area that normally receives 50 or 60 inches of rain spread throughout the year, then you can probably live through a dry month here and there without anything more than portable sprinklers.

It is not a big chore to keep the lawn green and the plants healthy by connecting up the hose to conveniently located high-pressure hose-bibbs. However, it is a different story if your area has lower rainfall and periodic, long dry spells. Or you may have a large piece of property with lots of lawn area and plants. In either of these cases, you should consider installing a permanent, underground sprinkler system.

SPRINKLERS

For large areas with well-drained soil and tolerant, compatible plant material, large diameter heads that water everything at once can often be used satisfactorily. Impact heads, commonly called *Rainbirds,* and gear or camdriven rotary heads with a radius from 25 to 40 feet are well-suited for lawns and slopes where the spray won't hit walls and windows. They usually cost less because fewer heads are required.

In most gardens, smaller stationary heads are preferred because of their more selective control. Here, lawns are usually put on separate circuits from ground covers and other areas having different watering requirements. Slopes and shaded areas should also be controlled separately. It wastes a lot of water if you have to turn on the sprinklers just because one spot in full sun dries out.

Pop-up type impact head rests flush with lawn when not in use. A mower can ride over it with no problem and there's nothing to trip on. Cost is about $20.

Water pressure raises the head clear of the lawn when in use.

Impact head is fine in a ground cover but is a hazard and a chore to trim around in a lawn. Cost is less than $10.

This is an unsightly and dangerous way to trim around a stationary lawn head.

A better choice is to use a pop-up type head that requires less trimming to keep grass clear of spray.

Stream-spray heads apply water like a gentle rain and minimize erosion.

Putting your shrub heads on a separate valve from lawn sprinklers permits less-frequent watering of shrubs and ground covers.

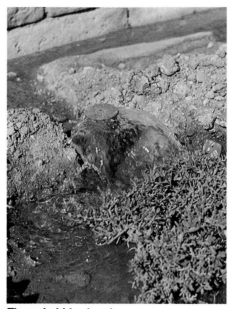

These bubbler heads save water because they apply it directly to the plant and not to the bare ground.

A gate valve at this fruit-tree bubbler permits precise control of the amount of water the tree receives.

The lawn around pop-up heads needs less-frequent trimming than lawn around stationary heads. Stream-spray heads throw out tiny streams of water from pin-point holes. They are useful for steep banks where erosion is a problem, or where pressure is too low for conventional heads.

It is better not to water shrub beds as often as lawns. Shrubs should be watered by bubbler or low-spray heads. This layout is relatively expensive because the heads have to be placed close together. Some small shrub areas can be watered with a hose. Other areas can be planted with drought-tolerant plants, using large watering basins. Thus, shrub heads are desirable, but you can get by without them.

The actual design of a sprinkler system can be done by a landscape architect, irrigation consultant, sprinkler contractor or homeowner. Generally, the sprinkler contractor designs on the ground as he installs. Simple systems with adequate pressure—50 pounds per square inch (psi)—can be laid out by the homeowner with the aid of a sprinkler catalog and a little free advice. Pressures exceeding 100 psi call for a pressure regulator to protect piping and prevent atomization of sprinkler spray.

Desirable features include triangular pattern, half and quarter heads spraying away from paving and structures, and control valves located conveniently out of spray. Ten stationary heads or three large-diameter heads are normally run on a 3/4-inch control valve and a 1-inch supply line. Low pressure, grade changes and other complicating factors indicate the need for professional advice on the layout.

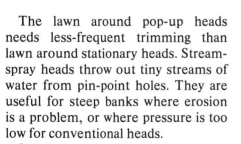

Connecting a portable sprinkler to the hose may not be automatic but it sure helps during a temporary dry spell.

PIPES

Galvanized steel piping used to be the standard material used for residential sprinkler systems. It is relatively cheap, readily available, strong and simple to install. It is also heavy to handle, subject to corrosion and requires special tools.

Plastic has taken over practically all sprinkler work. There is a wide range of different types to suit almost every situation. Rigid polyvinylchloride (PVC), schedule 40 or class 315 for pressure lines, and class 200 for "downstream" from the valves, is recommended for residential installations. It is impervious to corrosion, light-weight and can be worked with common household tools. Material runs slightly higher than galvanized steel, but installed costs are just about the same.

Plastic is strong, but handle it carefully. The only place it isn't advisable to use plastic is where it is exposed above grade, such as on a slope where you don't want to disturb the soil with a trench. In this case, galvanized steel is commonly used. Schedule 80 PVC is extra heavy and can be threaded for use as risers—or you can use galvanized steel risers instead.

Copper piping (type M) is serviceable, but is not used as much as in the

INSTALLING PLASTIC PIPE

Coat the end of the pipe with plastic pipe cement.

Coat the inside of the plastic fitting.

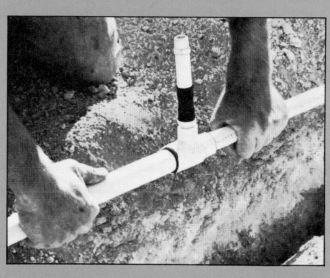

Slip the pipe into the fitting, making a quarter turn to spread the cement. Hold firmly for about a minute. Let joint cure overnight before turning on the water.

Flexible riser protects plastic pipe and fitting from breaking if head is removed.

Turn on water to flush out piping before sprinkler head is installed.

Existing manual valves can be converted to remote control by replacing the innards of the old valve with an electric solenoid type. The wires go to the automatic controller.

The weight of rainwater closes a switch that shuts off the automatic controller so sprinklers don't come on during a storm.

past. It costs more than either plastic or galvanized steel and is difficult for a homeowner to install without previous experience and proper tools.

AUTOMATIC TIMERS

Automatic controllers that operate on a time clock are valuable for large properties, homeowners who take frequent trips or those who do not otherwise get around to watering. Properly monitored and frequently reset to conform with weather changes, they are real water-savers. They are a life-saver in windy areas—you simply set the clock so they come on when the wind isn't blowing, usually in the very early morning when you'd hardly want to get up to do it.

Cost for including an automatic timer when installing a new system starts at about $300 for the simplest 3-valve type. Add $100 for each additional valve. Your material cost will be approximately one-half of this. Most existing systems can be converted to automatic simply by adapting existing valves and adding connecting wires from the new controller. For those whose main problem is forgetting to turn off the sprinklers, mechanical timers that automatically shut off the water can be added to existing valves. The cost for these is only about $25 per valve.

IS AN AUTOMATIC SYSTEM TRULY AUTOMATIC?

Not in the sense that you can just hook it up and then forget it. What the controller does is activate the sprinklers at the hour and day you choose, for the desired length of time. Repeat cycles allow them to come on more than once each day. Sophisticated controllers allow separate circuits, called *stations,* to activate on different days. This way, the lawn can be watered several times a week while the shrubs and ground cover can be set to come on only once during that period.

It is a mistake to set automatic controllers and then ignore them. If you do, the yard gets the same watering during a cool period as it does when it is hot and windy. Some people even neglect to allow for rain. The sprinklers just go merrily on their way in the midst of a storm. However, with reasonable attention, an automatic controller will save both water and gardening time.

COLD-CLIMATE FACTORS

In severe climates where the ground freezes, some precautions are advisable to protect piping and equipment. Slope piping slightly to a drain at the end of the line. When cold weather approaches, water should be drained from the lines after every sprinkling. It may be easier to bury the piping deep to protect it from freezing. Some plastic valves can be damaged by cold and should be wrapped. Or use frost-proof types.

RESTRICTIONS

Most building departments require plumbing permits for the installation of any sprinkler system. Anti-siphon devices are required to prevent back-siphonage of irrigation water into the potable water supply. Some plumbing codes call for separate high-pressure supply lines direct from the water meter to the sprinklers. Plastic is allowed for this use by most agencies if schedule 40 is used and it is buried at least 18 inches deep.

For a house under construction, an oversize service line to the house is needed if many sprinklers are to be run off it. When possible, it is advisable to increase the service line from the usual 1 inch to at least 1-1/2 inches, and to extend a 1-inch high-pressure spur to the back of the house.

Leaving convenient tees for future sprinkler connections is much easier than having to cut the line. Hose-bibbs that are part of the house plumbing system are usually unsatisfactory for permanent sprinkler connection. In most cases using hose-bibbs is not allowed by code.

ESTIMATING COSTS

To make a rough cost estimate for a sprinkler system, figure material costs, including pipe and fittings, at $7.50 per shrub head, $10 per pop-up lawn head, $25 per large-diameter head, $12.50 per manual control valve, 75 cents per lineal foot for 1-inch pressure lines. Double the prices for installed cost if you intend to have a contractor do it. Allow something extra for hard and rocky soil, high-pressure supply lines, long runs from valves to sprinklers and steep slopes.

DOING IT YOURSELF

Now that you know all about installation and the fact that you can save 50 percent on costs, perhaps you've decided that putting in the sprinklers yourself isn't such a bad idea. If so, here's a simple guide to follow.

Check your water line with a pressure gauge during the day in warm weather to approximate the minimum water pressure, and again at night for the maximum. Some water companies will give you this information over the phone. Consult a landscape architect or irrigation consultant for special procedures if the readings are below 50 psi or above 100 psi.

If you haven't already measured and made a plot of your yard as described in Chapter 2, do it now. Or you can just pace it off and make a rough plot, and rely more on ground layout.

Refer to the example plan on page 81 and draw a plan or rough sketch after deciding which areas you want covered and which ones should have separate valves. Select the type of heads best suited for each area and lay them out in a triangular pattern. The spacing is generally determined by taking 60 percent of the diameter of throw. For example, a head listed as a 10-foot radius would be 0.6 x 20-foot diameter, equaling 12-foot spacing.

There are two exceptions to this. Stream-spray heads are laid out in a square pattern and must throw from head to head. A 15-foot radius can have 15-foot spacing. The other exception is the group of slow-flowing irrigators described under "Drip, Trickle, Bubble and Ooze."

Combination valve and anti-siphon device satisfies plumbing code requirements in most areas. These are hidden behind a dwarf Chinese holly, but easily reached from the walk.

Complete the plan by establishing your high-pressure supply line to the valves. A 1-inch line is adequate for normal loads. You should be able to conveniently reach the valves from a paved area and turn them on without getting wet. If you install an automatic controller, the remote control valves don't *have* to be out of the sprinkler spray—but they may need occasional adjusting, so it is better if they are.

Before you start the actual work, show your plan to the building department and get a plumbing permit. They can advise you on what kind of back-flow prevention you need and other requirements.

Stake out all the piping, valves and heads on the site. Adjust the stakes indicating head spacing until it appears they will give full and even coverage without spraying all over everything.

Make an estimate of the materials, tools and equipment necessary to do the job, and purchase them so they'll be on hand when you need them. Include enough pipe, fittings and risers to allow for a few mistakes.

You can dig the trenches by hand if the ground is soft and if it is an average-size yard. A power trencher can be rented for hard soils and large projects.

Install the high-pressure supply lines and the valves. *Don't forget to turn off the water at the meter first.* It is doubtful that you'll find a convenient 1-inch tee to connect to. If the service line is plastic, it is easy to cut into and install a tee.

Galvanized steel or copper is more difficult. Look for a union to disconnect where the piping enters the house. If there isn't one, you may need a plumber. A gate valve that will enable you to shut off the sprinkler supply without disturbing the house can be included in the pipe just before the first valve. Putting in a hose-bibb wherever there isn't one nearby on the house is worth the few extra dollars.

Install the piping and risers. Turn on the valve so it flushes out the line and bubbles out the top as you put the heads on. This gets rid of most of the dirt that can cause clogging. Turn on each section and adjust the individual heads for best coverage and to minimize spray on paving and structure. If a head doesn't quite throw far enough, you can often insert a larger nozzle and avoid increasing pipe or valve size.

DRIP, TRICKLE, BUBBLE AND OOZE

Drip and trickle systems usually employ 5/16-inch-diameter flexible polyethylene tubing attached to a monitoring device, called an *emitter,* and running to the plant to be irrigated. Some emitters are plugged directly into rigid or flexible piping without the small tubing. The emitter allows a very low rate of water to pass through—usually 1 to 2 gallons per hour. The water soaks in slowly, minimizes runoff and evaporation, and the deep penetration encourages deep rooting.

This is a water service line where it enters the house. The hanging device is a pressure regulator. Anything to the right of it has too little pressure for conventional sprinklers, although it may be fine for drip types. The hose-bibb piping at the left is too small to connect to. What you have to do is break into the line somewhere between the meter and the shut-off valve on the vertical pipe and connect your sprinklers from that point.

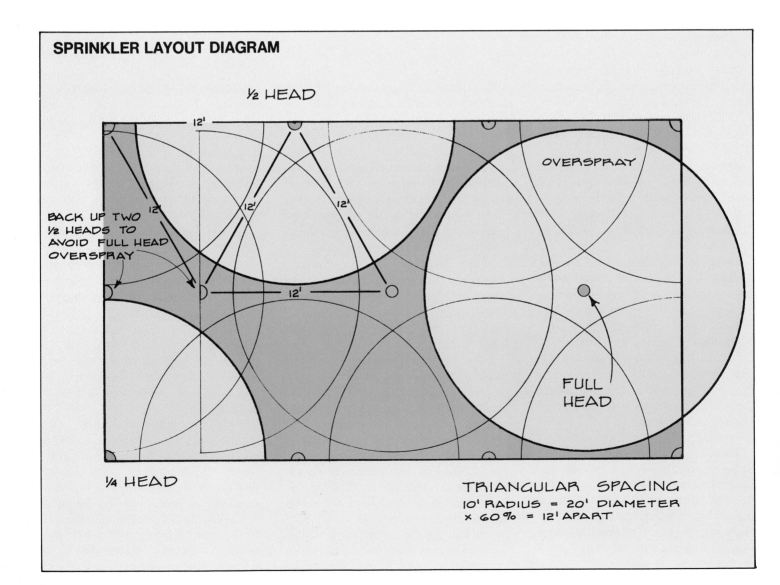

SPRINKLER LAYOUT DIAGRAM

½ HEAD

12'

BACK UP TWO ½ HEADS TO AVOID FULL HEAD OVERSPRAY

12' 12' 12'

12'

OVERSPRAY

FULL HEAD

¼ HEAD

TRIANGULAR SPACING
10' RADIUS = 20' DIAMETER
× 60% = 12' APART

SAMPLE IRRIGATION PLAN

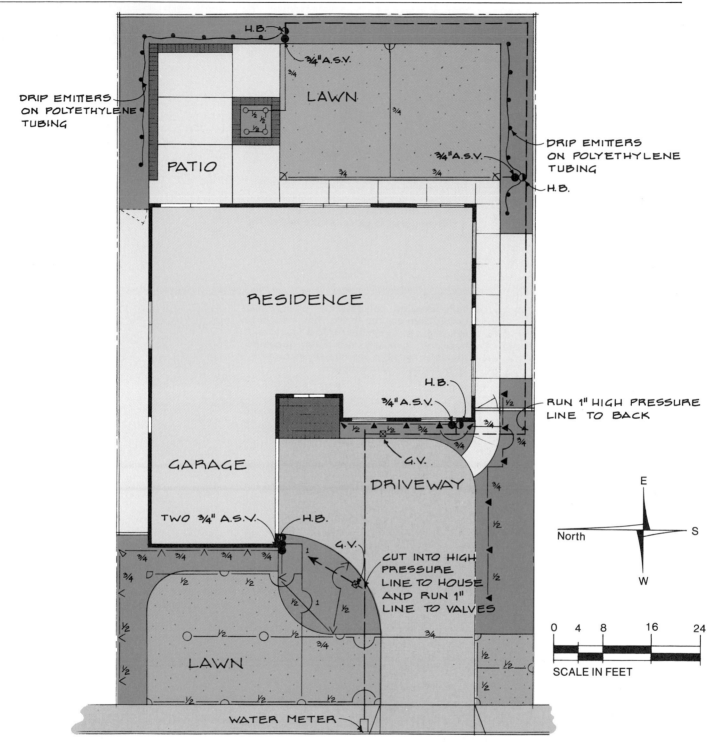

LEGEND

- – – – PVC Class 315 Supply Line—12" Deep
- ——— PVC Class 200 Sprinkler Line—8" Deep
- G.V. ⊠ Gate Valve
- A.S.V. ● Anti-Siphon Control Valve
- H.B. ◑ Hose-Bibb
- ⌐• Drip Emitter
- ⊢ Connection
- ⌐ No Connection

Low-Spray Shrub Heads—6' Radius Equals 8' Triangular Spacing
- ◤ 1/4 Head
- ▼ 1/2 Head

Shrub Heads—8' Radius Equals 10' Triangular Spacing
- △ 1/4 Head
- ∨ 1/2 Head

Lawn Heads—10' Radius Equals 12' Triangular Spacing
- ◠ 1/4 Head
- ⌒ 1/2 Head
- ○ Full Head

Impact Heads—30' Radius Equals 12' Triangular Spacing
- ⊠ 1/4 Head
- ⩗ 1/2 Head

Bubbler Heads—12" Radius
- ⊙ Full Head

Drip and trickle system kits are simple to install. Most attach to a hose-bibb and many don't even have to go underground. They come complete with directions and all the necessary equipment. You only have to decide what needs watering.

Bubbler heads flow at a much higher rate—about 1 gallon per minute for most kinds. The water doesn't spray, so it is easy to confine it where you want it. An earth basin or planter box works quite well. As with drip and trickle systems, water soaks in deeply when it is properly contained. Evaporation is less than with conventional spray heads.

Bubbler heads are installed in the same manner as sprinklers. The only difference is that they are either placed one for each shrub or tree, or approximately 5 feet apart in a floodable planter box.

An ooze system is made of perforated flexible pipe installed entirely underground. It is excellent for high-use areas such as putting greens and croquet courts. The old-time soaker hose is similar to ooze piping, except the soaker hose is used above ground.

Despite their meteoric rise in popularity, drip, trickle, bubble and ooze systems will not solve all irrigation problems. They're not suitable for all situations. Where saving water is a consideration, they reduce run-off and evaporation, and apply water only where it is needed.

The logical place to apply all of these methods is for individual trees and shrubs where you don't want to water the ground in between. Orchards, widely spaced trees on a hillside and a row of screening or windbreak plants are good examples. Used in the right place and properly installed and operated, they are valid alternatives to hose watering and conventional sprinkler systems.

Flexible, 1/2-inch-diameter polyethylene tubing is an alternative to rigid PVC. This is a slip-on clamp to close off the end of the line.

Sub'Terrain emitter plugs into 1/2-inch-diameter polyethylene piping and small tubes are run to the tree. Most drip systems can be connected to a faucet or a hose. A backflow preventer, pressure regulator and filter are normally incorporated at the point of connection.

This sophisticated emitter has 6 outlets and is attached to rigid PVC piping for permanence.

Here 7/32-inch polyethylene tubing is run in shallow trenches to connect emitters to plant basins.

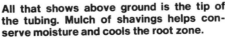

All that shows above ground is the tip of the tubing. Mulch of shavings helps conserve moisture and cools the root zone.

Left:
This drip kit attaches directly to the hose-bibb. It uses 5/16-inch polyethylene tubes connecting with even smaller emitter tubes at each strawberry plant.

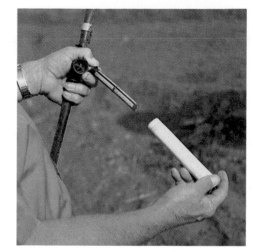

Right:
Filtering is essential for most emitters because of their very small openings. This filter is easily removable for cleaning.

Left:
Typical orchard emitter plugs directly into flexible piping at each tree.

Right:
This type of ooze piping, called *Nu Way*, has invisible pores that permit water to escape at a very slow rate. Installed underground, it can reduce water waste to practically nothing.

Left:
Roberts *Spot-Spitter* is attached to flexible polyethylene piping with smaller tubing and stuck into the ground at the base of the plant. A cross between a drip and regular head, it applies a small spray of water at a rate of 5 to 15 gallons per hour. It doesn't usually need a filter because the opening is large enough to avoid clogging.

Right:
Transparent tubing by *Thirst Quencher Systems* is practically invisible. You can control the flow at each plant with an adjusting screw.

Foolproof Plants

Now it is time to furnish your outdoor room. The suggestions and lists in this chapter are designed to help you select the best plants for your needs and location. These lists contain the kinds of plants that should be used for basic planting. Properly selected for a specific location, they will serve the intended purpose with a minimum of care and a low rate of failure.

There really isn't any such thing as a foolproof plant. Fortunately there are many rugged, reliable performers that come reasonably close. Obviously, the lists couldn't possibly include *every* plant that meets these requirements. If you know an outstanding performer, by all means use it if you wish. Likewise, if you are adventurous and like the challenge of growing temperamental or exotic plants, use them sparingly or hide them around the corner so that a possible dismal showing won't be a catastrophe.

GETTING THE MOST FROM YOUR PLANTS

In order to determine what plant to put where, you should first know what you want it to do for you. Keep in mind that plants have many important functions in addition to their natural beauty. Here are some common uses.

Shade—Usually thought of primarily as a tree to sit under or park a car under. You can also "air-condition" your house by planting trees to block the sun from the roof, walls and glass areas. A deciduous tree drops its leaves in winter, allowing sun to enter when it is appreciated most. Low-branching trees or tall shrubs can ward off devastating afternoon sun.

Dwarf red-leaf barberry, Chinese holly and juniper form an impenetrable barrier.

A majestic oak shades the roof and front of this Texas home.

Thick growth behind a concrete block wall gives privacy, breaks the wind and reduces traffic noise.

Flowering dogwood, Southern Indian azaleas and slash pines characterize this typically southern landscape scene.

Red oleander serves multiple purposes: privacy, screening, wind break and property barrier.

Herb border makes good use of a narrow planting bed.

Privacy—If the space is narrow, a clipped hedge may be necessary. However, careful selection can change a hedge into a screen of natural growth that requires less care. If privacy from a specific point, such as a neighbor's window, is the problem, a well-placed shrub or tree can often take care of it.

Screening—Mask a service area, blot out a bad view or hide a telephone pole with planting. Why look at a trailer or a meter or a pile of firewood when they can be hidden with plants?

Wind Break—Most properties do not have room for several rows of large trees, but sometimes an undesirable prevailing or seasonal wind can be modified with heavy planting. Large shrubs or small trees that extend above a solid fence are effective in breaking a wind down into a gentle breeze.

Traffic Barrier—Tough plants can encourage dogs, children and adults to walk where you want them, rather than cutting across lawn and planting beds. If the situation is severe, don't hesitate to use prickly or thorny plants.

Carpet—Lawn or lawn substitutes can provide a soft, safe, cool area to play or sit, and they look good at the same time. Selecting the right kind of lawn is just as important as picking out a shade tree.

Erosion, Mud, Dust and Fire Control—If you live on a hillside, erosion may be your first concern. Ground covers and shrub covers help cool the soil and the surrounding air. They also reduce glare.

Noise Reduction—The more plantings to absorb the sound, the quieter your garden will be. However, to block out the noise from a busy street or highway would take a forest several hundred feet thick, so don't expect a single row to be of much help.

Food and Flowers—You can grow cut flowers, herbs and vegetables in the traditional patch; or you can mix some effectively with ornamental shrubs. Many fruits look good enough to deserve a place anywhere in the garden.

Once you've decided what a plant is supposed to do, then you can think of what size it should be and what exposure and other conditions it will be subjected to.

CLIMATE ZONES

The South is a vast and diverse region. The many climate zones include arid plains to the west, the northerly forested mountains, the sub-tropical Gulf states and the eastern shore line from Virginia all the way down to the tropical tip of Florida.

Based on temperatures alone, they cover areas that never see frost to those that reach 0F every winter. The United States Department of Agriculture (USDA) map is helpful as a general guide. However, there can be wide variation within a few square miles. A south-facing hillside lot can easily be as much as 10° warmer in winter than one on the valley floor a stone's throw away. There are even warm and cold pockets within an individual yard. Extreme shifts in temperature are common in some areas, with frost at night followed by an 80F day.

The plants in the following lists should perform satisfactorily within their designated climate zones. Extreme conditions such as low-lying air drainage basins, high-altitude mountain areas, sites within the salt spray of the ocean and favored tropical spots call for careful checking of what plants thrive locally. You may want to find out if the local Cooperative Extension Service has developed a climate map for your state that breaks down the USDA zones into more detailed sub-zones.

EXPOSURE

There are few plants that will survive in all degrees of sunlight from deep shade to reflected sun. Most

PLANT HARDINESS ZONE MAP

Approximate Range of Average Annual Minimum Temperatures

ZONE 6	−10F to 0F (−24C to −18C)	
ZONE 7	0F to 10F (−18C to −12C)	
ZONE 8	10F to 20F (−12C to −7C)	
ZONE 9	20F to 30F (−7C to −1C)	
ZONE 10	30F to 40F (−1C to 5C)	

Based on information from the United States Department of Agriculture

have a definite requirement that must be satisfied. For simplicity, the four basic wall exposures of your house are a good guide.

The north side—*N*—is the coolest and shadiest. It gets direct sun only in the early morning and late afternoon for a short time during the longest summer days.

The east side—*E*—gets the morning sun, but is protected from the afternoon sun when temperatures are high. This is not the same as the filtered sunlight of a lath-covered porch or under a tree, but similar.

The south side—*S*—gets the most sun and is comparable to full sun out in the open. However, with a normal 3-foot overhang, the house wall is shaded during the hottest months because the sun angle is higher. During the winter, the wall is exposed to more sun because of the lower angle. The overhang also affords some frost protection during cold nights.

The west side—*W*—is probably the most difficult exposure to select plants for. It is cool in the morning and hot in the afternoon. In some areas, the reflected heat is enough to cook the leaves of many plants. Keeping an air space between the wall and the plant is advisable.

Obviously, all plants aren't planted directly against a wall and all houses aren't oriented exactly north and south. Another way to determine exposure is to equate *N* with full shade, *E* with partial shade, *S* with full sun and *W* with reflected sun. Nearby fences, neighbors' houses, trees, large shrubs and mountains may modify the amount of sun a plant will receive. Also, as your own trees reach maturity, a sunny spot may become a shady one.

Plants sometimes can adapt to more or less sunlight than is considered typical for the species. However, if *E* and *N* are indicated as the best exposures for a plant, this means it requires a shady situation. Trying to grow it against a west wall in a hot climate dooms it to failure. Likewise, a sun-loving plant listed as *S* and *W* will most likely dwindle away in the shade.

Caution: If a sun-loving plant is grown under partial shade conditions in the nursery, it may suffer if immediately planted in the sun. Try to duplicate the exposure it has been accustomed to or plant it during a cool season.

Provide protection for tender-barked trees such as dogwood, maple and pecan in hot climates until there is enough foliage to shade the trunk. Use a commercial product such as Spiral Wrap or TreeGARD, wrapping the trunk from the base of the tree to just below the lowest branches. This also offers some protection from dehydration, frost, rabbits, mice and boring insects. Try to avoid setting out any plant during a hot spell. Cool, overcast days are best for planting.

SELECTING PLANTS

The plants in these lists are easy to grow and will give consistent results in your landscape. They will tolerate a wide range of conditions and thrive under normal garden situations when given reasonable care.

The general organization of the lists is by type and expected approximate size at *young maturity.* This may take as little as one or two years for rapid growers, 5 to 10 years for most, and 20 years or longer for slow-growing trees.

Older plants may eventually exceed the listed size, especially when grown under ideal conditions. I've seen English boxwoods 10 feet high, camellias that have attained tree size, and a magnificent crape myrtle that was measured at 49 feet. But I still would not plant them with that height in mind.

Some plants can be used in a smaller space because they're slow-growing or narrow, and can be kept under control with a minimum amount of pruning. Varieties termed *compact* or *dwarf* will stay smaller—but not forever.

There is a certain amount of overlapping. If you're looking for a low shrub, you might also refer to medium shrubs, shrub covers and accents. Likewise, you might find a large tree to suit your needs also listed under medium trees or narrow-upright trees.

Arrangement is in order of tolerance to cold. This is true of most of the plant lists throughout the book. If you live in a severe climate, start at the top of the list first. Tender plants, and most of those that thrive in a mild climate, are at the bottom of the lists. The fascinating and unique tropical plants that can be grown only in Zone 10 and the warmest parts of Zone 9 are included in a special list on pages 118 through 121.

COMPATIBILIY

If you're consistent in your preferences, most of the plants you select will look good together. If you like pines, you probably also like junipers, nandina and podocarpus. The resulting combination is harmonious. If you happen to like everything, you may be tempted to use too many dif-

Landscape architect Eldon Russell created this subtle combination of Asiatic jasmine, liriope and Southern Indian azaleas.

FLOWERING TREES

Silk Tree/Mimosa, see page 102.

Purple-leaf Plum, see page 100.

Fringe Tree, see page 100.

Chinese Flame Tree, see page 102.

FLOWERING TREES

Many trees not only have handsome foliage and a pleasing shape, but the added bonus of flowers. These display especially dramatic blossoms. The plants below are arranged according to hardiness, with the most cold-tolerant at the top, and the most sensitive to cold at the bottom.

Fringe tree
Purple-leaf plum
Bradford pear
Dogwood
Goldenrain tree
Eastern redbud
Flowering cherry
Silk tree/Mimosa
Saucer magnolia
Southern magnolia
Chinese flame tree
Chinaberry/Pride of India
Texas mountain laurel
Crape myrtle
Jerusalem thorn
Cajeput/Punk tree
Umbrella tree
Royal poinciana

ferent kinds and end up with a hodge-podge of textures, forms and colors. A design based on simplicity, repetition and restraint is usually more pleasing than an overly complex one.

Horticulturally, the plants in the lists are quite compatible when placed according to their exposure requirements. They should grow together satisfactorily in normal soil when given similar care and watering. As you become further acquainted with their specific needs, you'll get to know that a certain one responds to more water, or that another needs an extra application of fertilizer once in a while.

You can assume the plants in the lists require regular amounts of rainfall and watering unless stated otherwise. Once a plant is well established and has a deep root system, it won't curl up and die if there's a temporary drought or if you miss a watering. Those especially able to withstand dryness are noted to be drought tolerant. If you live in an area where water conservation is a consideration, Chapter 14 discusses the subject in detail.

Outstanding features, special uses, important characteristics and additional species and varieties are listed in the right-hand column of the lists. All plants are evergreen unless termed deciduous. Especially slow or fast growers are indicated—all others have moderate growth rates. If good drainage or special soil conditions are required, these are so noted under *Culture*.

Now you're ready to use these lists of "old reliables" and pick those that appeal most to you.

MINIMUM TEMPERATURE

The first thing you need to know about a plant is whether or not it can survive the lowest temperatures likely to occur with some frequency in your area. If you're a newcomer, ask a local nurseryman or weather station expert what kind of temperatures can be expected at your site. The *approximate* sustained minimum temperature that a plant will tolerate is indicated by reference to zones corresponding to the USDA map on page 87. For convenience, zone adaptations as well as best exposure and culture are given for each plant.

OTHER FACTORS

If minimum temperature were the only factor, then *all* the plants could be used in Zone 10, all those withstanding 20F (−7C) could be used in Zones 9 and 10, and so on. This is only partially true. Some plants actually need *winter chilling* and will lose vigor in too warm a zone. There are also other climatic conditions that affect how well a plant will perform. Heat, wind, rainfall, humidity, salt-spray, fog and air quality are important. Where a plant is known to have requirements beyond minimum temperature or special tolerance, this is so noted.

USING THE LISTS

The best way to start is to go to a local nursery to familiarize yourself with the plants that are available. They're probably the best suited for your specific area. Take a drive and record those plants growing nearby that you recognize and like.

Now, refer to the lists and make a tentative selection based on your planting design. Try to stick with plants recommended for your zone or colder. If you're in a borderline area, you may want to try a few less hardy ones if they appeal to you. Double check that you've placed them all in the proper exposure.

Use the lists properly and you can avoid almost all the gardening problems that you see around your neighborhood. There is no need for you to make common mistakes such as planting a wide-spreading shrub close to a sidewalk, a large shrub in front of a view window or a giant tree where it will rip up paving and drop leaves all over the yard. The right plant in the right place—the first time—is what you're after.

Study the landscape plans at the end of Chapter 7 before deciding on your choices. Pay special attention to the plans based on the climate that's closest to your own. Obviously, you can't use all the plants shown on the plans—or even want to. But you should find at least several to your liking and be able to get the feel for proper use and spacing.

PLANT NAMES

Plants usually have two scientific or Latin names. They may look difficult to pronounce, but you can avoid costly mistakes if you are careful about them. The first word is the *genus* name. The second is the name of the *species*. A third name, which is not always included, is the *variety* or *cultivar* name. Cultivars are shown in quotes. Each scientific name designates only one type of plant, while the same common name can be applied to many different plants. You should be sure that both or all three names of a plant are exactly what you want.

To complicate matters, botanists are constantly reclassifying plants and changing the names back and forth. Often a nursery will continue to list a plant by its former name, so be prepared to run into some that have two or more scientific names. Note one major discrepancy: *Ligustrum lucidum*, glossy privet, with large, thin leaves, is often sold in the South as *Ligustrum japonicum*, Japanese privet, which has smaller and thicker leaves.

Ligustrum japonicum, left. *L. lucidum*, right.

TRUNKS AND SPANISH MOSS

It is not often a major factor in the selection of a tree, but there's no denying the distinctive beauty of certain trunks. Some, like the white birch, American sycamore and cajeput tree, are vertical accents of white in the landscape. Others, such as the slash pine, river birch, tulip tree and Southern live oak, have intriguing textures and a feeling of age. My favorite is the smooth bark of the crape myrtle that can be appreciated both with the eyes and with the fingers.

Spanish moss, *Tillandsia usneoides,* often enhances old branches of Southern live oak and other trees along the Gulf and where it is hot and humid. Rather than remove it, allow it to develop into hanging garlands of filmy gray for a uniquely southern effect.

Filmy garlands of Spanish moss decorate the branches of older Southern live oak and other trees in hot, humid areas of the South.

Distinctive mottled trunk of the American sycamore adds interest to the landscape.

Smooth, shiny bark of the crape myrtle is delightful to touch.

Striking trunk of the white birch makes a strong vertical accent in the garden.

LOW SHRUBS—18 inches to 3 feet

For small planting areas, foreground planting and in front of low windows. Space 2 to 4 feet apart. Also see Shrub Covers.

Common Name *Scientific Name*	Climate Zones Best Exposure/Culture	Description/Remarks Similar Species & Varieties
Dwarf Red-leaf Barberry *Berberis thunbergii* *'Crimson Pygmy'*	Zones 4-9 E, S, W. Withstands heat and some dryness. Best in well-drained soil with regular watering.	Deciduous. Small, spiny leaves with outstanding red color in sun. Slow, compact growth. *B. t. atropurpurea* similar, grows 4' to 6'.
Gold Coast Juniper *Juniperus chinensis* *'Gold Coast'*	Zones 4-10 E, S, W. Widely adapted. Subject to bagworms and red spider mites.	Yellow-tipped foliage makes good color contrast. Compact, does not sprawl. *J. c. 'Parsonii'*, similar growth habit, grayish green foliage. Photo page 93.
Dwarf Japanese Holly *Ilex crenata* varieties	Zones 6-9 N, E. More sun okay where cool. Subject to nematodes in sandy soil.	Small, shiny leaves, not prickly. Dense, compact growth. Blue-black berries on female plants. *'Helleri'*, *'Stokes'* and *'Convexa'* *('Bullata')* are most common varieties, with *'Helleri'* holly being the smallest. Can be clipped to limit size.
Dwarf Chinese Holly *Ilex cornuta 'Rotunda'*	Zones 6-10 N, E, S. Widely adapted. Salt tolerant.	Glossy, dark green, prickly holly foliage makes good barrier. Slow, thick growth; no berries. *I. c. 'Carissa'*, similar except leaves have smooth margins with single spine on tip. Photo page 93.
Dwarf Pyracantha *Pyracantha* variety	Zones 6-10 E, S, W. Widely adapted.	Small leaves, red berries in fall. *'Red Elf'* and *'Tiny Tim'* most common.
Satsuki Azalea *Rhododendron* hybrids	Zones 7-9 N, E. Well-drained acid soil and moisture. Mulch, do not cultivate.	Small leaves. Gumpo types have especially nice shiny foliage. Large, single flowers, bloom in early summer; white, pink, orange-red, red, striped and flecked. Kurume azaleas are similar, can be kept low, but will eventually reach 4' or more.
Dwarf Yaupon *Ilex vomitoria 'Nana'*	Zones 7-10 N, E, S. Widely adapted. Salt tolerant.	Small, shiny leaves; usually no berries. Compact, mounding form, excellent low hedge. *I. v. 'Stokes'* is even more compact. Photo page 93.
Box-leaf Euonymus *Euonymus japonica* *'Microphylla'*	Zones 7-10 S, W. Tolerates heat. Subject to scale and mildew. Needs good soil drainage.	Small, shiny, dark green leaves. Compact growth, makes good clipped hedge. Variegated form available. *E. japonica* has larger leaves, usually variegated, grows 6' to 8'.
Texas Ranger *Leucophyllum frutescens* *'Compacta'*	Zones 8-10 S, W. Heat and drought tolerant. Sandy soil best. Do not overwater in clay soils.	Small, silvery gray leaves; rose-purple flowers. *L. frutescens* grows to 6', tends to sprawl.
India Hawthorn *Raphiolepis indica*	Zones 7-10 E, S. Best in a cool location. Salt tolerant.	Leathery, dark green leaves. Clean appearance. Named varieties available with white to deep pink flowers in early spring, compact to open growth. Photo page 93.
Japanese Boxwood *Buxus microphylla* *japonica*	Zones 7-10 Poor winter foliage in Zone 7. N, E, S, W. Withstands heat and alkaline soil better than English boxwood.	Small, yellowish green leaves, usually with indented tip. Excellent low hedge, or unclipped for natural form. Harland boxwood, *B. harlandi*, is hardier to cold and more compact. Photo page 93.
Wheeler's Dwarf Tobira *Pittosporum tobira* *'Wheeler's Dwarf'*	Zones 8-10 N, E. More sun okay where cool. Subject to iron chlorosis.	Shiny, dark green leaves. Attractive texture; tailored and elegant. Slow growth, good in mass plantings. *P. tobira* has more open growth with creamy white fragrant flowers in spring, grows to 6' or more.

Dwarf Yaupon

India Hawthorn

Parson's Juniper

Dwarf Chinese Holly

Japanese Boxwood

Gold Coast Juniper

MEDIUM SHRUBS—3 to 6 feet
Consider these before using large shrubs that may require constant cutting back. Space 4 to 5 feet apart.

Common Name *Scientific Name*	Climate Zones Best Exposure/Culture	Description/Remarks Similar Species & Varieties
Rose *Rosa* varieties	Zones 3-9 E, S, W. Light shade okay in hot areas. Responds to fertilizer and water. Subject to aphids and mildew.	Deciduous. Grown for flowers rather than for foliage or form. Grandifloras and floribundas fit into landscape better than hybrid teas. Annual pruning necessary.
Spirea *Spiraea vanhouttei*	Zones 4-9 E, S, W. Widely adapted.	Deciduous. Blue-green leaves, arching branches. Plentiful clusters of white flowers in late spring. Dwarf red spirea *S. bumalda 'Anthony Waterer'* grow 2 to 3 feet tall.
Pfitzer Juniper *Juniperus chinensis* *'Pfitzerana'*	Zones 5-10 E, S, W. Widely adapted. Subject to bagworms and red spider mites.	Feathery, gray-green foliage; wide, arching growth. Numerous varieties. *'Mint Julep'* is bright green; semi-upright vase shape. *'Armstrongi'* has medium-green foliage, not as wide. *'Nick's'* is gray-green, more compact. Photo page 95.
English Boxwood *Buxus sempervirens*	Zones 5-9 N, E. Needs cool location, slightly acid soil.	Bright green, pointed leaves. Slow growth to eventual large, rounded form unless clipped. True dwarf Common Boxwood, *B. s. 'Suffruticosa'*, easily kept to 3 feet or less. Photos pages 147, 156.
Mugo Pine *Pinus mugo*	Zones 5-8 E, S, W. Slightly acid, well-drained soil with iron. Best where cool. Subject to pine tip moth.	Dark green needles. Slow, compact growth, will stay in container for years. Good way to repeat feeling of pines in smaller form. Photo page 95.
Dwarf Burford Holly *Ilex cornuta* *'Burfordii Nana'*	Zones 6-10 N, E. More sun okay where cool.	Glossy bright green leaves; red berries on female plants. Neat and refined appearance. Use regular Burford holly where large shrub is desired. Photo page 95.
Variegated Chinese Privet *Ligustrum sinense* *'Variegata'*	Zones 7-10 E, S, W. Widely adapted.	Semi-deciduous below 20F (−7C). Small green and white leaves. Usually clipped to control shape and size. Good hedge plant.
Goucher Abelia *Abelia 'Edward Goucher'*	Zones 7-10 E, S, W. Widely adapted.	Semi-deciduous below 20F (−7C). Small, shiny leaves, bronze with cold. Arching habit; small lavender flowers. Glossy abelia, *A. grandiflora*, has pinkish white flowers; hardier and larger. Photo page 95.
Sandankwa Viburnum *Viburnum suspensum*	Zones 8-10 N, E, S. Tolerates clay soil. Subject to aphids.	Large, oval, glossy green leaves; small white flowers marginally fragrant. Dense foliage, makes good screen or hedge. *V. tinus* is taller and narrower, best in full sun. Photo page 67.
Southern Indian Azalea *Rhododendron* hybrids	Zones 8-10 E. Well-drained acid soil. Protect from strong winds. Mulch, do not cultivate. Watch for lace bugs.	Nice green foliage; spectacular flowers in vivid colors. Growth habit and size differ with variety, most will surpass 6 feet with age. Kaempferi and Glenn Dale types are similar size, hardier north. Rhododendrons are large shrubs with large leaves and flowers; grow best in Zones 6-8. Photo pages 95, 185.
Variegated Tobira *Pittosporum tobira* *'Variegata'*	Zones 8-10 N, E. More sun okay where cool.	Green and white foliage; fragrant, small, creamy-white flowers. Has nice natural form or can be clipped.
Aralia *Fatsia japonica* *(Aralia sieboldii)*	Zones 8-10 N, E. Tolerates heavy shade. Rich, moist soil best. Subject to scale and aphids.	Large, tropical, dark green leaves. Cut back to renew when it gets leggy. Good atrium and container plant. Photo page 95.

Glossy Abelia

Aralia

Dwarf Burford Holly

Mugo Pine

Mint Julep Juniper

Southern Indian Azalea

LARGE SHRUBS—6 to 15 feet

Place carefully with ultimate size in mind. Plant away from walls and paving. Space 6 to 10 feet apart. Regular pruning can limit growth.

Common Name *Scientific Name*	Climate Zones Best Exposure/Culture	Description/Remarks Similar Species & Varieties
Pyracantha *Pyracantha coccinea*	Zones 5-10 E, S, W. Best on dry side. Needs iron. Subject to fireblight and red spider mites.	Small, dark green leaves; white flowers in spring; orange or red-orange berries in fall. Rangy and thorny. Good espalier. Many varieties. *P. koidzumii* has red berries, hardy to Zone 8. Photo page 156.
Silverberry *Elaeagnus pungens*	Zones 6-10 E, S, W. Heat, salt and drought tolerant.	Grayish green leaves with brownish overtones. Spiny stems. Sprawling habit but can be clipped or espaliered. Variegated types popular. *E. philippinensis* is graceful and weeping, hardy in Zones 9-10. Photo page 97.
Chinese Holly *Ilex cornuta*	Zones 6-10 N, E, S. Some foliage burn in hot sun. Subject to tea scale.	Prickly, holly leaves; red berries on female plants. Varieties include 'Burfordii', 'Dazzler' and 'Willow-leaf'. See low and medium shrubs for smaller forms.
Camellia *Camellia japonica*	Zones 7-10 E. Flower buds may freeze in Zone 7. Will grow N exposure, but flowers limited. Well-drained acid soil. Mulch, do not cultivate. Subject to petal blight.	Large, glossy, dark green leaves. Striking, white, pink, red and variegated flowers October to May, depending on variety. Good container plant. *C. sasanqua,* smaller leaves; single flowers in fall are less subject to frost; willowy growth easily trained as espalier. Photo page 97.
Fraser Photinia *Photinia fraseri*	Zones 7-10 E, S, W. Takes heat well. Good mildew resistance. Subject to fireblight.	Reddish spring and fall color; white flowers in spring. Also grown as small tree and espalier. *P. glabra,* similar; *P. serrulata,* larger; both subject to mildew. Photo page 97.
Ternstroemia (Cleyera) *Ternstroemia japonica*	Zones 7-10 N, E. Well-drained acid soil. Mulch, do not cultivate.	Oval, polished leaves with bronzy green new growth; inconspicuous fragrant flowers in early summer. Slow-growing, elegant foliage shrub. Plant grown as *Cleyera japonica* throughout the South appears to actually be ternstroemia. Cleyera is similar, except it grows taller, has larger leaves, flowers in the fall. Photo page 97.
Oleander *Nerium oleander*	Zones 8-10 E, S, W. Use 'Hardy Red' in coldest areas. Likes heat. Drought tolerant. Tolerates salt and alkaline soil.	Narrow, dark green leaves; white, pink, yellow and red flowers throughout summer. All parts are poisonous. Sometimes grown as a small tree. 'Mrs. Roeding' and 'Petite' series are medium shrubs. Photos pages 86, 187.
Japanese Privet *Ligustrum japonicum*	Zones 8-10 N, E, S, W. Widely adapted. Salt tolerant.	Glossy, thick, dark green leaves; white flowers in late spring. Excellent hedge, or prune out for small, multi-trunk tree effect. *L. j.* 'Texanum' is more compact, can be kept under 6 feet. 'Silver Star' is variegated form. 'Suwannee River' very compact. Photos pages 66, 90, 181.
Compact Carolina Laurel Cherry *Prunus caroliniana* variety	Zones 7-10 E, S, W. Tough, but responds to good care.	Shiny, light green leaves. Small, creamy-white flowers, inedible black "cherries." 'Compacta' and 'Bright-'n-Tight' make good screens or hedges. *P. caroliniana* becomes a small tree.
Glossy Privet *Ligustrum lucidum*	Zones 8-10 N, E, S, W. Widely adapted. Tolerates dryness.	Large, thin, medium green leaves. Odor of white flowers objectionable to some. Sprouts from base for tall screen or hedge. Can be pruned out to make a small tree. Not as attractive as Japanese privet, but fast and tough. Photo page 97.
Wax Myrtle *Myrica cerifera*	Zones 7-10 E, S, W. Tolerates sandy soils and salt spray. Wet or dry okay.	Narrow, green leaves; small flowers and berries. Tough screen or wide hedge. Prune to reveal silver-gray trunks, and use as a small tree. Photo page 97.

Silverberry

Sasanqua Camellia 'Yuletide'

Ternstroemia (Cleyera)

Glossy Privet

Wax Myrtle

Fraser Photinia

UPRIGHT SHRUBS—for narrow places

Most shrubs grow about as wide as they do high. Here are some that can be kept narrow with a minimum of effort.

Common Name *Scientific Name*	Climate Zones Best Exposure/Culture/Height	Description/Remarks Similar Species & Varieties
Oregon Grape *Mahonia aquifolium*	Zones 5-8 N, E. More sun okay where cool. Slightly acid soil best. Watch for looper caterpillar. Height: 4' to 6'	Holly-like, leathery leaves on vertical stalks, turn purplish red in cold. Yellow flowers in spring, blue-black, grape-like fruit. 'Compacta' makes good shrub cover at 2'. *M. beali* has broad, gray-green leaves, Zones 7-9. *M. fortunei* has fern-like leaves, needs shade, Zones 8-9. Photo page 99.
Twisted/Hollywood Juniper *Juniperus chinensis* 'Torulosa' (J.c 'Kaizuka')	Zones 5-10 E, S, W. Widely adapted. Height: 10' to tree	Dark green foliage, richest in coastal areas. Striking, irregular shape. Grows to tree size with age, but can be held below 10' with pruning. Many other upright forms of junipers available. Photo page 99.
Wintergreen Barberry *Berberis julianae*	Zones 6-10 E, S, W. Widely adapted. Height: 4' to 6'	Semi-evergreen in coldest areas. Large, dark green leaves; red fall color. Small, yellow flowers in spring. Makes a thorny barrier. *B. julianae* 'Nana' is a dwarf form.
Heavenly Bamboo *Nandina domestica*	Zones 6-10 N, E, S. Loses leaves in cold winters. Slightly acid soil, plus iron and moisture. Height: 3' to 6'	Pinkish, light green, ferny foliage; red fall color. White flowers, red berries on older plants. Multiple stems, naturally narrow. 'Compacta' is lower and thicker growing. See shrub covers for 'Harbour Dwarf.'
Lily-of-the-Valley Shrub *Pieris japonica*	Zones 6-9 N, E. Well-drained acid soil, moisture. Height: 4' to 6'	Dark green, glossy leaves; bronze-pink new growth. Drooping panicles of tiny white flowers in spring. Slow growth. Photo page 99.
Wilson Holly *Ilex altaclarensis* 'Wilsonii'	Zones 7-10 N, E. More sun okay where cool. Height: 8' and more	Large, shiny, spiny, dark green leaves; red berries in winter on female plants. Polished and neat. Usually with several main upright branches; can also be trained as a small tree.
Yew Pine/Japanese Yew *Podocarpus macrophyllus*	Zones 7-10 N, E, S. Well-drained, slightly acid soil. Height: 6' to 12' and more	Narrow, dark green leaves. Slowly becomes a tree if not pruned. Good against chain link. *P. m. maki*, slower, denser growth; shorter leaves not as dark green. Both make handsome container plants. Photo page 99.
Holly-leaf Osmanthus *Osmanthus heterophyllus*	Zones 7-10 N, E, S. Tolerates clay soil. Height: 3' to 8'	Holly-like, dark green leaves; small, fragrant flowers. Size depends on variety. 'Gulftide' to 8', 'Rotundifolius' to 5', 'Variegatus' slow and compact to 3' with creamy-white leaf edges. Good barrier screens and hedges. Photo page 99.
Golden Bamboo *Phyllostachys aurea*	Zones 7-10 E, S, W. Height: 10' and more	Light green, narrow leaves. Slow to start, then grows rapidly. Remove old canes to control height. Spreads if roots aren't controlled. Photo page 99.
Japanese Aucuba *Aucuba japonica*	Zones 7-10 N, E. Tolerates heavy shade. Well-drained, rich soil best. Height: 4' to 6'	Large, toothed, dark green leaves. Bright red berries on female plants. Fairly slow growing, can be kept small. Many varieties, including dwarf, narrow-leaved and variegated. Photo page 99.
Curlyleaf Ligustrum *Ligustrum japonicum* 'Rotundifolium'	Zones 8-10 N, E. Height: 4' to 5'	Twisted, thick, dark green leaves bunched closely together. Slow growing. Often sold as *L. j.* 'Coriaceum'.
Sweet Viburnum *Viburnum odoratissimum*	Zones 8-10 E, S. Subject to aphids. Height: 6' to 10'	Large, long, bright green, "varnished" leaves. Fragrant flowers in late spring followed by small red to black berries. *V. japonicum* has rounder, less glossy leaves, grows broader. Not as choice a plant. The name, *V. macrophylla*, is sometimes applied to Sweet Viburnum, but is actually a synonym for *V. japonicum*.

Lily-of-the-Valley Shrub

Yew Pine

Twisted Juniper

Japanese Aucuba

Golden Bamboo

Holly-leaf Osmanthus

Mahonia Beali

SMALL TREES—10 to 20 feet

Some are merely large shrubs trained into trees. Others will eventually grow more than 20 feet tall unless pruned. Use them where you want something taller than a shrub, but where space is limited.

Common Name *Scientific Name*	Climate Zones/Culture	Description/Remarks Similar Species & Varieties
Fringe Tree *Chionanthus virginicus*	Zones 4-9 Partial shade where hot. Well-drained acid soil.	Deciduous. Magnificent, airy, greenish white flowers cover tree in late spring. Yellow fall color. Photo page 101.
Purple-leaf Plum *Prunus cerasifera* *'Atropurpurea'*	Zones 5-10 Okay in lawn, but not constant wetness.	Deciduous. Several varieties with purple foliage; white or pink flowers in spring. Small plums a nuisance on paving. Photo page 131.
Flowering Cherry *Prunus serrulata*	Zones 5-8 Well-drained soil.	Deciduous. Many varieties with various growth habits; white to deep pink flowers in spring. *'Kwanzan'*, outstanding with large, double, rosy-pink flowers.
Flowering Dogwood *Cornus florida*	Zones 5-9 Partial shade where hot. Well-drained acid soil with moisture. Subject to fungus diseases and canker.	Deciduous. Breathtaking white or pink flowers in spring. Scarlet berries with red fall color. Japanese Dogwood, *C. kousa*, blooms early summer, has large ornamental fruit. Photo page 100.
Japanese Black Pine *Pinus thunbergiana*	Zones 7-10 Top kill from early fall freezes in Zones 5 and 6. Widely adapted.	Rich, dark green needles. Can be kept small indefinitely by pinching out new growth in spring. Most attractive as an irregular, picturesque specimen. Photo page 101.
Japanese Maple *Acer palmatum*	Zones 6-9 Partial shade with moisture. Protect from hot, dry winds.	Deciduous. Lobed leaves, bright green to purple, finely cut in some varieties. Red fall color. Slow and well-behaved.
Saucer Magnolia *Magnolia soulangiana*	Zones 6-9 Acid soil with coolness and moisture.	Deciduous. Large, cup-shaped flowers, white to purple, appear before large leaves in late spring. Often grown as a large shrub.
Yaupon *Ilex vomitoria*	Zones 7-10 Tolerates heat, salt and alkaline soils.	Small, shiny leaves; red berries in fall on female plants. Prune out for multi-trunk tree or grow as a large shrub. Photo page 101.
Crape Myrtle *Lagerstroemia indica*	Zones 7-10 Tolerates dryness. Full sun and good air drainage minimizes mildew; Indian Tribe series have good resistance.	Deciduous. Small leaves, bronzy in spring and orange-red fall color. Profusion of large white, pink, red, lavender or purple flowers in late summer. Beautiful bark can be featured by pruning as a multi-trunk tree. Dwarf varieties used as medium shrubs. Photo page 101.
Texas Mountain Laurel *Sophora secundiflora*	Zones 8-10 Tolerates hot sun and alkaline soil if well drained.	Dark green, clean foliage. Fragrant, blue flowers in spring. Best pruned out as a multi-trunk tree. Slow growth and difficult to transplant from wild. Photo page 100.
Loquat *Eriobotrya japonica*	Zones 8-10 Foliage will sunburn in very hot areas. Subject to fireblight.	Large, dark green leaves. Yellow, edible fruit develops only when winter flowers not killed by frost. Single- or multi-trunk tree, espalier or lush background shrub. Photo page 162.
Pineapple Guava *Feijoa sellowiana*	Zones 8-10 Withstands dryness well.	Gray-green leaves; tan bark, small red flowers. Best as a multi-trunk specimen or large shrub. *'Coolidge'* has good fruit and is self-fertile.

Texas Mountain Laurel

Fringe Tree

Japanese Black Pine

Flowering Dogwood

Crape Myrtle

Yaupon

MEDIUM TREES—20 to 30 feet

In time, most of the following will grow taller than 30 feet in a favorable climate. However, they can serve in a normal-sized yard for many years without taking over if properly pruned. Keep 10 feet or more away from house walls.

Common Name *Scientific Name*	Climate Zones/Culture	Description/Remarks Similar Species & Varieties
River Birch/Red Birch *Betula nigra*	Zones 2-9 Needs moisture. Okay in lawn. Tolerates poor drainage.	Deciduous. Graceful, weeping foliage; pinkish brown flaking bark. Usually branches out low to ground into several trunks. European white birch, *B. pendula,* has striking white bark, not as tolerant of heat; subject to borers. Photo page 103.
Fruitless Mulberry *Morus alba* variety	Zones 4-10 Withstands heat, alkaline soil and dryness.	Deciduous. Large, glossy, dark green leaves. Fast grower. Classic umbrella shade tree. Heavy shade and surface roots make gardening near it difficult. Photo page 17.
Red Maple *Acer rubrum*	Zones 4-9 Appreciates moisture. Tolerates poor drainage.	Deciduous. Typical maple leaves with red petioles. Red flowers in early spring. Yellow and red fall color. Fast growth to 30' and more. Photo page 103.
Eastern Redbud *Cercis canadensis*	Zones 5-9 Rich, well-drained soil with moisture best, but adaptable.	Deciduous. Heart-shaped leaves; rose-purple flowers along the branches in early spring. 'Alba' has white flowers. Yellow fall color. Photo page 103.
Silk Tree/Mimosa *Albizia julibrissin*	Zones 6-9 Best in heat with ample water, but will survive anywhere. Subject to mimosa webworm and wilt.	Deciduous. Ferny foliage; pink flowers in summer. Slow to start, then fast. Low, spreading shape; also multi-trunk. Drops leaves, flowers and pods; suffers wind and ice storm damage.
Evergreen Elm *Ulmus parvifolia* *(U.p. 'sempervirens')*	Zones 6-10 Widely adapted. Tolerates alkaline soils and dryness. Caterpillars like it. Resistant to Dutch Elm diseases.	Semi-evergreen in warm climate. Small, shiny, bright green leaves. Weeping habit requires careful pruning. 'Brea' and 'Drake' are more upright. Photo page 103.
Chinese Flame Tree *Koelreuteria bipinnata* *(K. integrifoliola)*	Zones 7-10 Tolerates alkaline soils and dryness.	Deciduous. Dark green leaves. Clusters of yellow flowers in summer, followed by showy pinkish capsules. Goldenrain tree, *K. paniculata,* is hardier to Zone 5, but not as ornamental. Photo page 103.
Cedar Elm *Ulmus crassifolia*	Zones 7-10 Tolerates alkaline clay soils and dryness. Okay in lawn.	Deciduous. Small, rough leaves; yellow fall color. Eventually a large tree but not wide spreading. Superior to Siberian Elm, *U. pumila,* where hardiness is not a factor.
Chinaberry/Pride of India *Melia azedarach*	Zones 8-10 Tolerates heat, alkaline soils and drought.	Deciduous. Dark green lacy foliage; lavender flowers in early summer; yellow berries are poisonous. Rapid growth. Brittle and dirty. Texas umbrella tree, *M. a. 'Umbraculifera',* is smaller, dome-shaped. Photo page 103.
Jerusalem Thorn *Parkinsonia aculeata*	Zones 8-10 Heat, salt and drought tolerant. Alkaline soil okay.	Deciduous. Sparse, pendulous foliage, with tiny leaves. Spiny branches; yellow flowers in spring and continuing. Not tailored, best for casual setting.
Chinese Tallow Tree *Sapium sebiferum*	Zones 8-10 Best in slightly acid soil with moisture.	Deciduous. Roundish leaves move in slightest breeze. Brilliant red, orange and yellow fall color. Round-headed; fast-growing. Photo page 103.

Eastern Redbud

Red Maple

Cedar Elm

River Birch

Texas Umbrella Tree

Chinese Tallow Tree

Chinese Flame Tree

Evergreen Elm

LARGE TREES—30 feet and over

Use these trees with caution. They require considerable room, cast a lot of shade and can drop enormous quantities of leaves when mature. Keep 15 feet or more away from house walls.

Common Name / *Scientific Name*	Climate Zones/Culture/Height	Description/Remarks / Similar Species & Varieties
Sugar Maple / *Acer saccharum*	Zones 4-8. Widely adapted. Height: 80' and more	Deciduous. Large, maple leaves. Yellow and red fall color. Fast growth. Silver maple, *A. saccharinum,* smaller to 50', fast growing and brittle. Photo page 105.
Weeping Willow / *Salix babylonica*	Zones 4-10. Best with some winter cold. Likes lots of water. Subject to borers and caterpillars. Height: 30' and more	Briefly deciduous. Narrow leaves, graceful weeping habit. Needs pruning for clearance beneath. Fast growth. Roots are invasive. Relatively short-lived. Photo page 105.
Cottonwood / *Populus deltoides*	Zones 5-10. Needs ample water for best growth. Subject to borers. Height: 60' to 100'	Deciduous. Large, triangular leaves; yellow fall color. Rapid growth, but brittle and relatively short-lived. Invasive roots. Male trees are cottonless. Several other species similar. Photo page 105.
Tulip Tree / *Liriodendron tulipifera*	Zones 5-10. Best in acid soil with moisture. Height: 60' to 100'	Deciduous. Large, light green leaves; yellow fall color. Greenish yellow flowers in spring; pretty but difficult to see high up on old trees. Pyramidal form. Photo page 105.
American Sycamore/Buttonwood / *Platanus occidentalis*	Zones 5-9. Widely adapted. Needs water. Subject to anthracnose fungus. Height: 60' to 80'	Deciduous. Large leaves; poor fall foliage appearance. Attractive peeling bark with creamy-white patches. Fast, upright growth. Photos pages 91, 179.
Red Oak / *Quercus shumardi*	Zones 5-9. Well-drained, alkaline soil. Height: 50' and more	Deciduous. Typical oak leaves; red and orange fall color. *Q. rubra* and *Q. coccinea,* also called red oak, are hardier to cold, prefer slightly acid soil. Photo page 105.
Pecan / *Carya illinoinensis*	Zones 6-9. Deep, well-drained soil best. Apply zinc sulphate where deficient. Okay in lawn. Tolerates heat. Height: 50' and more	Deciduous. Long, narrow leaflets. Plant locally adapted varieties for nuts. Good shade tree, but litters. Photo page 105.
Deodar Cedar / *Cedrus deodora*	Zones 7-10. Appreciates good soil and water, but accepts adverse situations. Height: 50' and more	Bluish green-gray needles. Fast growth to broad pyramid. Allow sweeping lower branches to remain for best effect. *C. atlantica glauca* is silvery-blue, can be trained as irregular specimen. Photo page 105.
Southern Magnolia / *Magnolia grandiflora*	Zones 7-10. Deep, rich soil with moisture. Apply Epsom salts to supply magnesium sulphate. Height: 60' and more	Large, lustrous, dark green leaves. White fragrant flowers 8" diameter in early summer. Red seedpods in fall. Slow to grow and requires care in transplanting. Broadly pyramidal; best when allowed to branch to the ground. *M. g. 'St. Mary'* is smaller, makes good small tree or espalier. Photos pages 130, 152.
Southern Live Oak / *Quercus virginiana*	Zones 7-10. Wide adaptation, but responds to warmth, good soil and ample water. Height: 60' and more	Smooth-edged, glossy leaves. Moderately slow, eventually reaching 60' with wide spread. Smaller in Texas and westward. Often garlanded with Spanish moss in Gulf states. Magnificent, long-lived tree. Photo page 91.

Cottonwood

Tulip Tree

Deodar Cedar

Weeping Willow

Red Oak

Sugar Maple

Pecan

105

NARROW, UPRIGHT TREES—for grouping, rows and windbreaks

Although some of these trees grow very tall, they can be used in almost any garden because of their narrow spread. Planting in groups or groves 10 to 20 feet apart will further limit lateral growth. Many make good windbreaks and privacy screens when planted in rows 6 to 10 feet apart.

Common Name *Scientific Name*	Climate Zones/Culture/Height	Description/Remarks Similar Species & Varieties
Lombardy Poplar *Populus nigra 'Italica'*	Zones 4-10 Widely adapted. Subject to borers and poplar canker. Height: 40' and more	Deciduous. Triangular, light green leaves; yellow fall color. Very fast columnar growth. Common windbreak and country road tree. Suckers and roots are invasive. Short-lived.
Ginkgo/Maidenhair Tree *Gingko biloba*	Zones 5-10 Okay in lawn. Height: 50' and more	Deciduous. Odd-shaped, light green leaves; yellow fall color. Slow growth; narrow in youth, old trees more spreading. Photo page 107.
Bradford Pear *Pyrus calleryana* *'Bradford'*	Zones 5-9 Okay in lawn. Resistant to fireblight. Height: 25' to 30'.	Deciduous. Shiny, dark green, oval leaves; yellow, orange, red fall color. White flowers in early spring. Small fruit inedible. Natural pyramidal habit. Good large espalier. *P. 'Aristocrat'* has rounder form. Sand pear, *P. pyrifolia,* more irregular, hardier to cold. Photo page 107.
American Sweet Gum *Liquidambar styraciflua*	Zones 5-10 Acid soil wih moisture best. Good lawn tree. Needs iron in alkaline soils. Height: 50' and more	Deciduous. Maple-like leaves; variable red, yellow, orange, purple fall color. Narrow pyramidal form. Round, spiny fruit can be a nuisance. Chinese sweet gum, *L. formosana,* more likely to develop good fall color in Deep South, not as tall. Photo page 107.
Tupelo/Pepperidge/Sour Gum *Nyssa sylvatica*	Zones 5-9 Tolerates wet soils; okay in lawn. Height: 30' to 50'	Deciduous. Dark green, glossy leaves; glowing red fall color. Moderately slow growth. Photo page 164.
Lusterleaf Holly *Ilex latifolia*	Zones 7-9 Partial shade best. Height: 15' to 50'	Large, shiny, dark green leaves with spiny edges. Yellow flowers; red berries in clusters. Use as tall screen or pyramidal tree. American holly, *I. opaca,* has similar uses. *'East Palatka'* very fast grower. *'Foster's No. 2'* good hybrid.
Bald Cypress *Taxodium distichum*	Zones 6-10 Acid soil with ample water; withstands swampy conditions. Height: 60' and more	Deciduous. Lacy foliage; new growth light green; bronzy fall color. Broad pyramidal form. Photo page 107.
Italian Cypress *Cupressus sempervirens* *'Glauca'*	Zones 7-10 Widely adapted. Tolerates dryness. Height: 40' and more	Dark, blue-green foliage. Narrow column. Can be sheared to keep smaller. Bold skyline silhouette. Plant 3' to 4' apart for windbreak. Photo page 107.
Common China Fir *Cunninghamia lanceolata*	Zones 7-9 Appreciates coolness. Height: 30' to 40'	Broad, spiny needles on thickly layered branches. Symmetrical cone shape, often with several trunks. *C. I. 'Glauca'* has blue-green foliage, is hardier to cold. Photo page 107.
Slash Pine *Pinus elliottii*	Zones 8-10 Acid soil with moisture. Subject to pine tip moth. Height: 50' and more	Long, dark green needles. Fast growth. Cuban pine, *P. Caribaea,* is similar, also called slash pine, less hardy to cold. Loblolly pine, *P. taeda,* similar, hardy to Zone 7. Photo page 84.
Australian Pine/River She-oak *Casuarina cunninghamiana*	Zones 9-10 Takes dry or wet soil, but not direct salt spray. Height: 50' and more	Long, needle-like "leaves." Graceful, hanging branches. Pine-like appearance. Good windbreak, hedge or grove tree. Minimal suckers from this species. *C. lepidophloia,* dense and attractive, but suckers badly; grafted trees highly desirable. *C. equisetifolia* is common ocean shore-line tree in Zone 10. Photo page 107.

Bald Cypress

Italian Cypress

Common China Fir

Ginkgo

American Sweet Gum

Bradford Pear

Australian Pine

107

GROUND COVERS

These are usually purchased as rooted cuttings, 50 to 100 per flat, or in bundles of divisions. Plant small ground covers 6 to 12 inches apart, larger types 12 to 24 inches apart.

Common Name *Scientific Name*	Climate Zones/Best Exposure Culture/Height	Description/Remarks Similar Species & Varieties
Japanese Spurge *Pachysandra terminalis*	Zones 4-8 N, E. Difficult in heat. Well-drained, acid soil with moisture. Height: 6" to 12"	Shiny, light to dark green leaves with serrated edges. Occasional, fragrant white flowers in summer. Neat-appearing with beautiful, uniform texture. Good under trees. Photo below.
Periwinkle *Vinca minor*	Zones 4-8 N, E. More sun okay where cool. Acid soil with moisture. Height: 3" to 6"	Small, shiny dark green leaves on trailing stems; blue, purple or white flowers in spring and summer. *V. major* has larger, oval leaves, grows to 18", tolerates more heat, sun and dryness. Hardy only to Zone 6. Variegated forms of both available. Photo below.
Carpet Bugle *Ajuga reptans*	Zones 4-9 N, E. Dormant in winter in coldest zones. More sun okay where cool. Moist, well-drained soil. Subject to fungus and nematodes. Height: 3" to 6"	Dark green leaves; upright blue flowers in late spring. Will tolerate some traffic. Mow to renew. *'Purpurea'* has bronze foliage. Photo page 109.
Goldmoss Sedum/Stonecrop *Sedum acre*	Zones 4-9 E, S, W. Winter die-back in coldest zones. Well-drained soil. Drought and heat tolerant. Height: 3" to 6"	Tiny, light green leaves; yellow flowers in late spring. Good in rock gardens, between stepping stones and small areas. *S. anglicum,* similar with dark green leaves, pinkish white flowers.
Hall's Honeysuckle *Lonicera japonica* *'Halliana'*	Zones 4-10 E, S, W. Deciduous in coldest zones. Widely adapted. Drought and heat tolerant. Height: 18" to 30"	Dark green leaves; fragrant white to yellow flowers in late spring. Fast, vigorous and invasive. Best for slopes and large areas. Also grown as a vine. *L. j. chinensis* or *'Purpurea'* is easier to control, has purplish leaves. Photo below.
English Ivy *Hedera helix*	Zones 5-9 N, E. More sun okay where cool. Salt tolerant. Widely adapted, but responds to good soil with adequate moisture. Height: 12" to 18"	Dark green leaves. Slow to start. Cut back to renew. Spreads by long runners; also grown as a vine on chain link, clinging to masonry or hanging over a wall. Many varieties available. Baltic ivy is hardiest to cold. Hahn's ivy smaller with light green leaves. Photo below.

Japanese Spurge

Aaron's Beard

Periwinkle with Hahn's Ivy

Purple Honeysuckle

Mondo Grass

Common Name *Scientific Name*	Climate Zones/Best Exposure Culture/Height	Description/Remarks Similar Species & Varieties
Purple-leaf Winter Creeper *Euonymus fortunei* 'Colorata'	Zones 5-8 N, E, S. Widely adapted. Tolerates heat and dryness. Subject to euonymus scale. Height: 12" to 18"	Dark green leaves; reddish purple in winter. Fast, spreading growth; good for slopes and large areas. Cut back to renew. Common winter creeper, *E. f. radicans*, has small, dark green leaves; can be used as a vine.
Aaron's Beard/St. Johnswort *Hypericum calycinum*	Zones 5-9 E, S. Deciduous in coldest zones. Widely adapted; will grow under trees, with water or dryness. Height: 12" to 18"	Light green leaves; bright yellow flowers in summer. Spreads rapidly by underground stems. Cut back to renew. Photo page 108.
Mondo Grass/Monkey Grass *Ophiopogon japonicus*	Zones 6-10 N, E, S. Well-drained, slightly acid soil. Height: 6" to 12"	Arching, narrow, grass-like, dark green leaves. Spreads slowly by underground stems to form a solid mat. Cut back to renew. Photo page 108.
Big Blue Lilyturf *Liriope muscari*	Zones 6-10 N, E, S. Widely adapted. Watch for slugs and snails. Height: 12" to 18"	Arching, wide, grass-like, dark green leaves; violet flowers in summer. Several varieties available. Cut back to renew. Creeping lilyturf, *L. spicata*, is hardy to Zone 4; grows lower, can be mowed. Photo below.
Asiatic Jasmine *Trachelospermum asiaticum*	Zones 7-10 Freezes back in cold winters. Well-drained soil. Height: 6" to 12"	Glossy green leaves; occasional fragrant, cream-colored flowers in late spring. Best when kept sheared to even height several times a year. Photo below.
Ferns *Athyrium, Dryopteris,* *Nephrolepis, Cyrtomium* species	Zones 4-10 Dormant in winter in coldest zones. Exposure and hardiness according to type. Most prefer part shade and moisture. Height: 6" to 24"	Graceful, filmy foliage. Ferns are often overlooked as a ground cover. Great for under trees for a woodsy, natural effect. Photo below.
Algerian Ivy *Hedera canariensis*	Zones 8-10 N, E. More sun okay where cool. Withstands heat but appreciates moisture. Salt tolerant. Height: 18" to 24"	Large, shiny green or variegated leaves. Fast, invasive growth. Best for slopes and large areas. Spreads by long runners; also grown as a vine on chain link, clinging to masonry or hanging over a wall. Cut back to reduce build-up and to renew. Photo below.

Asiatic Jasmine

Carpet Bugle

Big Blue Lilyturf

Algerian Ivy with Lavender Lantana

Ferns

SHRUB COVERS—12 to 24 inches

Similar to ground covers except woodier and usually slower to cover. More likely to discourage traffic. Makes an interesting transition between flat areas and taller shrubs. Usually planted from 1-gallon cans—some are available in flats but will take longer to cover.

Common Name *Scientific Name*	Climate Zones/Best Exposure Culture/Height & Spacing	Description/Remarks Similar Species & Varieties
Prostrate Juniper *Juniperus horizontalis* variety	Zones 3-10 E, S, W. Well-drained soil. Subject to red spider mites. Height: 6" to 18" Spacing: 4' to 5' apart	Many low-spreading varieties. *'Bar Harbor'* is gray-blue with open growth; *'Wiltoni'* is slow and very low with silver-blue foliage; *'Plumosa'* has fine foliage that turns plum color in fall.
Japanese Garden Juniper *Juniperus procumbens* *'Nana'*	Zones 4-10 E, S. Avoid extreme heat. Subject to red spider mites. Height: 6" to 12" Spacing: 3' to 4' apart	Fine-textured, blue-green needles; tight growth. Slow, but choice. Use Tamarix juniper, *J. sabina tamariscifolia*, for faster, wider spread and more tolerance to heat. Photo page 111.
Bearberry Cotoneaster *Cotoneaster dammeri*	Zones 5-9 E, S, W. Tolerates clay soil if not over-watered. Subject to fireblight disease. Height: 6" to 12" Spacing: 4' to 5' apart	Small, shiny, dark green leaves; tiny white flowers in spring; red berries in fall. Flat, trailing branches root as they go. *'Lowfast'* grows rapidly. *'Skogsholmen'* is taller and more irregular. *C. horizontalis*, semi-deciduous with glossy leaves, flat layered branches. *C. glaucophylla*, silvery gray leaves to 3' high. Many other types available.
Shore Juniper *Juniperus conferta*	Zones 6-10 E, S, W. Sandy soil best; salt tolerant. Subject to red spider mites. Height: 12" to 18" Spacing: 4' to 5' apart	Light green foliage, trailing habit. *'Blue Pacific'* is bluer, denser, tolerates heat better.
Harbour Dwarf Heavenly Bamboo *Nandina domestica* *'Harbour Dwarf'*	Zones 6-10 N, E, S. Loses leaves in cold winters. Needs iron, slightly acid soil, regular moisture. Height: 18" to 24" Spacing: 2' to 3' apart	Pinkish, light green, ferny foliage; red fall color. Dense and spreading. Another low grower. *N. d. 'Nana'*, has coarse purplish leaves. Spreads very slowly. Subject to mildew; not choice. Photo page 111.
Lavender Cotton *Santolina chamaecyparissus*	Zones 7-10 S, W. Alkaline soil okay. Do not overwater. Drought tolerant. Height: 12" to 18" Spacing: 2' to 3' apart	Fine, dense, aromatic whitish-gray leaves; yellow flowers in summer. Mounding form; clip to keep neat. *S. virens* has bright green leaves, makes interesting contrast with gray-foliaged plants.
Prostrate Rosemary *Rosemarinus officinalis* *'Prostratus'*	Zones 8-10 E, S, W. Good drainage; alkaline soil okay. Tolerates heat and drought. Height: 18" to 24" Spacing: 2' to 3' apart	Narrow, dark green, aromatic leaves are used in cooking. Tiny blue flowers appear over several seasons, attract bees. Also used to drape over walls. Common rosemary has upright growth habit to 4', is hardier to cold. Photo page 111.
Cast Iron Plant *Aspidistra elatior*	Zones 8-10 N, E. Tolerates heavy shade. Shelter from wind to protect leaves. Height: 18" to 24" Spacing: 2' to 3' apart	Large, dark green leaves arise from base to 2' high. Slow growth. Good container plant. Variegated form available. Photo page 111.
Confederate/Star Jasmine *Trachelospermum jasminioides*	Zones 8-10 E, S. West okay where cool. Appreciates good care and moisture. Height: 12" to 18" Spacing: 2' to 3' apart	Shiny, dark green leaves; covered with white fragrant flowers in summer. Needs pinching back to encourage compact growth. Slow to start. Also grown as a small, twining vine with support. Photo page 111.
Lavender Lantana *Lantana sellowiana*	Zones 9-10 S, W. Do not overwater, drought tolerant. Height: 12" to 24" Spacing: 3' to 4' apart	Dark green leaves; lavender flowers most of the year. Fast, trailing growth, roots along the stems. Trailing hybrids and low shrubs with white, yellow, orange and multi-colored flowers popular, but not quite as hardy to cold. Photo pages 109, 111.
Sprenger Asparagus *Asparagus densiflorus* *'Sprengeri'*	Zones 9-10 E, S. Tolerates dryness. Height: 18" to 24" Spacing: 2' to 3' apart	Light green ferny foliage; red berries. Great pot and hanging basket plant. Compact form has denser foliage. Photo page 155.

Lavender Lantana

Cast Iron Plant

Harbour Dwarf Heavenly Bamboo

Japanese Garden Juniper

Confederate Jasmine

Prostrate Rosemary

VINES

Perhaps the most difficult to use correctly of all types of plants, vines can be the most striking. Provide adequate support to suit the specific method of climbing. Allow time for training. Also see Large Shrubs for those trainable as espaliers.

Common Name *Scientific Name*	Climate Zones/Best Exposure Culture/Height	Description/Remarks Similar Species & Varieties
Lady Banks' Rose *Rosa banksiae*	Zones 2-10 S, W. Widely adapted; almost trouble free. Height: 20'	Deciduous in cold zones. Shiny, dark green leathery leaflets; few or no thorns; small white or yellow double flowers appear late spring to summer. Excellent arbor climber or against a fence. Also many hybrid tea climbers. Photo page 113.
Hybrid Clematis *Clematis* hybrids	Zones 2-9 E, S. Best with roots in shade, top in sun. Plant deep in well-drained lime soil, with heavy mulch. Height: 10' to 20'	Deciduous. Dark green leaflets; spectacular flowers in white, pink, purple, red and mixed color up to 8" across in spring or summer. Rapid twining habit good for post, fence or trellis. Pruning methods vary with type. *C. armandii* is evergreen, hardy to Zone 7. Several good native species worth consideration. Photo page 113.
Virginia Creeper *Parthenocissus quinquefolia*	Zones 3-9 N, E. South okay where cool. Appreciates water. Height: 40'	Deciduous. Sawtooth leaflets in fives; reddish yellow fall color. Clinging tendrils will climb walls; use as deep ground cover. Best on masonry walls— it may damage wood houses. Boston Ivy, *P. tricuspidata*, is semi-evergreen with glossy three-lobed leaves, tighter growth. Photo page 113.
Grape and Muscadine *Vitis labrusca, V. rotundifolium V. vinifera*	Zones 4-10 S, W. Select variety for zone. Well-drained soil. Allow to dry out between deep waterings. Height: 20'	Deciduous. Large, lobed leaves; summer fruit. Fast growth once roots are established. Good for large arbor or train on horizontal wires. Prune and train according to variety. Muscadine is well adapted to the South, seldom bothered by insects or diseases. Many types available.
Common Trumpet Creeper *Campsis radicans*	Zones 4-10 S, W. Widely adapted. Height: 40'	Deciduous. Divided leaflets; large, orange-red trumpet flowers in summer. Rampant grower clings with aerial rootlets; spreads by root suckers. *C. tagliabuana 'Mme. Galen'* has salmon-red flowers; is better behaved. Do not plant on wood houses.
Chinese Wisteria *Wisteria sinensis*	Zones 5-10 E, S, W. Well-drained, slightly acid soil with iron and moisture. Reduce spring fertilizer and water on old plants to encourage blooming. Height: 40'	Deciduous. Long leaflets; hanging clusters of fragrant violet or white flowers in late spring. Twining vines that develop large trunks with age; excellent on a sturdy pergola. Often trained as a large shrub or small tree. Japanese wisteria, *W. floribunda*, has longer flower clusters to 18".
Coral/Trumpet Honeysuckle *Lonicera sempervirens*	Zones 5-10 E, S. Widely adapted. Height: 20'	Semi-deciduous in cold zones. Oval, bluish green leaves; long, tubular coral flowers in summer, attract hummingbirds but not fragrant. Twining growth. Shrubby without support. Photo page 113.
Evergreen Smilax *Smilax lanceolata*	Zones 7-10 E, S. Height: 20'	Dark green leathery leaves, stiff stems; dark red fruit in early summer. Spreads underground. Foliage good for flower arrangements.
Carolina Jessamine *Gelsemium sempervirens*	Zones 7-10 E, S, W. Widely adapted. Height: 15' to 20'	Shiny, light green leaves; fragrant yellow trumpet flowers in winter and early spring. Cut back twining growth to renew. All parts are poisonous. Well-behaved and controllable. Photo 113.
Cat's Claw *Macfadyena unguis-cati*	Zones 8-10 E, S, W. Likes heat. Height: 20' to 30'	Loses leaves in coldest areas. Glossy green leaves in pairs; yellow trumpet flowers in early spring. Climbs rapidly and clings to masonry walls with claw-like tendrils. Cat's Claw may damage wood houses.
Coral Vine/Rosa de Montana *Antigonon leptopus*	Zones 8-10 E, S, W. Likes heat and water. Height: 30' to 40'	Dies to roots with frost, grows back in spring. Large, heart-shaped leaves; rose-pink sprays of flowers in summer until frost. Fast growth, climbing by tendrils on fences, trellises, over shrubs and up trees. White variety sometimes available. Photo page 113.

Hybrid Clematis

Carolina Jessamine

Virginia Creeper

Lady Banks' Rose

Coral Vine

Coral Honeysuckle

ACCENTS

To liven up an entrance, break the monotony of a ground cover and add a little sparkle where it is needed. Almost any plant that has a striking form, contrasting texture, brightly colored foliage or outstanding flowers can serve as an accent. Use with discretion or they may overwhelm the landscape and appear out of place.

Common Name *Scientific Name*	Climate Zones/Best Exposure Culture/Height	Description/Remarks Similar Species & Varieties
Bearded Iris *Iris* in variety	Zones 4-10 E, S, W. Well-drained soil. Do not over-water. Height: 1' to 3'	Perennial, dormant in winter. Size depends on variety. Stiff, sword-shaped leaves. Orchid-like flowers in many colors and forms, spring and summer. Divide every 3 or 4 years in late summer. Plant rhizomes shallow. Louisiana irises well-adapted to lower Gulf. Photo below.
Plantain Lily *Hosta* species	Zones 4-9 N, E. Needs organic soil and summer moisture. Watch for slugs and snails. Height: 12" to 18"	Perennial, dormant in winter. Handsome leaves, 6" to 12" long, green or variegated, some with ribs or wavy margins. White, blue or lavender flowers on tall stems in summer. Large numbers of species and varieties. Can be planted 12" to 18" apart for shady ground cover.
Adam's Needle *Yucca filamentosa*	Zones 4-10 E, S, W. Well-drained, sandy soil. Heat and drought tolerant. Height: Stemless to 3'	Evergreen perennial. Stiff, narrow, bluish green leaves with curly threads on edges. Very tall, creamy spikes of flowers in summer. *Y. flaccida* is similar, with less rigid leaves.
Daylily *Hemerocallis* species	Zones 5-10 E, S, W. Best in well-drained soil with water during blooming season. Height: 1-1/2' to 3'	Perennial, some evergreen in warmest zones. Light green, arching, strap-shaped leaves. Large flowers, many varieties in yellow, orange, red, pink, white and blends, mostly early summer to fall. Plant bulbs shallow in casual groupings 24" apart for ground cover. Photo page 115.
Pampas Grass *Cortaderia selloana*	Zones 6-10 E, S, W. Widely adapted. Salt, alkali, heat and drought tolerant. Height: 10' and more	Evergreen grass, will die back in winter in coldest zones. Narrow, arching, sharp-edged leaves. Striking, whitish plumes on 5' stalks in fall. Single specimen or plant 6' apart as a windbreak. Rapid, overwhelming growth. Should be cut back in winter to renew—wear heavy gloves. Photo 187.
Variegated Liriope *Liriope muscari* variety	Zones 6-10 N, E, S. Watch for slugs and snails. Height: 12" to 18"	Evergreen perennial. Arching, wide, grass-like leaves, edged in white or yellow. Violet flowers in summer. Good accent, border or ground cover. *'Silvery Sunproof'* tolerates considerable sun. *L. gigantea* has dark green leaves, grows to 3' high. Photo page 115.

Hosta

Bearded Iris

Nipponlily

Common Name *Scientific Name*	Climate Zones/Best Exposure Culture/Height	Description/Remarks Similar Species & Varieties
Curveleaf Yucca *Yucca recurvifolia* *(Y. pendula)*	Zones 7-10 E, S, W. Widely adapted. Salt, alkali, heat and drought tolerant. Height: 6' and taller	Evergreen perennial. Blue to gray-green, strap-shaped leaves with sharp spine on tip curve gracefully downward. Single or multi-head trunks, can be cut back to reduce height. Striking, white flower clusters on 3' stalks in summer. Spanish bayonet, *Y. aloifolia*, has stiff, sharply pointed leaves, is more tree-like. Photo page 187.
Nipponlily *Rohdea japonica*	Zones 7-10 N, E. Best in organic soil with moisture. Height: 12" to 18"	Evergreen perennial. Broad, arching, strap-shaped leaves, dark green or variegated. Cream flowers; red berries. Slow growing. Good shady groupings, groundcover or in a container. Photo page 114.
Sotol *Dasylirion* species	Zones 8-10 E, S, W. Well-drained soil. Salt, alkali, heat and drought tolerant. Height: 3' to 5'	Evergreen perennial. Narrow leaves to 3' long with small spines on margins. Slow growth, stemless or with short trunk. Very tall, neat-appearing flower stalks. Several species native to Texas.
Century Plant *Agave americana*	Zones 8-10 E, S, W. Widely adapted. Salt, alkali, heat and drought tolerant. Height: 6'	Evergreen perennial. Stiff, fleshy, blue-green, sword-shaped leaves with toothed margin and sharp tip. Very tall, striking, flower stalks on plants at least 10 years old, then dies back to basal sprouts. Variegated form and smaller species also common.
Sago Palm *Cycas revoluta*	Zones 8-10 N, E. More sun okay where cool. Well-drained rich soil with moisture. Subject to scale. Height: 3' and taller	Evergreen, palm-like plant. Shiny, dark green leaves recurve downward. Very slow growth; will stay less than 3' for many years. Usually the most expensive plant in the nursery. Good container plant. *C. circinalis,* is faster, taller, lusher. Hardy in Zone 10 only. Photo page 155.
Holly Fern *Cyrtomium falcatum*	Zones 8-10 N, E. Well-drained acid soil with moisture. Height: 18" to 24"	Evergreen fern. Shiny, dark green, leathery, coarse fronds. Common name refers to holly-like appearance of leaflets. Plant 18" apart for shady ground cover.
Fancy-leafed Caladium *Caladium bicolor*	Zones 9-10 E. Thrives in warm shade, rich organic soil. Height: 2' to 3'	Perennial, dormant in winter. Giant, arrow-shaped leaves on long stalks. Exotic foliage in white, red, pink and mixed colors. Use in mass plantings or containers. Grow in colder zones by lifting tubers in winter, but needs summer heat. Photo below.

Tulips

Daylily

Variegated Liriope

Fancy-leafed Caladium

PALMS

A palm lends a distinctive touch to the landscape. Large or small, sun or shade, there's a palm for almost every situation. Low winter temperatures limit range, but careful selection and placement in a protected spot can extend use into the coldest parts of Zone 8. Palms appreciate soil with a high organic content, and establish best during summer. Can be planted deep for anchorage and to induce new root growth from the buried trunk.

Common Name *Scientific Name*	Climate Zones/Culture/Height	Description/Remarks Similar Species & Varieties
Mediterranean Fan Palm *Chamaerops humilis*	Zones 8-10 Hardiest of all. Withstands dryness, but responds to regular watering. Height: 6' to 12'	Bluish gray-green, fan-shaped leaves. Slow growing, can be used as a shrubby accent. Develops multiple trunks with age. Good scale for average garden. Does well in a large container. Photo page 117.
Fortune Windmill Palm *Trachycarpus fortunei (Chamaerops excelsa)*	Zones 8-10 May freeze below 10F (−12C), but usually recovers. Best with moisture. Height: 15' to 20'	Dark green, fan-shaped leaves; slender, hairy brown trunk. Narrow, upright growth; fits easily into small garden. Plant 4' to 5' apart with trunks angled slightly outward for clump effect. Photo page 117.
Pindo Palm *Butia capitata (Cocos australis)*	Zones 8-10 Withstands dryness, but responds to regular watering. Height: 10' to 20'	Gray, arching, feather-like fronds; thick trunk. Slow growth, can be used as low tree about as wide as high. Form and color make it a good accent.
Cabbage Palm *Sabal palmetto*	Zones 8-10 Borderline in colder areas of Zone 8. Widely adapted. Tolerant of salt and soggy soils. Height: 20' and more	Dark green, fan-shaped leaves; slender criss-cross or smooth trunk. Fairly rapid, narrow upright growth. Good in groups. Dwarf palmetto, *S. minor*, and Saw palmetto, *Serenoa repens*, are trunkless to 3' high. Several other native species of varying size, hardiness and appearance. Photo page 117.
Needle Palm *Rhapidophyllum hystrix*	Zones 8-10 Prefers part shade and moisture. Height: 5'	Dark green, fan-shaped leaves, silvery below. Short trunk covered with black spines. Slow growing, developing several trunks with age.
Canary Island Date Palm *Phoenix canariensis*	Zones 9-10 Withstands dryness or moisture. Salt tolerant. Height: 40' and more	Long, green, feather-like fronds recurve downward. Orange, date-like fruit somewhat ornamental, but also a nuisance. Stout trunk and wide spread make it too large for most gardens. Photo page 117.
Mexican Fan Palm *Washingtonia robusta*	Zones 9-10 Salt tolerant. Okay in lawn. Height: 50' and more	Bright green, fan-shaped leaves; slender trunk. Covered with a skirt of dead leaves, or cleaned-off for criss-cross or smooth effect. Rapid growth, soon gets too tall for average garden. Best in groups.
Chinese Fountain Palm *Livistona chinensis*	Zones 9-10 Tolerates considerable shade. Height: 20' and more	Dark green, fan-shaped leaves, weeping on ends. Slow growth, takes years to develop a trunk; can be used as a lush foliage shrub. Photo page 117.
Queen Palm *Arecastrum romanzoffianum (Cocos plumosa)*	Zones 9-10 Likes moisture, okay in lawn. Protect from wind. Height: 25' and more	Long, light green, feather-like fronds arch gracefully. Slender, attractive, gray-tan trunk. Best in groups. Photo page 117.
Saw Cabbage Palm *Acoelorrhaphe wrightii (Paurotis wrightii)*	Zones 9-10 Needs moisture and iron. Okay in lawn. Height: 20' and more	Bright green, fan-shaped leaves. Very slender, many multiple trunks. Nice as silhouette specimen with lower foliage cleaned out.
Pigmy Date Palm *Phoenix roebelinii*	Zones 9-10 Prefers partial shade in hot areas with ample moisture. Height: 6' to 12'	Shiny, dark green, gracefully arching, feather-like fronds. Slender trunk. Slow growth. Excellent container or patio plant. Photo page 117.

Chinese Fountain Palm

Canary Island Date Palm

Pigmy Date Palm

Cabbage Palm

Mediterranean Fan Palm

Queen Palm

Fortune Windmill Palm

TROPICAL PLANTS

Exciting and flamboyant, tropical plants conjure up dreams of white, sandy beaches with their fragrant flowers, lush foliage and exotic fruits. Some of these may survive in protected spots of Zone 9, but most need the heat, plentiful rain and temperatures above freezing found only in Zone 10.

Common Name *Scientific Name*	Best Exposure/Culture Height & Spacing	Category/Description/Remarks Similar Species & Varieties
Wedelia *Wedelia trilobata*	E, S, W. Salt tolerant. Height: 6" to 12" Spacing: 12" to 18" apart	Ground cover. Shiny, light green leaves, trailing habit. Yellow flowers in spring and summer.
Purple Heart *Setcreasea pallida*	E, S. Well-drained soil. Watch for slugs and snails. Height: 12" to 18" Spacing: 12" to 18" apart	Ground cover and accent. Long, bright purple leaves and stems. Trailing habit; brittle if walked on. Dramatic, but garish. Wandering Jew, *Tradescantia* and *Zebrina* are similar with green, variegated and colored leaves; vigorous and invasive.
Oyster Plant *Rhoeo spathacea* *(R. discolor)*	E, S. Well-drained soil. Watch for slugs and snails. Height: 12" to 18" Spacing: 12" to 18" apart	Ground cover and accent. Sword-shaped leaves, green on top, bright purple below. Good container plant and hanging basket. Photo page 119.
Dwarf Natal Plum *Carissa grandiflora* 'Tuttlei'	N, E, S, W. Salt tolerant. Height: 18" to 24" Spacing: 3' to 4' apart	Shrub cover. Shiny, dark green, oval leaves; thorny stems; white, fragrant flowers; red edible fruit. Neat and tailored. Several other low varieties. *C. grandiflora* looks identical, is a large shrub. Photo page 119.
Coontie *Zamia integrifolia*	E, S. Withstands some dryness, but better with moisture. Salt tolerant. Height: 2' to 3' Spacing: 2' to 3' apart	Shrub cover and accent. Dark green, palm-like leaves. Slow growth. Good companion plant for palms.
Coral or Fountain Plant *Russellia equisetiformis*	S, W. Salt tolerant. Height: 3' to 4' Spacing: 3' to 4' apart	Shrub cover. Trailing, bright green stems with tiny leaves; coral-red, tubular flowers most of the year. Interesting filmy texture, effective with boulders. Good hanging basket plant.
Allamanda *Allamanda cathartica*	E, S. Salt tolerant. Height: 10' to 20' Spacing: 4' to 5' apart	Vine or shrub. Leathery, bright green leaves; large golden yellow flowers all year. Can be pruned as a hedge. Variety 'Hendersonii' most common, purple form also known. A plant called purple allamanda is actually India rubber vine, *Cryptostegia grandiflora.*
Bougainvillea *Bougainvillea species*	S, W. Salt tolerant. Blooms best when slightly dry. Height: 20'	Vine or shrub. Dark green leaves; thorny branches; dazzling flower bracts of magenta, purple, red, orange, white and mixed colors through most of the year. Rapid growth, needs training and support. Transplant with care. Some varieties suitable for large pots. Photo page 119.
Ceriman or Split-leaf Philodendron *Monstera deliciosa* *(Philodendron pertusum)*	E. Rich, moist soil. Height: 20'	Vine. Giant, leathery, dark green, deeply cut leaves; calla-like flowers become alligator-skinned edible fruit—must be fully ripe to avoid irritating crystals. Grows against a wall or on a tree trunk.
Croton *Codiaeum variegatum*	E, S. Well-drained soil with moisture. Height: 5' to 10' Spacing: 3' to 4' apart	Shrub. Wide range of leaf shapes, sizes and colors, depending on variety. Outstanding foliage accent shrub; colors include green, red, yellow, brown, pink and mixtures. Photo page 121.
Ixora *Ixora coccinea*	E, S. Acid soil with iron and moisture. Height: 5' to 10' Spacing: 3' to 4' apart	Shrub. Dark green, leathery leaves. Red flower clusters most of the year. Yellow flowering and dwarf forms sometimes available. *I. macrothrysa* has larger flowers and leaves. Photo page 119.

Bougainvillea

Dwarf Natal Plum

Umbrella Tree

Ixora

Oyster Plant

Dwarf Poinciana

119

Tropicals

Common Name *Scientific Name*	Best Exposure/Culture Height & Spacing	Category/Description/Remarks Similar Species & Varieties
Candle Bush *Cassia alata*	S, W. Well-drained soil. Salt tolerant. Height: 5' to 10' Spacing: 5' to 6' apart	Shrub. Shiny, bright green, compound leaves, partially defoliates in winter. Bright yellow, candle-like flowers, late winter through spring. Rapid, rangy growth; cut back drastically in fall to renew. Photo page 121.
Beefsteak or Copper Leaf *Acalypha wilkesiana*	E, S, W. Well-drained soil with moisture. Subject to beetle damage. Height: 5' to 10' Spacing: 4' to 5' apart	Shrub. Large, colorful leaves, usually reddish copper, but many varieties with dark red, green, yellow, and mixed colors. Good accent specimen, screen or clipped as a hedge. Chenille Plant, *A. hispida*, is smaller with green leaves and long, hanging, furry red flowers. Photo page 121.
Hibiscus *Hibiscus rosa-sinensis*	S, W. Well-drained, slightly acid soil with iron and moisture. Height: 6' to 20' Spacing: 5' to 8' apart	Shrub. Shiny, dark green leaves; large flowers most of the year, in red, pink, white, yellow, orange and mixed colors. Many varieties, from compact hedge types to tall, tree-like forms. 'LaFrance' is vigorous screen with pink flowers. *H. tiliaceus* is a small, seashore tree. Photo page 121.
Silver Buttonwood *Conocarpus erectus sericeus*	S, W. Salt and wind tolerant. Height: 10' Spacing: 5' to 6' apart	Shrub. Silvery-gray, oval pointed leaves. Excellent seashore plant. Use as natural screen or can be clipped as a hedge. Button mangrove, *C. erectus*, has green leaves, often reaches tree size.
Sea Grape *Cocoloba uvifera*	E, S, W. Salt and wind tolerant. Height: 10' to 20' Spacing: 6' to 8' apart	Shrub and small tree. Large, round, leathery, green leaves with red veins, new growth mahogany color. Hanging clusters of grape-like fruit on female trees, mostly used for jelly and wine. Excellent seashore plant. Use as screen or train into low-branching tree or espalier.
Roxburg Fig *Ficus auriculata* *(F. roxburghii)*	E, S, W. Rich soil with moisture. Protect from wind. Height: 10' to 20'	Large shrub or small tree. Huge, textured, rich green, oval to round leaves with reddish new growth. Fiddleleaf fig, *F. lyrata*, has large, fiddle-shaped leathery leaves; use as small tree or container plant.
Umbrella Tree *Schefflera actinophylla* *(Brassaia actinophylla)*	E, S. Rich soil with moisture. Height: 20' and more	Small tree. Large, shiny, light green leaves in horizontal rosettes. Upright multiple trunks. Exotic red flowers look like octopus tentacles. Fast growth. Also good container plant and indoors with plenty of light. Photo page 119.
Screw Pine *Pandanus* species	E, S, W. Tolerates salt and soggy soil. Height: 20' and more	Small tree. Long, dark green or variegated sword-shaped leaves with prickly margins. Pineapple-like fruit on female plants. Slender trunks with palm-like heads of foliage; large, bizarre prop roots. Photo page 121.
Royal Poinciana *Delonix regia*	S, W. Well-drained soil. Salt tolerant. Height: 30' to 40'	Medium tree. Dark green, finely cut leaves; dazzling, bright orange-red flower clusters cover tree in summer. Fast growth, picturesque horizontal habit. Photo page 121.
Mango *Mangifera indica*	S, W. Well-drained soil. Most are subject to anthracnose fungus; some resistant varieties available. Height: 30' and more	Medium tree. Long, hanging, dark green narrow leaves; new growth bronze. Wide range of fruit types. Choose from endless list of named varieties—seedlings are usually poor quality. Can be pruned out to make an attractive shade tree. Juices may cause skin rash on sensitive persons.
Cajeput or Punk Tree *Melaleuca quinquenervia* *(M. leucadendra)*	S, W. Tolerates salt, wind and soggy soil. Height: 30' and more	Narrow, upright tree. Pale green leaves with parallel veins; creamy-white flower spikes several times a year. Striking white bark and hanging branches give a birch-like effect. Most effective with multiple trunks or can be planted 6' apart as a windbreak. Photo page 131.
Coconut Palm *Cocos nucifera*	E, S, W. Sandy soil with moisture. Tolerates salt and wind. Height: 50' and more	Palm. Long, shining, feather-like fronds. Green, orange or brown coconuts. Gracefully curving trunks. Most common beach tree. Especially susceptible to lethal yellows disease. Use resistant dwarf Malaysian types for new plantings. Photo page 121.

Candle Bush and Beefsteak

Royal Poinciana

Croton

**Hibiscus and
Coconut Palm**

Roxburg Fig

Screw Pine

Foolproof Planting 7

Here is where all your selections from the plant lists are put to use. But selecting plants is not enough. Once you've developed a planting plan similar to the ones at the end of this chapter, you must then provide a proper environment for the plants.

PLANTING SEASON

What is the best time of year for planting? Throughout the South, fall and early spring are ideal for most broad-leaved evergreens and conifers. Even mid-winter is okay in mild areas where severe winds and freezing temperatures are not a problem. This allows time for roots to develop and the plants to get settled before being subjected to the heat of summer.

Newly set-out plants are less apt to dry out during the cool months, so supplemental watering is less of a chore. Wait until late spring for plants that are subject to frost damage so they have a full season to become established before being exposed to the rigors of winter. This is especially important for tender tropicals and plants that are borderline in your zone.

Generally, it is best to avoid the extremes of winter and summer. There are exceptions. Heat-loving palms and bamboos prefer warm soil for root growth. They're usually happier when planted from June to October. Warm-season grasses such as bermuda, centipede, St. Augustine and zoysia, along with dichondra, also belong in this category. Any plants set out in the heat of the year will require extra watering in the absence of rain.

Deciduous shade and fruit trees, roses, berries and deciduous shrubs are often sold bare-root. They are normally available in January and February and should be planted at that time, preferably before leafbuds have begun to open.

SOIL PREPARATION

It would be great if topsoil were always stockpiled at the start of construction and then replaced when the house is finished. Unfortunately, many sites are stripped bare and you end up with poor soil, or the soil may have been poor to begin with. In some extreme cases it may be advisable to

Steer manure should be mixed with organic material to avoid an excess of salt.

bring in good quality topsoil—if available. Usually, the addition of organic material and fertilizer to existing soil is less expensive. The problems of imported weeds and diseases, and a drastic change in soil texture, or *interface,* is also avoided. When topsoil is brought in, blend it with the native soil by deep spading or rototilling rather than just laying it on top.

Weeds are a good indicator of soil quality. If you have a lush crop of various types, desirable plants should grow just as well. If the neighbors' yards are thriving, so should yours. But be sure to ask them if they had to make extensive modifications to get everything to grow.

In the absence of weeds and nearby landscapes, it is difficult to tell what your soil is like by just looking at it. The safest thing to do is to have the Cooperative Extension Service at your state university or a private soil lab do a soil test. Along with the test you'll get specific recommendations as to what should be added to your soil before planting. A soil test can also determine if there is a nematode problem—better to find out in the beginning so you can treat the soil and avoid susceptible plants.

The first determination will be whether the soil is acid or alkaline. This is expressed on a pH scale from 1 to 14. Neutral is 7.0—anything higher is alkaline, anything lower is acid. Most plants prefer a slightly acid soil in the range from 6.0 to 6.5. However, most southern soils are too acid and need to be "sweetened" by the addition of dolomitic lime.

Good planting practices and proper plant selection pay off in results like this Atlanta garden designed by landscape architect Edith Henderson, FASLA.

Some areas with low rainfall or alluvial soil are too alkaline. The pH must be lowered by the addition of soil sulphur or magnesium sulphate for optimum growth of most plants.

Sound complicated? The technical chemical relationships are. Unless you want to become an expert in soils, it is easiest to adhere to the recommendations of a soil test, or to follow proven local practices. Rough quantities often used are 80 to 100 pounds of dolomitic limestone per 1,000 square feet for acidic soil or 20 to 30 pounds of soil sulphur per 1,000 square feet for alkaline soil. Include 200 pounds of agricultural gypsum per 1,000 square feet for tightly compacted alkaline clay soil.

For lawn and relatively flat ground cover areas, a good basic application is a mix of 3 to 4 cubic yards of organic material, 250 pounds of organic fertilizer such as processed sewage sludge, and 35 pounds of balanced fertilizer (8-8-8) for each 1,000 square feet. Rototill or dig the mix 6 inches deep by hand. For very poor soils such as sub-soil or pure sand, the amount of organic material should be increased.

At a cost of approximately 10 to 15 cents per square foot for all materials, this treatment will loosen clay soils, increase the water-holding capacity of sandy soils and provide humus, nitrogen, phosphorus and potassium.

Incidentally, adding sand to clay soils is not very effective unless a large amount is used and dug in deeply. Extra organic material is better unless you have a cheap source of salt-free sand nearby.

The organic material should not rob the soil of nitrogen as it decomposes, should be low in salt content and free of weed seeds, insects and diseases such as nematodes and fungi. Composted sawdust and shavings, ground pine bark and rice hulls are excellent organic materials. Nitrogen fertilizer should be added when necessary to replace any nitrogen lost during decomposition.

Sphagnum peat moss is a good amendment but usually costs considerably more. Mushroom compost and composted manure cost less, but often have a fairly high salt content.

They're safer to use in well-drained soils. Fresh manure can damage tender plant roots, and may smell unpleasant.

Buying the organic material by the truckload is advisable for quantities of more than 5 cubic yards. If you can find a bulk source, you can save 50 percent or more over the sack price.

COMPOST

The ideal way to get organic material is to produce it yourself by composting. This is not generally possible for a new garden, but once it is established you can make good use of your leaves and trimmings instead of burning or hauling them away. Compost is excellent for vegetable gardens and mulching.

If soil depth is limited by an impermeable layer such as rock, caliche or hardpan, this should be broken through by drilling or excavating to permit root penetration. A minimum of 12 inches of soil is desirable for lawn and ground cover, 24 to 36 inches for shrubs, and 36 to 60 inches for trees. Raised planting beds and containers are called for when it is impractical to provide these minimum depths.

Ground covers on steep banks and shrubs and trees are normally treated individually by incorporating materials directly in the planting hole rather than in the entire area. Don't worry about having a minimum depth of soil throughout the entire yard. You need it only at each individual planting hole.

PLANTING

There are many formulas for planting. The "fish-with-the-corn-seed" of the American Indians was reportedly quite successful, but a trifle impractical today. Old-time gardeners have mysterious ingredients that they insist are essential for proper growth. In fact, nearly everyone has a favorite planting method—and most of them work.

Even though every variety of plant has specific individual needs, these needs are not always critical. Most plants will do reasonably well if basic requirements are met. The planting

directions in this chapter have proven to be satisfactory for almost all plants. They are simple, economical and practically foolproof.

The key to success is blending the original soil on the site with added organic material. Roots grow more easily into the surrounding soil. Drainage is better via capillary action when the existing soil and the backfill around the new plant are similar. Otherwise, an "underground pot" is created and roots and water stay confined within the planting hole.

Drainage is the crucial factor. Here is a simple test. Dig the plant hole and fill it with water. If the water is still there several hours later, additional measures are needed, assuming the soil wasn't thoroughly wet when you dug the hole.

Use a post hole auger or large drill to dig two or more *chimneys* several feet deep in the bottom of the hole. *Don't* fill them with sand or gravel. Believe it or not, this will actually impede water flow because of the change in soil texture. Instead, fill the chimneys with the prepared backfill as shown on page 125.

With proper watering techniques, drainage should now be adequate unless excess water accumulates every time it rains or the sprinklers are turned on. In this case you'll have to choose tolerant plants and raise

Overgrown variegated holly osmanthus in a 1-gallon can is a real bargain. Loosen roots prior to planting.

them higher than the surrounding grade. You can also try to correct the overall drainage situation by better surface flow and installing underground drain lines. Very few plants thrive in a swamp.

The size of the plant at the time of planting is closely related to the problem of growth rate and spacing. If your budget permits, relatively large plant material can be used and properly spaced. Slower growing plants can be chosen without having to wait years for their development. However, most landscape budgets don't allow this. Large individual plants not only cost more, so does the labor for planting them.

There is much to be said for plants in smaller sizes because many transplant better when young. The price chart on this page shows sizes and costs of various classes of plants.

Many nurseries sell some of their plants balled-in-burlap, called *b/b*. The price is usually slightly higher than a similar size plant grown in a container. In my opinion it doesn't matter whether a plant is b/b or container grown, as long as you obtain a healthy, well-rooted plant.

Many deciduous plants are available bare-root during the winter at a price considerably less than for container-grown plants. In addition to greater choice and lower cost, other advantages of bare-root plants are that they are lighter and therefore easier to handle. There is also no problem of incompatible soil types that can occur when b/b and containers are planted into a different native soil.

It is fun to shop for bargains, but when purchasing plants at supermarkets and discount house "nurseries," the advice and reliability of an experienced nurseryman is usually lost. Beware of overgrown specials with root problems. Conversely, beware of undersize plants not yet grown in the can-size offered. Sometimes 1-gallon plants are sold in 5-gallon cans at 5-gallon prices.

To avoid mix-ups in identification, be sure of the plant you want or look for the wholesaler's tag. If you know what you're after, a $1.39 1-gallon plant on sale may be just as good as one selling for $3.00.

Plant Prices

Class of Plant	Usual Size	Approximate Price Retail	Approximate Price Installed
Perennial	1 quart	$ 1.50	$ 2.50
Most shrubs and vines	1 gallon	$ 3.00	$ 5.00
Special shrubs	5 gallon	$ 10.00	$ 16.00
Most trees	5 gallon	$ 12.50	$ 25.00
Special trees	15 gallon	$ 50.00	$ 75.00
Specimen trees	24-inch box	$200.00	$250.00
Ground cover	flat	$ 10.00	$ 15.00

But how can you know what you are after? Generally, a good plant will appear healthy, young and vigorous. As you examine more plants, you will begin to notice differences in color and form that indicate health and vigor. Shrubs should have a nice shape. Trees should have a stout trunk and sturdy framework.

Stick your finger down into the soil to feel if there are roots circling directly around the main stem or trunk.

Sometimes when a seedling is transferred to a new pot, its roots are directed in a circle. This can seriously limit growth and could eventually choke the plant, which is more important than if the plant appears to be *root-bound,* or too big for its container.

Actually, most plants are okay if the container is full of roots, as long as they're not kinked, circling or girdling. Loosen the outside roots and spread them out when planting and

HOW TO PLANT A SHRUB

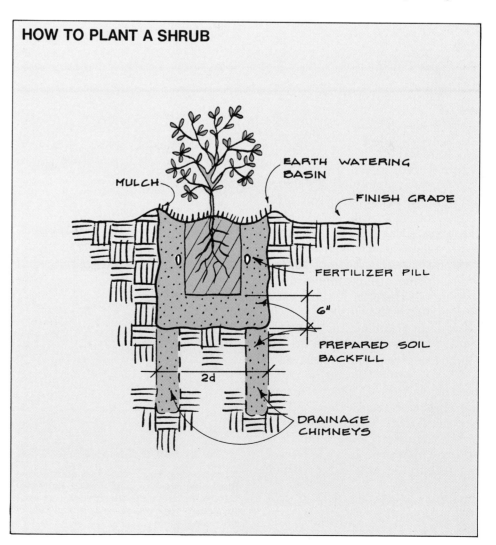

they'll soon grow into the surrounding soil.

STEPS IN PLANTING

● Modify the soil pH level as necessary. This was described under "Soil Preparation."

● Excavate the hole for the plant to approximately twice the diameter of the plant's root ball and 6 to 12 inches deeper.

● Check the drainage as described on page 124. If drainage is poor, dig chimneys.

● Mix soil for backfill. A mixture of 1/4 organic material, 1/4 processed sewage sludge and 1/2 soil excavated from the plant pit works well. A half cup of superphosphate per cubic foot of backfill helps stimulate root growth without burning. Recent research indicates that in *very good* soil, growth is just as good or better, without special backfill.

● Backfill the bottom of the hole so the plant will be at the same level as it was in the nursery can. Tamp the backfill firmly to prevent settling. Raise above grade in soggy soils and for sensitive plants such as azaleas and camellias.

● Remove the plant from its container, taking care not to break the root ball. You should loosen any roots that look bound, but be careful not to damage the root system.

● Set the plant in position. Fill the pit with soil mixture and tamp soil firmly around the root ball. Place time-release granules, such as Osmocote, or slow-release fertilizer pills, such as Nitroform, next to the root ball according to the manufacturer's directions. Avoid chemical fertilizers that can injure tender new roots.

● If you are planting a tree, carefully remove any existing stake. If the tree is incapable of supporting itself, drive two 2x2 stakes of treated or decay-resistant wood, or 1-inch-diameter steel pipes at the outside edges of the plant pit. Secure the tree loosely to permit movement in the wind. Large trees may have to be guy-wired to prevent rocking the root ball or tipping over.

● Build a temporary earth watering basin at the outside edge of the plant pit. Install a mulch of organic material, bark chunks or stone approximately 2 inches thick.

● Soak the plant by filling the basin several times. Add vitamin B-1 or other transplanting hormone such as Hormex or Superthrive. This reduces transplanting shock and stimulates root growth. Don't allow the root ball to dry out. Unless there is ample rainfall, supplementary watering will be necessary until roots have spread into the surrounding soil.

● If the plant has an exceptionally large amount of foliage in proportion to the size of the root ball, reduce the

Jute mesh is held in place with special oversize staples. Ground cover is then planted in small openings.

Hydroseeding large slopes is much easier than planting individual plants by hand. Shrubs and trees can be planted from containers before hydroseeding, or included in the seed mix.

leaf surface by thinning out and pruning back.

GROUND COVER AND SLOPE PLANTING

For gentle slopes that are easy to mow, lawn is usually the best choice. Steep slopes, along with narrow areas, rocky soil and heavy shade are prime candidates for a ground cover or shrub cover.

If the soil preparation materials can be tilled into the entire area without creating an erosion problem, the plants will spread and fill in faster. Otherwise, individual pockets should be dug, similar to those needed for shrubs and trees, except smaller.

Flats or bundles of ground cover plants should be treated with care. It is best to plant in slightly moist soil and to water immediately to prevent the roots from drying out. Supplementary irrigation will be necessary until the plants are well established if rainfall is insufficient. Weed control is crucial. Light applications of liquid or pelletized fertilizer (at monthly intervals) will speed growth.

Consider *hydroseeding* application instead of conventional ground cover for large banks. See page 141. Cost is approximately 10 cents per square foot for a minimum area of 5,000 square feet. Mixes containing grasses, clover, crown vetch and various flowers are presentable and will naturalize under favorable conditions.

Vinca major is a reliable, long-lived ground cover suitable for flat areas or slopes.

PLANTING TREES

Follow the basic steps suggested on page 128 for planting. If you buy your tree wrapped in burlap, loosen the twine or wire and open the burlap at the top of the root ball before you fill the hole.

If you purchase a bare-root tree, make sure the roots are plump and fresh. If they are dry, soaking them in water overnight before planting should help. After you place the tree in its pit, work the soil around the roots and tamp it down carefully. Then stake the tree and soak the roots using a water basin. After this initial soaking, be careful not to overwater. Bare-root trees are dormant and need less water. When the weather warms, you can begin watering regularly.

Staking is an important part of tree planting. It is often overlooked until windstorms break branches or blow trees over. Ideally, a nursery tree will have a stout trunk, called *heavy caliper,* and will require no support at all.

Low-branching and pyramidal trees such as sweet gum, crape myrtle, birch, ginkgo and many conifers can often get by without staking. Trees with *small caliper,* flexible trunks and a heavy head of foliage, are usually grown with a stake at the nursery and cannot stand without help. Large trees may have to be anchored with guy wires to prevent tipping over.

Remove the nursery stake and tie the trunk loosely between two sturdy stakes. Allow the trunk to flex with the wind and gain strength. This is like exercise for the tree. Rigid constraint keeps the tree a cripple, dependent on the stakes like crutches. When a big blow comes, the entire head of the tree can snap off if it has nowhere to bend. Thinning the foliage allows wind to pass through, reducing the "sail" effect.

Rubber or plastic ties should be used so the bark isn't chafed or the trunk cut into by thin wires. When guy wires are used, attach them to the trunk or heavy branches in three places. Run the wires at a 45° angle to sturdy stakes driven into firm ground. Encase the wires with sections of hose wherever they touch the bark. Mark the wires with plastic flags so people don't trip on them.

As the tree develops, you should enlarge its watering basin. The area next to the trunk should be kept relatively dry to prevent disease, but the outside diameter of the basin should be at least as wide as the *drip line* of the tree, the point where most rain rolls off the tree's leaves.

Enlarging the basin beyond the drip line will encourage root growth, as will deep watering. Roots will only grow where there is water. Too small a basin will inhibit growth and shallow watering will produce shallow roots. In either case, the tree will not grow as strong as it should. Once the tree is well established, remove the earth basin entirely—except in low-rainfall areas where too much water is not a problem.

WEED CONTROL

The best time to control weeds is *before* any planting is done. This is especially important in ground cover and lawn areas. Existing weeds and those germinated when the soil is soaked are easy to eliminate. Keeping the area moist for several weeks will usually bring a good crop.

Most broad-leaved weeds and grasses can be hoed off or rototilled into the soil. Perennial broad-leaf weeds should be sprayed with a 2,4-D mix or Round-up or Kleen-up. Johnson, bermuda and other deep-rooted perennial grasses should be sprayed with dalapon, also called Dowpon, or Round-up or Kleen-up several weeks before cultivating. Two applications are sometimes necessary.

Eliminating existing weeds is only part of the problem. Most soils will still contain many weed seeds. For extreme situations, use either of two temporary soil sterilants. They will kill weed seeds without affecting future planting.

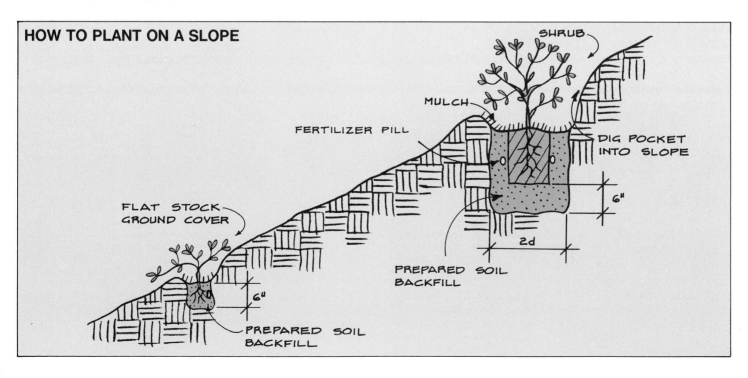

HOW TO PLANT ON A SLOPE

SHRUB

MULCH

FERTILIZER PILL

DIG POCKET INTO SLOPE

FLAT STOCK GROUND COVER

PREPARED SOIL BACKFILL

6"

2d

PREPARED SOIL BACKFILL

6"

HOW TO PLANT A TREE

Holes are dug after tree locations have been laid out. Mix approximately 25 percent organic material, 25 percent processed sewage sludge and 50 percent excavated soil for the backfill mix. Fill bottom to receive plant ball and tamp *firmly*.

Metal can should be cut on all four sides. Plastic containers are tapered and plant can be gently tapped out if well rooted. Handle the root ball with care. If it breaks, apply transplanting hormones and you may help it recover from the shock.

Set plant to grade. Backfill part way and put fertilizer pills in place before filling the rest of the way.

Firm the soil against the root ball so there are no air spaces.

Make a large earth basin and fill with a 2-inch-deep mulch of organic material.

Stake as necessary. This Leyland cypress practically supports itself, so a temporary single stake was used. Fill basin with water several times to make sure entire root area is saturated.

This tree-staking method allows the trunk to move in the wind and gain strength as it grows.

• *Cyanimid,* calcium cyanamide, is applied at the rate of 50 pounds per 1,000 square feet raked in 1 inch deep. Keep moist for two weeks and allow to dry out for another two weeks before planting. Material cost is about 2 cents per square foot. A bonus feature is that nitrogen is left in the soil.

• *Vapam* is applied at the rate of 2-1/2 gallons per 1,000 square feet in a water solution and allowed to dry out for three weeks before planting. Cost is also about 2 cents per square foot. It also gives some control of nematodes and soil diseases.

Both should be applied after all other soil preparation has been completed. Keep them outside the dripline of existing trees and shrubs. Treated areas should be planted as soon as the waiting period is over to avoid reinfestation. Effectiveness is highest in warm weather, often disappointing in extremely cold or hot weather.

Important: Be sure to read labels carefully and follow the manufacturer's directions when applying any chemicals.

NEMATODES

Where soil nematodes are a serious problem, drastic measures may be necessary. In areas where there are no existing trees and shrubs, methyl bromide or a nematocide can be used before any planting is done. These chemicals are hazardous to handle and should be applied only by licensed personnel on the recommendation of a cooperative extension agent or landscape professional. Vapam is relatively easy to apply and may give some control.

USING PLANTING PLANS

On the following pages are planting plans based on the lot plans in Chapter 2. They will give you some hints for plant selection. Follow the steps below and use the plant lists in Chapter 6 to select the best plants for you.

First, give some thought about what purpose you want a plant to serve. Next, decide on the general category, size and placement. Then determine if the plant is adapted to your climate and whether it will have the proper exposure.

Now zero in on use and function once again. If a medium tree is needed for quick shade, a golden rain tree would be a better choice than a slower growing and more upright Bradford pear. If you want a large shrub that can be easily kept from getting too wide, yew pine would win hands down over oleander.

In many situations, the choice is not critical. You may be able to use almost any plant that is suited to your climate and exposure. This is where you can begin to combine plants for a pleasing composition of color, form and texture. Perhaps you can throw in a bit of seasonal interest with a tree that develops fall color, or a few flowering shrubs. If you're interested in fragrance, consider Southern magnolia, jasmine, honeysuckle, osmanthus, pines and roses. Also, try to group plants according to their watering needs so you don't have to drag out the hose to soak a few thirsty shrubs in the far corner of the yard.

Don't sacrifice utility for the sake of color. There's no need for every plant in your garden to be a heavy bloomer. However, many of the plants in the foolproof lists are both reliable *and* flowering. If you want more color, consider using annuals, bulbs and perennials in addition to the basic planting.

What is fascinating about planting design is that the requirements are challenging, the possibilities unlimited and the rewards tremendous.

NURSERY CONTAINER SIZES

Nursery plants are sold in many different sizes—from 1-quart perennials and bedding plants to large trees in boxes or barrels. Most containers are made of plastic or steel. Some nurseries sell plants *balled-in-burlap* (b/b). See pages 124 to 128 for tips on planting various types.

Balled-in-burlap Mugo pine.

1-gallon dwarf sword fern and 1-quart chrysanthemum.

5-gallon *'Mint Julep'* juniper and wax-leaf privet. Concrete blocks are 6 inches high.

Southern magnolia trees in 24-inch boxes.

7-gallon Wilson holly.

15-gallon crape myrtle.

STYLING YOUR LANDSCAPE

Plants help set the tone or style of your landscape. Carefully placed trees and accents add interesting color, contrast and texture to the scene. Plants help establish mood and feeling. The well-planned landscapes on this page may give you some good ideas.

Intricate, twisting branches of the Southern live oak symbolize the romance and nostalgia of the South.

Red and white colors of this Richmond home are echoed in the azaleas and dogwood tree.

Tall, upright form of a multi-trunk cajeput tree adds interesting dimension to this residence.

Plantings of white birch and ground cover give an inviting, woodsy feeling to this walk.

Stately appearance of this Dallas house is enhanced by the well-trimmed hedge and colorful planting beyond. Landscape architects: Lambert's.

Smooth bark and interesting branching pattern of the coral tree make it an ideal specimen near front entrance.

Contrasting gray and green of two junipers makes a neat, attractive driveway planting.

PLANTING PLAN—Interior Lot

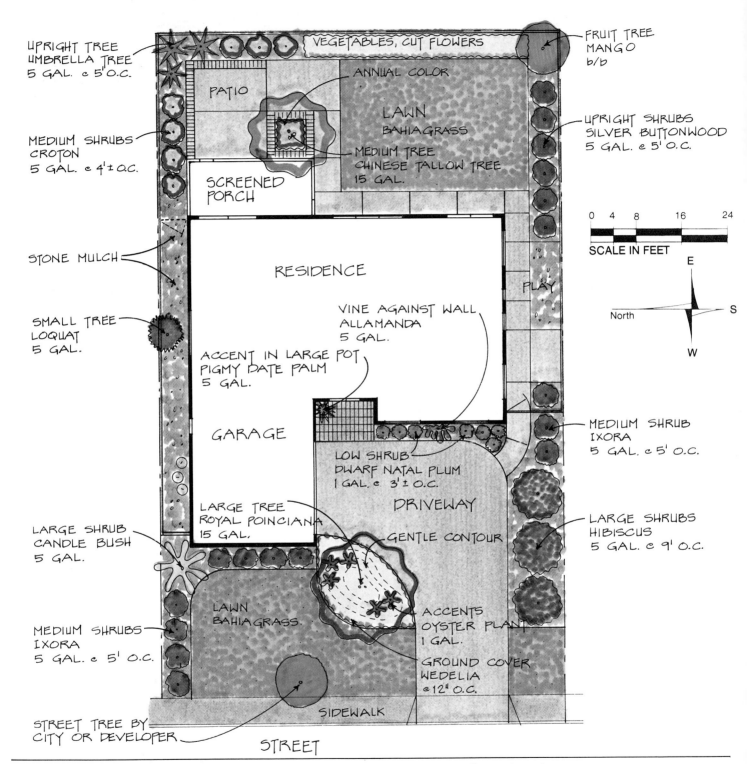

Zone 10—Tropical Climate

- Approximate average annual minimum temperature 30F to 40F (−1C to 5C). Frost rare.
- Near the coast, but away from direct salt spray.
- Many sunny days, high summer heat, warm nights and high humidity.
- Prevailing coastal winds with occasional windstorms.

Planting Considerations

- Plants thrive in the tropical climate and coastal conditions.
- Simple, orderly plant placement and selection are appropriate to the overall design.
- Small container sizes are used to stay within a modest budget.
- Bahiagrass withstands anticipated heavy use and is well-adapted to the climate.

PLANTING PLAN—Corner Lot

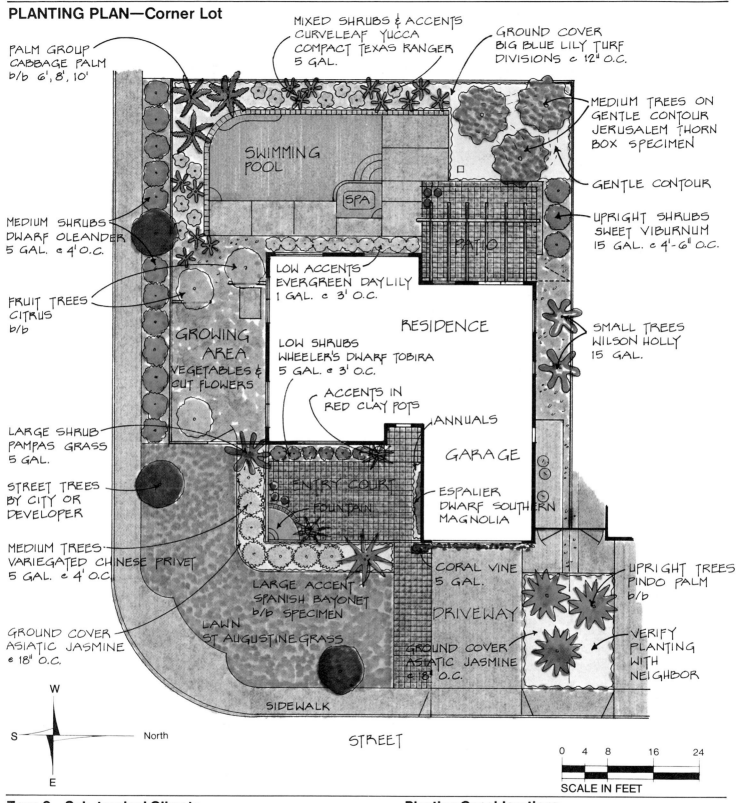

PALM GROUP
CABBAGE PALM
b/b 6', 8', 10'

MIXED SHRUBS & ACCENTS
CURVELEAF YUCCA
COMPACT TEXAS RANGER
5 GAL.

GROUND COVER
BIG BLUE LILY TURF
DIVISIONS @ 12" O.C.

MEDIUM TREES ON
GENTLE CONTOUR
JERUSALEM THORN
BOX SPECIMEN

SWIMMING
POOL

SPA

GENTLE CONTOUR

UPRIGHT SHRUBS
SWEET VIBURNUM
15 GAL. @ 4'-6" O.C.

MEDIUM SHRUBS
DWARF OLEANDER
5 GAL. @ 4' O.C.

FRUIT TREES
CITRUS
b/b

LOW ACCENTS
EVERGREEN DAYLILY
1 GAL. @ 3' O.C.

RESIDENCE

PATIO

SMALL TREES
WILSON HOLLY
15 GAL.

GROWING
AREA
VEGETABLES &
CUT FLOWERS

LOW SHRUBS
WHEELER'S DWARF TOBIRA
5 GAL. @ 3' O.C.

ACCENTS IN
RED CLAY POTS

LARGE SHRUB
PAMPAS GRASS
5 GAL.

ANNUALS

GARAGE

STREET TREES
BY CITY OR
DEVELOPER

ENTRY COURT

FOUNTAIN

ESPALIER
DWARF SOUTHERN
MAGNOLIA

MEDIUM TREES
VARIEGATED CHINESE PRIVET
5 GAL. @ 4' O.C.

LARGE ACCENT
SPANISH BAYONET
b/b SPECIMEN

CORAL VINE
5 GAL.

UPRIGHT TREES
PINDO PALM
b/b

GROUND COVER
ASIATIC JASMINE
@ 18" O.C.

LAWN
ST. AUGUSTINEGRASS

DRIVEWAY

GROUND COVER
ASIATIC JASMINE
@ 18" O.C.

VERIFY
PLANTING
WITH
NEIGHBOR

W   North
S
E

SIDEWALK

STREET

0   4   8   16   24
SCALE IN FEET

Zone 9—Sub-tropical Climate

- Approximate average annual minimum temperature 20F to 30F (−7C to −1C). Some light frost.
- Some coastal influence.
- Many sunny days, high summer heat, warm nights and high humidity.
- Occasional high winds.

Planting Considerations

- Heat-loving plants with tolerance of a few degrees of frost are used throughout.
- Palms, red clay pots and color accents carry out a *Spanish-Mediterranean* theme.
- Ample budget allows for 5-gallon and larger shrubs and several specimen trees.
- St. Augustinegrass will be green almost all year; thrives in high summer heat.

PLANTING PLAN—Cul-de-sac Lot

Zone 8—Moderate Climate

- Approximate average annual minimum temperature 10F to 20F (−12C to −7C).
- Summer heat and winter cold.
- Little coastal influence. Both high and low humidity.
- Occasional high winds.

Planting Considerations

- Plants sensitive to frost are avoided.
- Most plants have a casual quality and are placed in clumps and groups for a natural feeling.
- Modest-size plants fit in with the average budget.
- Hybrid bermudagrass lawn will withstand considerable wear; can be overseeded when dormant for winter color.

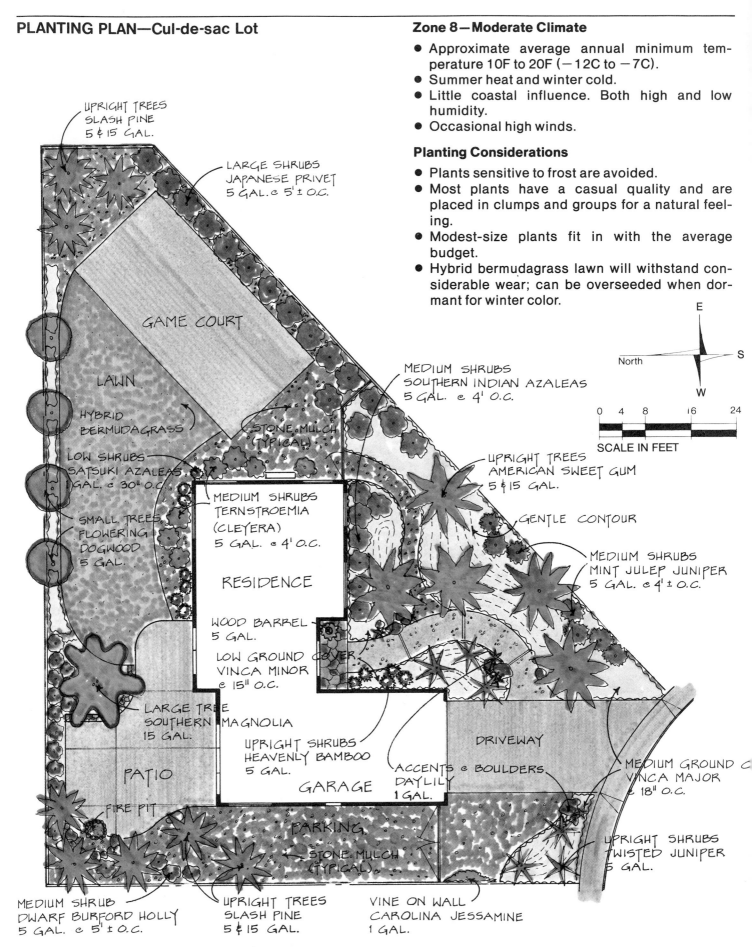

UPRIGHT TREES
SLASH PINE
5 & 15 GAL.

LARGE SHRUBS
JAPANESE PRIVET
5 GAL. @ 5'± O.C.

GAME COURT

LAWN

HYBRID
BERMUDAGRASS

LOW SHRUBS
SATSUKI AZALEAS
GAL. @ 30" O.C.

SMALL TREES
FLOWERING
DOGWOOD
5 GAL.

STONE MULCH
(TYPICAL)

MEDIUM SHRUBS
SOUTHERN INDIAN AZALEAS
5 GAL. @ 4' O.C.

UPRIGHT TREES
AMERICAN SWEET GUM
5 & 15 GAL.

MEDIUM SHRUBS
TERNSTROEMIA
(CLEYERA)
5 GAL. @ 4' O.C.

RESIDENCE

GENTLE CONTOUR

MEDIUM SHRUBS
MINT JULEP JUNIPER
5 GAL. @ 4'± O.C.

WOOD BARREL
5 GAL.

LOW GROUND COVER
VINCA MINOR
@ 15" O.C.

LARGE TREE
SOUTHERN MAGNOLIA
15 GAL.

UPRIGHT SHRUBS
HEAVENLY BAMBOO
5 GAL.

DRIVEWAY

ACCENTS @ BOULDERS
DAYLILY
1 GAL.

MEDIUM GROUND C
VINCA MAJOR
@ 18" O.C.

PATIO

FIRE PIT

GARAGE

PARKING

STONE MULCH
(TYPICAL)

UPRIGHT SHRUBS
TWISTED JUNIPER
5 GAL.

MEDIUM SHRUB
DWARF BURFORD HOLLY
5 GAL. @ 5'± O.C.

UPRIGHT TREES
SLASH PINE
5 & 15 GAL.

VINE ON WALL
CAROLINA JESSAMINE
1 GAL.

E
North
S
W

SCALE IN FEET
0 4 8 16 24

PLANTING PLAN—Condo Lot

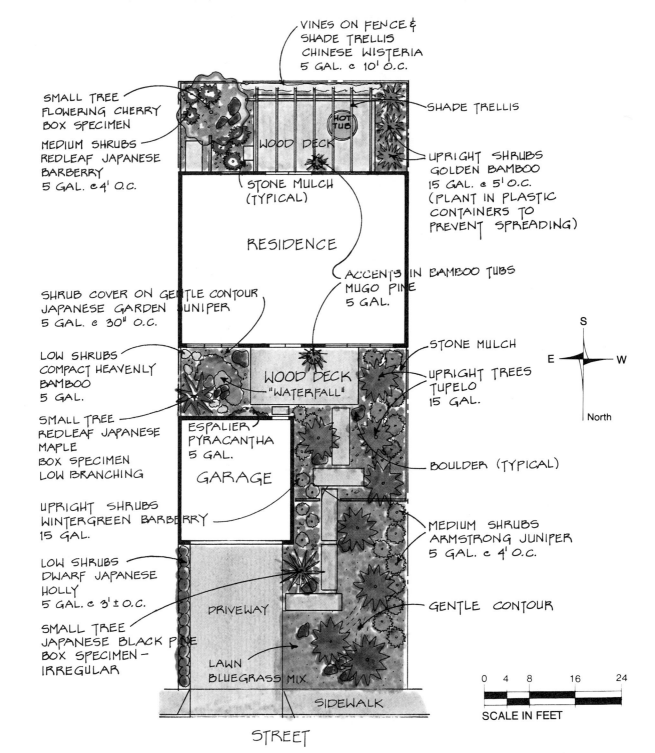

VINES ON FENCE &
SHADE TRELLIS
CHINESE WISTERIA
5 GAL. @ 10' O.C.

SMALL TREE
FLOWERING CHERRY
BOX SPECIMEN

MEDIUM SHRUBS
REDLEAF JAPANESE
BARBERRY
5 GAL. @ 4' O.C.

SHADE TRELLIS

WOOD DECK

HOT TUB

UPRIGHT SHRUBS
GOLDEN BAMBOO
15 GAL. @ 5' O.C.
(PLANT IN PLASTIC
CONTAINERS TO
PREVENT SPREADING)

STONE MULCH
(TYPICAL)

RESIDENCE

ACCENTS IN BAMBOO TUBS
MUGO PINE
5 GAL.

SHRUB COVER ON GENTLE CONTOUR
JAPANESE GARDEN JUNIPER
5 GAL. @ 30" O.C.

LOW SHRUBS
COMPACT HEAVENLY
BAMBOO
5 GAL.

STONE MULCH

WOOD DECK
"WATERFALL"

UPRIGHT TREES
TUPELO
15 GAL.

SMALL TREE
REDLEAF JAPANESE
MAPLE
BOX SPECIMEN
LOW BRANCHING

ESPALIER
PYRACANTHA
5 GAL.

GARAGE

BOULDER (TYPICAL)

UPRIGHT SHRUBS
WINTERGREEN BARBERRY
15 GAL.

MEDIUM SHRUBS
ARMSTRONG JUNIPER
5 GAL. @ 4' O.C.

LOW SHRUBS
DWARF JAPANESE
HOLLY
5 GAL. @ 3' ± O.C.

SMALL TREE
JAPANESE BLACK PINE
BOX SPECIMEN—
IRREGULAR

DRIVEWAY

LAWN
BLUEGRASS MIX.

GENTLE CONTOUR

SIDEWALK

STREET

S
E — W
North

0   4   8   16   24

SCALE IN FEET

Zone 7—Severe Climate

- Approximate average annual minimum temperature 0F to 10F (−18C to −12C).
- Wide temperature variation common within 24-hour period.
- Periods of low humidity.
- Strong, seasonal winds.

Planting Considerations

- Hardiest plants from the top of the lists are used throughout.
- Conifers, bamboo, irregular forms, boulders and contours enhance an *Oriental* motif.
- Feature plants are of specimen size. Key shrubs are 15-gallon size in accordance with ample budget.
- Low maintenance achieved with rugged plants, stone mulch and a limited lawn area.

It is hard to imagine what our neighborhoods would look like without lawns. They provide the continuity that links individual landscapes into a harmonious whole. And there is no better surface to play and romp on. Grass also helps control erosion and dust, reduces noise and glare and has a significant overall cooling effect. A lawn of some type is usually the best landscape treatment for large, open, level areas.

How much care you need to give it, and how much it costs depends on the soil, climate, type of grass and whether you want a casual meadow or a manicured carpet. There are many choices.

In general, the cool-season grasses are best for the cooler areas of Zone 7 and northward. Warm-season grasses are most successful in Zones 9 and 10. Zone 8 is the transition area where either kind might do well—or poorly. Carefully check out what performs well locally and select the type that best fits your needs. Seed, sprigs, stolons, plugs and sod that are *certified* will guarantee purity and are worth the slight additional cost.

COOL-SEASON GRASSES

Best planting time: fall and spring.

Bluegrass—*Poa pratensis*

There is a confusing number of bluegrass varieties. More than 40 are currently being marketed. *Fylking, Adelphi* and *Baron* are outstanding, but your nurseryman or extension agent may recommend other varieties for your particular climate. Usually two or more are combined rather than planting singly. Rough bluegrass, *Poa*

Verdant expanse of bluegrass-mix lawn explains its popularity, but it does require constant care and lots of water to look this good.

trivialis, is valuable for moist, shady areas; *Sabre* is a selected variety worth looking for.

Uniformity, fine texture, ability to withstand normal wear and rich, green color explains the popularity of bluegrass. It will grow in full sun or light shade. For best performance, it requires good soil, slightly on the acid side. It requires supplemental watering during dry spells, regular fertilization, and a good program of weed, insect and disease control. Sow seed at 2 to 3 pounds per 1,000 square feet.

When not to use a lawn? Steep slopes are difficult to mow. No grass thrives under trees with heavy shade and root competition. Rocky soils may cost too much to improve enough to support a lawn. Small, narrow strips are difficult to mow and edge. In these cases, a ground cover or shrub cover would most likely be a better choice.

Where rainfall is low, periodic droughts common and irrigation water limited, lawn areas should be reserved for use and viewing adjacent to the house. Fringe areas can be covered with bark chips, pine needles, gravel or similar materials. Drought-tolerant plants can be added where desired. If there is native vegetation, consider cleaning it up a bit. Enjoy a woodsy effect instead of tearing it out to install a high-maintenance lawn.

Mowing height is normally 1-1/2 to 2 inches. Some varieties will withstand shorter mowing.

Fescue—*Festuca elatior*

Tall fescue is valuable for the warmest parts of Zone 7 and the coldest parts of Zone 8. These areas are too hot in summer for bluegrass and too cold in winter for the warm-season grasses. Tall fescue tends to bunch when planted with other grasses, so it should comprise at least 60 percent of a mixture. Or, better yet, sow it alone at 8 to 10 pounds per 1,000 square

In many situations, there's just no substitute for a beautiful lawn.

There's nothing quite like a rolling lawn. This is *Tifgreen* hybrid bermudagrass. It requires first-class maintenance to look first class, but will survive even if totally neglected. Landscape architect: Ken Smith.

feet. *K-31* is the most common variety for southern conditions.

Tall fescue is tough. It stands wear and hot weather well. It is reasonably drought tolerant, thrives in most soils, takes a little shade and is not overly susceptible to insect and disease. About its only drawback is the coarse texture.

Varieties *Rebel* and *Falcon* are finer textured and perform well in the transition zone from Philadelphia south to Atlanta. Cool fall weather is best for planting, but with careful watering it can be planted in spring or other times of the year. Mowing height is 2 to 2-1/2 inches.

Creeping red fescue, *Festuca rubra,* is fine-textured and is often added to a bluegrass mix because it is more shade tolerant. Try it as an unmowed slope or ground cover for a casual, natural effect. It also makes a good winter overseeding for dormant, warm-season grasses such as bermuda and St. Augustine. Sow at 4 to 5 pounds per 1,000 square feet. *Penn-lawn* and *Jamestown* are two good varieties.

Ryegrass — *Lolium* species

Annual ryegrass is often used to overseed dormant warm-season grasses, sown at 5 to 6 pounds per 1,000 square feet. Mow low in spring to encourage the permanent, warm-season grass to take over again.

Old-fashioned perennial ryegrass

Common bermudagrass. The hybrids are finer textured.

makes a coarse, bunchy, inferior lawn. New, improved, fine-bladed hybrids, such as *Pennfine, Manhattan, Yorktown II* and *NK-200,* are compatible with bluegrass. They add toughness and disease resistance when 2 or 3 pounds per 1,000 square feet are included in the mix.

These new hybrids can also be used to overseed common bermudagrass. If mowed at 1-1/2 to 2 inches, they will persist fairly well throughout the year in all but the hottest climates.

WARM-SEASON GRASSES

Best planting time: late spring and early summer.

Bermudagrass — *Cynodon dactylon*

The various bermudagrasses are

Main drawback of bermudagrass is the winter dormancy period in all but the warmest areas. Overseeding and spraying with lawn dye are common practices for maintaining a year-round green appearance.

tolerant of heat, drought, poor soil, alkalinity, salt and heavy traffic. Insect and disease resistance are generally good. They require frequent mowing and nitrogen fertilization. They build up considerable thatch, go dormant in winter except in frost-free areas, need full sun for best performance and spread into nearby planting beds.

St. Augustinegrass is at its best in Zones 9 and 10, and is also used in Zone 8 when winter dormancy is not too objectionable.

Blade width of St. Augustinegrass is similar to tall fescue and carpetgrass.

Common bermudagrass makes a fairly presentable lawn when given reasonable care. When it invades and combines with other grasses, the result is a varied texture that is objectionable if you're looking for a classic carpet. Sow 1 to 2 pounds of seed per 1,000 square feet. Mow often to a 1-inch height to prevent formation of seed heads.

Hybrid bermudagrasses are often used for high-quality lawns. They require more care, but have a more pleasing color and texture than common bermudagrass. *Tifway (T419), Tiflawn (Tifton 57)* and *Tifgreen (T328)* are three of the best.

I prefer *Tifgreen* because it has the finest texture, although it does require a little higher maintenance than the others.

The hybrids set no viable seed, so they must be sodded or planted from sprigs or plugs spaced 6 to 12 inches apart. Hybrids can also be planted from stolons spread at the rate of three bushels per 1,000 square feet. Mow 3/4-inch high at least once a week during the growing season. Annual dethatching is advisable to prevent excessive build-up.

St. Augustinegrass— *Stenotaphrum secundatum*

This is perhaps the most common grass throughout the lower South,
thriving in both sunny and partially shady locations. It makes a thick sod, is coarse in texture, and tolerates traffic fairly well. Best growth is with ample water in a fertile, well-drained soil. But St. Augustinegrass is not overly fussy and will persist in salty soils. Surface runners are easy to keep out of nearby planting beds.

Unfortunately, St. Augustinegrass is susceptible to brown patch, leaf spot, St. Augustine decline, chinch bugs and white grubs. *Floratam* variety is recommended for its resistance to St. Augustine decline and chinch bugs. It is not as cold tolerant and is less shade tolerant than other varieties.

Sod St. Augustinegrass or plant from sprigs or plugs at 12 inches apart. Mow to a height of 2 to 3 inches. St. Augustine eventually gets very thick and must be dethatched on a regular basis. Excessive fertilizer encourages thatch build-up.

Zoysiagrass— *Zoysia* species

If you want a smooth, even-textured lawn that is really tough, this is the grass for you. It withstands low temperatures and wear. It tolerates partial shade and is subject to little disease and insect damage. It gets by on normal watering, doesn't take over planting beds, and is thick enough to crowd out weeds and other grasses.

There are two drawbacks. Zoysiagrass establishes very slowly. Plugs may take several years to cover an area completely. Sprigs in rows at 6 inches apart will take at least a full year. Stolonizing at 5 bushels per 1,000 square feet may establish a little faster under ideal conditions. This is where sod may be worth the added expense, especially if a relatively small area is involved. Although cold-tolerant, zoysiagrass will turn brown after the first frost and is slow to come out of dormancy in the spring.

Emerald (Z. japonia X Z. tenuifolia) and *Meyer (Z-52, Z. japonica)* are most common, although Manilagrass *(Z. matrella)* is used where tolerance to salt spray is a factor. Mow 3/4 to 1-inch high. Annual dethatching is necessary if you want a billiard-table effect.

Centipedegrass— *Eremochloa ophiuroides*

In relatively frost-free areas with poor acid soils, this grass is a good low-maintenance choice. It requires less mowing than other grasses and chokes out weeds. It withstands dry spells well, needs little fertilizer, doesn't invade planting areas and tolerates as much shade as St. Augustinegrass. Disease and insect resistance are good from Texas along the Gulf to southern Georgia and northern Florida. Diseases are a problem south of Orlando. Centipedegrass will winterkill in heavy frost.

In alkaline soils or with high fertilization, *iron chlorosis* will occur,

This meticulously maintained 'Emerald' zoysia lawn of C.M. Einhorn in Atlanta even looks good when it is dormant.

Slow-growing zoysiagrass is a good choice for between stepping stones.

Centipedegrass thrives in poor, acid soils.

Bahiagrass is a warm-season grass that looks more like a cool-season type.

Small, heart-shaped dichondra leaves indicate that it isn't a grass at all. However, it serves well as a lawn under the right conditions. The coin is from Thailand.

necessitating treatment with iron chelates or sulphate. Sow seed at 1/2 pound per 1,000 square feet. Sprig at 6 inches apart, or lay solid sod. Mow infrequently to 1-inch height.

OTHER GRASSES

Carpetgrass — *Axonopus affinis*

This is low-growing and coarse-textured, somewhat similar in appearance to St. Augustinegrass. Valuable for frost-free areas with wet, sandy, acid soils where low maintenance is desired. It will tolerate a little shade, is relatively free of insects and disease, and withstands normal but not heavy traffic.

Carpetgrass is planted from seed at the rate of 3 to 5 pounds per 1,000 square feet. Sprig at 6 to 12 inches apart. Mow frequently at 1-inch height to prevent formation of undesirable seed heads.

Bahiagrass — *Paspalum notatum*

Admittedly bahiagrass doesn't look as good as bluegrass, but in Florida and along the Gulf where cool-season grasses won't grow, it is a reasonable substitute. Bahiagrass is relatively free of insects and disease, thrives in sandy soils, tolerates some salt and drought and is wear-resistant.

Argentine is a deep-rooted, wide-bladed variety. *Paraguay* and *Pensacola* are fine-bladed types. Plant from seed at 3 to 5 pounds per 1,000 square feet. Mow weekly during the growing season 2 inches high with a sharp mower to cut off tough seed heads.

Dichondra — *Dichondra caroliniana*

Dichondra is not a grass, but grown as a ground cover or lawn substitute. It gets a little brown when temperatures fall below 25F (−4C) and may be damaged below 20F (−7C). The interesting texture, bright green color, and infrequent mowing to a 1-inch height are chief advantages. Slightly acid soil is best. Continual moisture and regular fertilization are required for best appearance. It will take some foot traffic and light shade.

Constant vigilance is necessary to keep dichondra free from invading bermudagrass, spotted spurge and oxalis. It has a remarkable tolerance of diphenamid, which is sold as Enide or Dymid to help control germinating weed seeds. Diphenamid can be applied at time of planting.

The real problems are snails, flea beetles, nematodes, cutworms and fungus diseases. Where these are prevalent, dichondra should be limited to small areas such as between stepping stones. Sow seed at 2 to 3 pounds per 1,000 square feet or plant plugs 6 to 12 inches apart. Sodding is a common practice where sod is available.

INSTALLING YOUR LAWN

Installing a lawn isn't as much fun as planting shrubs and trees. But it can be satisfying and you can save a fair amount of money if it is done properly. Soil preparation, pH modification and weed control are the same wheth-

er the lawn is seeded, sprigged, stolonized, plugged or sodded. All are described in Chapter 7. Once they're completed and any water piping or sprinklers are installed, you're ready to begin. You should also check pages 49 and 50 for grading and drainage information.

Most nurseries will lend or rent mechanical seeders and rollers if you buy the materials from them. Cost and type of grass will determine which method of installation is best for you. Don't forget to allow 10 to 15 cents per square foot for normal soil preparation. Add the following per square foot: seeded lawns 10 to 15 cents; sprigging 15 to 25 cents, depending on spacing; stolonizing 20 to 30 cents; and sodding 25 to 50 cents. Sod prices vary considerably with type and locality. These are all contractor prices. Do it yourself and save at least 50 percent.

SEEDING

● Drag the area using a 4-foot-long 2x4 with approximately 50 pounds of weight added on top. This helps avoid low spots. The soil should be moist, but not muddy.
● Prepare the seed bed by raking

lightly. Rocks over 1/2 inch in diameter should be removed.
● Sow the seed at the rate prescribed on the package. Don't sow seed when the wind is blowing. Use a mechanical seeder for even distribution. Rake the seed in very lightly, so it is covered no more than 1/4 inch deep. Include 30 pounds of 8-8-8 commercial fertilizer per 1,000 square feet if not previously applied.
● Top dress or cover the seed bed lightly with organic material approximately 1/4 inch deep. This equals 1/2 cubic yard per 1,000 square feet. Nitrolized sawdust, peat moss or commercial top dressings are good. Don't use material with high salt content, such as manure.
● Roll with a water-filled lawn roller.
● Water to thoroughly saturate the mulch and keep it moist until seeds have germinated. If rainfall is insufficient, be prepared to water several times a day in hot weather for the first few weeks. If you have sprinklers, turn them on for short periods to avoid washing away the seeds.

HYDROSEEDING

Large lawn areas are often installed

using a spray-on method called *hydroseeding*. Seed and fertilizer are combined with a wood fiber, making a slurry similar to a thin papier-mache. Advantages are built-in mulch for the seed, good erosion control—especially when a binding additive is used—and sometimes lower cost than hand-seeding when sufficient area is involved.

SPRIGGING

As noted previously, most warm-season grasses cannot be sown as seed. Instead, a living piece or *sprig* of hybrid bermuda, zoysia, centipede or St. Augustine grass is inserted and compacted in the soil with a portion extending above ground. A light top dressing is advisable but is not as crucial as with seed.

The closer sprigs are planted together, the faster the coverage will be. For fast-growing hybrid bermudagrass, 12 inches apart is acceptable. However, 6 inches is better for all grasses, and essential for slow-growing zoysia. Use only fresh, moist sprigs and don't allow them to dry out. Avoid overwatering or sprigs may develop waterborne diseases. Coverage time varies

Sodding costs about twice as much as a seeded lawn, but saves a lot of hassle. This dichondra will be rolled for better root contact and to level the surface.

Some folks get downright carried away with their lawn—even put it on the roof.

from 30 days for bermuda under ideal conditions to two years for zoysia.

STOLONIZING

Stolonizing is similar to sprigging. *Stolons,* living pieces of grass, are distributed evenly over the surface and pressed into firm contact using a special ridged roller. Or, they can be lightly covered with a thin layer of soil. Top dressing and water are applied immediately to prevent drying out.

Only bermudagrass and zoysiagrass are normally installed by stolonizing. The advantage over sprigging is that time needed for coverage is reduced

considerably, and a more even surface is obtained.

SODDING AND PLUGGING

The best way to avoid erosion and eliminate weeding, watering and care of tender seedlings is to install a ready-made carpet of *sod.* It looks good immediately, and is ready for normal traffic after a few weeks. Lay the pieces on slightly moist soil that has been properly prepared and leveled. Butt the joints tightly and roll lightly before watering thoroughly.

If you're doing a large area, or if it is a really hot day, water small areas as

they're laid, rather than waiting until it is all finished. This way the sod won't dry out. Top dressing is not used, except a thin layer of fine sand can be used after the lawn is established to level minor unevenness. Look for new sod-growing techniques where the grass is grown in easy-to-handle mesh and mats.

Plugs are 2-inch squares of sod planted 6 to 12 inches apart. Disadvantages are time needed for full coverage and tendency to bumpiness. Plugs are often used in existing lawns with the hope that the new type of grass will miraculously take over the

Gentle slopes are easy to mow. In most cases, lawn is more serviceable than a ground cover.

White birch trees thrive in a lawn, and the light shade they create helps the lawn thrive too.

less desirable existing types. Sometimes it works, but usually the results are slow and irregular.

BUT YOU'VE ALREADY GOT A LAWN

What can you do to improve an existing lawn that looks poor, but isn't bad enough to tear out?

● First, mow it short to approximately 1/2 inch. Rake deeply to expose some soil. If existing thatch is thick, *verti-cut* it with a rented machine and remove all the debris.

● Soak thoroughly for several days.

● Aerate by removing cores of soil with a hand or power aerator.

● Remove any weeds that come up. If there are many broad-leaved weeds, apply a 2,4-D mixture of Trimec or Trex-San. Wait a week for it to do the job.

● If common bermudagrass is prevalent throughout the old lawn, why not join it rather than fight it? It looks quite presentable during the warm months, and responds well to water and fertilizer.

● Seed according to directions on pages 138 to 140.

● Another alternative is to spray the actively growing, unmowed lawn with Round-up or Kleen-up to eliminate all weeds and grasses, including bermudagrass. Wait a week, remove thatch with a verti-cutter so that approximately 25 percent bare soil is exposed. Then replant as for a new lawn.

INSECTS AND DISEASES

This book is not big enough to thoroughly cover the insects and diseases that attack lawns. Depending on where you live and what kind of lawn you have, you're likely to encounter chinch bug, sod webworms, armyworms, grubs, brown patch, dollar patch or St. Augustine decline at some time or another. With luck, you will not encounter all of them.

As discussed in Chapter 13, "Maintenance," some anticipatory chemical applications are advisable in many situations. Diagnosis is often difficult and products are constantly changing. If you have a good lawn-care service, ask what treatments they're using. If you do your own mowing, look to your nurseryman or extension agent for help. Once you get to know the problem and what to do about it, you can probably take care of it yourself as part of routine maintenance.

HOW ABOUT TREES?

It is often desirable to plant trees in a lawn for shade and appearance. Select a type that will tolerate lawn watering and will not cast dense shade or develop surface roots. Be sure the tree isn't planted in a low spot or it doesn't settle after planting. If your soil drains poorly, it is a good idea to plant the tree on a gentle rise or contour to avoid continually wet roots. Relatively shallow watering encourages surface rooting. Use a root feeder or soil soaker once in a while to provide deep moisture.

Some of the trees most compatible with lawns include purple-leaf plum, Southern magnolia, birch, cabbage palm, sweet gum, tulip tree and dogwood. See the plant lists in Chapter 6 for additional information.

Instant Landscaping 9

There are several advantages in starting out with small plants. They're easier to install, cost less and often establish themselves better than larger ones. After five years, the 98-cent special will probably be as big as if you'd started with a $27.50 specimen. But there are situations where an instant effect is worth paying the premium.

The average length of stay in a house is less than five years. Most families move out just about the time the planting starts to look nice. It is frustrating to see all your expense, hard work and loving care benefit the new owners rather than yourself. Even if you don't sell within five years, there is little use and enjoyment of an unshaded patio, a back yard with no privacy and a bleak and barren landscape.

Most homeowners do not have the budget to imitate the exterior decorating of model homes and commercial buildings. But we *can* borrow some of the techniques that transform a blank area into a full-grown garden overnight.

A common mistake is to rely entirely on plants. Use a solid fence instead of a hedge if immediate privacy is desirable. A shade trellis cools a patio the day it is finished. You don't have to wait years for a tree to grow. Planter boxes, low walls, benches and other landscape construction help make up for small plants.

TREES

Large trees are the backbone of instant landscaping. Field-grown or container specimens are generally available in heights up to 10 feet. This is far from a full-grown tree, but it is a step in the right direction. Cost and height vary greatly with the type of tree. A relatively slow-growing Southern magnolia will be smaller and more expensive than a rapid-growing weeping willow. Usually you can get a fairly respectable tree for $100 to $200, including planting.

Trees taller than 10 feet are often available in major metropolitan areas—for a price. Don't plan on installing a large balled-in-burlap or boxed tree yourself. Even a ten-footer can weigh up to half a ton and often requires a big truck with a winch to set it in place.

Brownish tan boulders were selected to complement the bark mulch. Black pine is from a 15-gallon container that cost about $40 to $50 retail.

What about large slash pines, cedar elms, Southern live oaks and other *bargains* wrenched from the ground rather than grown in a nursery? If handled with reasonable care, many can survive the shock of being moved and you end up with a large tree for a relatively low price. The catch is that there is little guarantee against failure. It is always best to deal with a reputable landscape company or nursery and have a clear understanding as to what the guarantee covers.

Instead of buying larger sizes to start with, you can select rapid-growing plants such as glossy privet, *'Lowfast'* cotoneaster, coral vine, Chinaberry, pampas grass, or *'East Paltka'* holly for a *delayed* instant effect. This is especially valid for a shade tree, screening shrub or vine, shrub cover or windbreak. There's no point in waiting 10 years for results. However, many fast growers are relatively short-lived and soon outgrow their location, necessitating excessive pruning or even removal. Use them with caution and allow plenty of room.

Another bargain is to buy large bare-root deciduous trees such as sycamore, pecan, maple or mulberry. The timing must be right because the planting season is limited to two or three months during winter when the trees are dormant. Only a few nurseries carry bare-root trees in large sizes. It is the least expensive way to get good-size trees the first season. Most of these are "softwood" types and are generally not as desirable as slower-growing "hardwoods."

SHRUBS

Rather than buy all shrubs balled-in-burlap or in 5-gallon containers,

This shade trellis turned a dull blank wall into an inviting entranceway.

THE ART OF INSTANT LANDSCAPING

Monday morning: Bare dirt without even a weed.

First, the walks were poured and sprinklers installed. Organic material was spread and then contractor John Rooney rototilled it into the soil.

Next, plant holes were dug. A heavy steel digging bar is helpful for hard soils.

It took two strong men to handle this boxed Fortune windmill palm. It weighed over 500 pounds.

Sod arrives in rolls like carpet.

Sod should be laid as fast as possible so it can be watered before it starts to dry out. Edges must be trimmed to fit, so it takes several workers to get the job finished quickly enough.

Friday afternoon: The finished yard after adding a few well-placed trees and shrubs to the sod lawn. Bare ground was covered with bark chunks. Other areas were covered with stone mulch, dichondra sod and flowers.

concentrate on a few of the most important ones. Some larger plants installed near the front door or patio can help tremendously. One $50 shrub in the right place can impart a lushness as soon as it is planted. Balance the budget by using 1-gallon sizes for the less important places.

GROUND COVERS

Most ground covers take one or more seasons before they actually cover the ground. They don't qualify for an instant effect. With some ground covers, such as Japanese spurge, *Vinca minor* and English ivy, you can speed things up by planting as closely together as 9 inches, and by making sure they get proper care. A better way is to cover the bare areas with a bark or stone mulch. This will eliminate mud and dust, besides looking good right away.

SOD LAWNS

Installing a lawn from sod is another technique often used when immediate results are desired, The advantage over seed is definitely short-term. Within six months, a seeded lawn should look just as good. However, sod does eliminate the crucial germination period when watering may be required three, four or five times a day. It also reduces erosion and weeds to a minimum, and can be walked on in a few weeks rather than several months from seed.

Frankly, the biggest reward of all is impressing your friends and neighbors. It will shock them to see your bare dirt transformed into a green carpet within a few hours!

When you take into account the labor for watering, weeding, reseeding bare spots and cleaning-up nuisance erosion, sod doesn't cost that much more than seed. Soil preparation and grading are identical for both. Contractor's price for seeding 1,000 square feet is $150 to $200. Laying sod would be $300 to $400. The extra cost is often worth it for a small lawn. Of course, the cost difference does become significant when you want to cover large areas.

OTHER TOUCHES

Boulders, driftwood, sculptures and

These balled-in-burlap English boxwood are priced at $15 apiece. This is expensive if you're planting a long hedge, but two or three in key locations may be desirable.

similar features can help dramatize a new landscape. Earth sculpture or contouring is another effective, relatively low-cost method often employed in model home landscaping. If you have excess soil, it might even save money to use it for contours rather than having it hauled away.

Container plants can be used to put foliage at just the right spot. Yew pine, twisted juniper, various hollies, aralia and camellia are good subjects for large pots or wooden tubs. In many cases they can be seen from both inside and outside the house. Hanging baskets such as Sprenger asparagus, spider plant and creeping Charlie are especially effective because they are usually at eye level.

A few spots of color finish things off. These flowers were planted closely together from 4-inch pots. The zigzag walk is more interesting than the usual straight version.

Bark mulch is a good way to cover the bare ground until the shrubs grow.

Don't haul away large rocks and boulders. They can be used as dramatic accents in both lawn and planting areas.

LIGHTING

Don't overlook nighttime viewing. This is when most entertaining occurs and when you want things to look special. A few well-placed lights that emphasize the biggest plants and outstanding features can make a newly planted yard appear much better than it really is.

Garden lighting can be divided into two main classifications: practical lighting for use, safety and security; and ornamental lighting for beauty and interest. Whenever possible, the two types should be combined so the lighting is both useful and beautiful.

The need for practical lighting is easy to determine. Steps, walks, house numbers, driveways, patios, swimming pools, game courts and other areas likely to be used at night obviously need illumination. Purely ornamental lighting is more open to personal preference and can even be left out entirely.

Up-lighting is where the light is at ground level and shoots upward. This is effective at the base of the object to be featured. Usually the light is placed in front of the object to be highlighted. Sometimes the light can be in back, such as with a specimen tree, which can create an interesting silhouette. The main problem is placing the light so it will not be seen directly, and only shines on the object to be illuminated.

Down-lighting is any type of lighting that is directed downward. It can be above, below or at eye level. The larger the area to be covered, the higher the light must be. The problem of glare is encountered as soon as eye level is reached. This can be solved with placement, shields or filters.

Outdoor fixtures must be waterproof, except low-voltage types, and should be of rugged construction. A hidden light source need not be a beautiful fixture, but where the fixture itself is seen, it should have a scale and design appropriate to the setting. Costs range from $10 to over $100, depending on size, type and quality. Junction boxes, as required by electrical codes, are distracting and should be hidden if possible, or replaced with an approved underground type.

Partially sunken floodlight unobtrusively up-lights a pine tree. The hood and grille help reduce glare.

Brick pilaster lights define entry drive and provide safety and security.

Wood lamp was designed and installed between railroad ties. Plastic was used instead of glass because it costs less and is easier to handle. Light source is a low-voltage floodlight.

Low-voltage wood light by Sylvan Designs costs approximately $15.

This driveway light is both practical and attractive. The bold scale of the heavy timbers is just right for the style of this house.

An 18-watt, low-voltage floodlight highlights the shape of this tree and creates a tranquil mood.

An old-fashioned gas light adds charm to this Dallas garden designed by landscape architect Lambert's.

This waterproof 120-watt transformer is plugged into an exterior outlet. No permit or electrician is required.

plus the actual fixture price. Costs for long conduit runs, breaking through walls and difficult access should be added to the basic figure.

LOW-VOLTAGE LIGHTING

You can probably see the handwriting on the wall. Except where high wattage is needed, such as for a game court or security floodlighting, low-voltage lighting has many advantages over 110-volt, and is probably the way you should go. Eight 18-watt low-voltage lights use less energy than one 150-watt floodlight. Because the candlepower is also lower, the effect is more subtle. Low-voltage lighting is safe to handle and doesn't require a building permit.

No special tools or skills are required to install low-voltage lights. The wires can be buried directly in the same trench as sprinkler piping, hung on a wall or fence or laid on the surface. Because they require no conduit, placement is easily changed for best effect. They can be added to an existing planting with a minimum of disturbance and an existing circuit can usually be used without danger of overloading. Floodlights can be installed flush with the ground or partially buried.

The cost is significantly lower than 110-volt lighting. Kits consisting of six lights, a waterproof transformer and 100 feet of wire are priced under $100. A wide range of fixtures is available in addition to floodlights, such as hanging lights, path lights and wood lanterns.

It is handy to be able to switch on lights from inside the house. If you already have an exterior outlet that is switched from inside, just plug the transformer in and you're all set. For an exterior outlet that is not switched, you can get a transformer with a built-in timer for an extra $10 or so. Another way is to drill a hole through the garage wall and install the transformer inside with a switch, or just plug it in when you want to turn on the lights.

The typical 120-watt transformer will handle six 18-watt lights. If you want more than six, use two transformers. Also available are 200-watt and 300-watt transformers for 11 and 16 lights, respectively.

Placement of garden lighting is best done at night, after construction and planting have been completed. Some experts advise working with extension cords, shifting fixtures until the desired effect is achieved. The difficulty with this method is that trenches for conduits then have to be dug through the existing planting, and some damage is likely to occur. One way of avoiding this is to install waterproof outlets before planting and use plug-in type fixtures on short cords. Another way is to use a low-voltage system that is easy to move around.

All electrical work, except low-voltage lighting, requires a permit and inspection. Because of the danger involved, and the tools and experience that are necessary, all but the low-voltage types are best installed by an electrical contractor. It is possible for the homeowner to do the trench digging and other unskilled labor. The contractor can do the electrical hookup. If you're running 110-volt lines, you might as well include some waterproof outlets and stub-outs for any future work.

Costs vary considerably for installation of garden lighting and individual fixtures. Outlet boxes for 110-volt lighting cost about $25 each. Conduits cost at least $1.50 per lineal foot, plus switches, fixtures and connection charge. This is assuming the work will be done by a contractor. A rough way to estimate is to allow $50 per outlet,

Small Spaces 10

Most of the ideas and information in this book apply whether you have a rambling ranch, normal-size city lot or a condominium with a tiny plot of land. If you want to include as many amenities as possible and your outdoor space is limited to a small area, it takes extremely careful planning.

When an area is very small, such as an atrium or enclosed court, the first decision is whether or not it is only to look at or if it can also be used for dining, entertaining and lounging. If you have two such areas, sometimes one can be devoted entirely to planting and the other to outdoor activities. If there's only one, then the major portion of it may have to be paved and planting space severely limited.

Container plants, espaliers, vines and hanging baskets are good ways of getting the maximum amount of greenery in a small space. Dwarf shrubs such as Wheeler's dwarf tobira, compact nandina, dwarf burford holly and red elf pyracantha are valuable for small beds. Narrow, upright shrubs and trees are also likely candidates for a walled-in patio, as discussed in Chapter 6.

Heat is often intensified and sun/shade patterns change drastically with the seasons in an area enclosed by high walls. North-facing areas may never receive any direct sunlight. A southern exposure can be a real problem. Plants must be chosen carefully or given special protection to survive the changing conditions of the season. Container plants can be moved to receive more or less sun as needed. Check the exposure column on the plant lists in Chapter 6 to make sure a

Enclosed atrium was treated as a pleasant scene, not an outdoor activity area. Design: Ken Smith, ASLA.

Owner-builder Dan Paul followed landscape architect Edith Henderson's plan to create an intimate sitting area.

This New Orleans courtyard serves double duty as an entrance and an activity area.

This carefully scaled Japanese garden makes the most of a small area.

A narrow patio is made to appear larger by a clever lattice wall treatment. Landscape architect: Steve Coenen, New Orleans.

Southern magnolia can be trained as a bold, large-scale espalier. Look for the cultivar, 'St. Mary'. It is easier to keep small.

Just because the front yard of this mobile home is only 6 feet wide doesn't mean it isn't important to the owner. Upright-growing twisted junipers are a good choice to shade the front windows and soften the look of the structure.

This narrow planting area appears larger because of the receding gray color of the fence and foliage of the blue Atlas cedars.

Landscape architect C.C. Pat Fleming extended the decking to gain space for poolside dining and enhanced the view with an airy wrought-iron railing.

shade plant doesn't end up cooking against a sunny wall.

Balconies and small decks are the most restrictive of all. Planting has to be limited to containers and hanging baskets. Pots that hang on the outside of a railing save precious interior space. Built-in planter boxes may look better than a row of pots, but unless carefully constructed, they leak and warp. And they can be very heavy. One way to avoid the problem is to build a simple sturdy box just the right size for the pots to fit inside. This also makes it easy to remove the plants for washing off and leaching, and for replacement if they dwindle and fail.

The water is recirculated to spew out of a bamboo pipe and make a splashing sound on the rocks.

Squint your eyes a little and this miniature scene appears to be a mountain stream. Design and installation by landscape contractor Jim Keener.

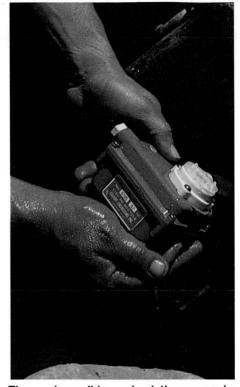

Tiny, submersible recirculating pump is only 1/30 horsepower and uses little energy. Reservoir is a 24-inch-diameter fiberglass plant container sunken into the ground.

SETTING THE SCENE

Scale of design is an elusive and intriguing consideration. Some Japanese gardens suggest distant mountains and infinite space in a confined area. One method is to accentuate perspective by placing large-textured, bright green plants near the viewer and fine-textured, grayish and purple plants at the far wall. This assumes you'll always be viewing it from the same spot. Otherwise, it could backfire and make the space appear smaller than it really is when seen from the other end.

Plants that are miniature versions of larger plants help achieve a spacious quality. A large shrub such as a wax myrtle or an old yaupon holly pruned to look like a multi-trunk tree can sometimes fool the eye. A grove of golden bamboo thinned out to widely spaced canes can appear to be a forest. Companion plants should have small leaves, such as nandina, tobira and juniper, so as not to break the spell. One century plant or yucca would blow the whole deal. Small boulders, 2x4 wood decking on edge, tiny peb-

Furniture selection is especially important in confined areas. These webbed chairs don't overpower this small patio.

bles and a mossy ground cover complete the scene—and that's what it truly is.

SPECIAL TOUCHES

Back to reality and practicality. Built-in seating and storage is one way to make the most of a limited space. Avoid heavy-framed wood furniture. The thinness of wrought iron is more appropriate. Even a glass tabletop helps the illusion. If there's a chance for a see-through fence panel without sacrificing privacy, this is the ideal place for it. Wrought-iron gates give security along with an airy quality.

Small water features can be used in any size garden, but are especially appropriate for miniature ones. A recirculating fountain operating on a 1/30 horsepower submersible pump requires very little water and power to operate. The sound of the water is more apt to be heard in an enclosed space and the visual effect is greatly appreciated at close range.

The same applies to works of art. Sculpture in full-round, mobiles, murals and bas-reliefs are often more at home in a small area than out in the

No room for a full-size fountain? Here's a pleasant-sounding waterfall that extends only 2 inches from the wall.

My neighbor's fence is only 5 feet away, so I built a shelf outside our kitchen window for a constantly changing display of flowers.

Landscape architect Eldon Russell found these old wood columns and used them to feature a sculpture at the home of Mr. and Mrs. Ronnie Finger.

What to do with a tiny dining room atrium? Water sheets down the ceramic wall and glistens at night when illuminated by a hidden light.

Bas-reliefs are made to order for garden walls. This one is an assembled clay piece by Nancy Smith.

This "natural creek" is actually tucked into a 15-foot space between house and property line.

open. This doesn't mean that large artwork has no place in a normal-size garden. It is just that smaller ones are more within the average budget and are better protected from vandalism, theft and the elements in a secured space.

Driftwood, mineral rocks, artifacts and other collected items that have a special meaning to the owner are also fun to include in a mini-garden.

Good workmanship is crucial in a tiny area. Flaws show up like cigarette burns in white carpeting. Because smaller quantities are involved, everything can be done more carefully without taking forever. It is difficult to find contractors to install very small jobs. There's little profit involved. This is where a do-it-yourselfer can build a masterpiece.

CONTAINER PLANTS

Container plants are valuable for relieving expanses of paving. They introduce foliage and color where planting directly in the ground would be impractical or impossible. Patios, atriums, courts, porches and balconies are such places. A few carefully selected and well-placed plants in appropriate containers can create the feeling of a garden in an otherwise barren area.

Exotic plants will often thrive within protective walls when they wouldn't have a chance out in the open. Plant collections such as bonsai, epiphyllums, cacti and succulents, herbs and cymbidiums are also

A protruding beam is a natural for hanging baskets. Sprenger asparagus looks delicate and ferny, but is a toughie in Zones 9 and 10.

A protected patio is a good spot for a hanging basket like this cold-tender common spider plant.

Ninety-nine cent chrysanthemums are set inside pots for a temporary front door display. They'll be planted in the garden after blooming.

Landscape architect Gregory Catlow selected a handsome container for a specimen sago palm to achieve a stately effect.

best grown in containers where they can receive proper care and be appreciated at close range.

Almost any plant can be grown in a container, at least for a short period of time. However, there are certain plants that adapt much better to this type of culture and are reasonably permanent. Some of the best include twisted juniper, yew pine, jade plant, mugo pine, camellia, cast iron plant, aralia, black pine, hollies and sago palm. Spider plant, *Vinca major,* sasanqua camellia, creeping Charlie and Sprenger asparagus are excellent hanging-basket plants.

Another approach is to use the container as a holder and set the plant inside, leaving it in its nursery container. Bulbs, annuals, perennials and flowering shrubs can be used in this way as a kind of living bouquet. Slip a 1-quart plastic pot or 1-gallon can into a slightly larger ceramic pot or wood tub and simply replace it when it is through blooming. Five-gallon-size shrubs and trees with seasonal features can be used in a similar manner.

Ample root room in the container is critical for most plants. Palms, bamboo, bonsai, dwarf conifers and most succulents are exceptions. A 16-inch size is sufficient if you're starting out with a 5-gallon-size plant, and it is not too heavy to move around. Larger shrubs and small trees in 15-gallon size need a 24-inch or larger container. They're quite heavy, so don't count on shifting them around very often.

Soil mix should be a packaged type or made from 50 percent organic material and 50 percent sandy loam,

with added nutrients and minerals. Commercial, lightweight mixes are fine for small plants, but larger shrubs and trees benefit from some sandy loam soil for better root anchoring.

Drainage holes are essential, but staining of paving can be avoided by leaching out the soil several times before moving the pot into place. Saucers are available for all but the largest pots. Cut a piece of heavy plastic to put under wood containers that have any metal that can rust.

The container should not only be the proper size but also appropriate to the setting. For example, red clay looks good with stucco and tile, wood tubs with wood siding and shake roofs. Containers don't have to be all the same kind, but too many different types in a small area can be disturbing. Often, a simple pot will show a plant to better advantage than one that attracts attention to itself.

There are many containers available, including clay, wood, concrete and plastic. Cost ranges from about $5.00 for small, mass-produced clay pots and redwood tubs, to $50 or more for larger and fancier ones. Half-barrels with a diameter of 24 inches that sell for $10 to $15 are real bargains.

Firethorn pyracantha is one of the best plants for espaliering. This is an especially interesting treatment.

English boxwoods flank a carefully trained Bradford pear espalier. Landscape architect: Edith Henderson, FASLA.

ESPALIERS

When you have a big, blank wall and only 12 inches of planting space, consider an espalier to alleviate the bareness. The term *espalier* seems to have an intimidating effect on many people. Perhaps they're picturing a perfectly trained specimen in the classic European style. Actually, an espalier can be any plant flattened to grow against a wall or fence. Often, plants are much easier to take care of this way. Design considerations usually dictate the shape of the espalier.

Pre-trained plants on a trellis are available from most nurseries. The price is high—about $25 for a 5-gallon size. You can develop your own by selecting a somewhat one-sided plant and doing a little pruning. Some kind of support is necessary for most plants. A trellis, plastic-coated wires, pegs or nails can be used. When using a trellis, get one large enough or easily expandable to allow for future growth. Holding the plant away from the wall 6 inches or so allows air circulation and lessens the possibility of damage from reflected heat.

In the accompanying box are some of the best-suited plants for both formal and informal espaliering. Try espaliering fruit trees to gain a tasty harvest in a small space. Many fruits are available in dwarf forms. Most vines can be used in this manner.

Refer to the plant lists in Chapter 6 for climate, exposure and additional information. As with most of the

other plant lists in the book, the plants most resistant to cold are first, and those least resistant are at the end.

MAINTENANCE

Overall maintenance is greater and more exacting for container plants than for the same ones growing in the ground. Watering is critical. The water supply can be quickly exhausted during a hot day. When it is gone there isn't any more. Larger containers have more root room and more reserve. Small clay pots and hanging baskets are the most demanding.

Setting one pot inside another and

filling the space between with sphagnum moss cuts water loss considerably. A little garden soil in the mix described earlier also helps retain moisture better than a lightweight, very fast-draining mix. Conversely, oversaturation easily occurs in pots with no drainage. Harmful salts accumulate and must be leached out periodically by heavy watering. Light, frequent fertilization is necessary to replace nutrients lost through this leaching. Root pruning and repotting are also necessary as the plant outgrows its container.

PLANTS FOR ESPALIERS

The plants in this list are arranged according to hardiness. The most cold-tolerant are at the top, and the most sensitive at the bottom.

Rose
Pyracantha
Silverberry
Deciduous fruit trees
Bradford pear
Cotoneaster
Twisted juniper
Willowleaf holly
Dwarf Southern magnolia
Fraser photinia
Camellia
Citrus
Sea grape

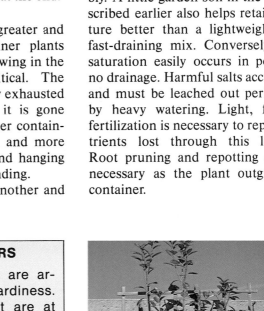

You can purchase pre-trained espaliered plants like this Fraser photinia if you don't want to attempt it yourself.

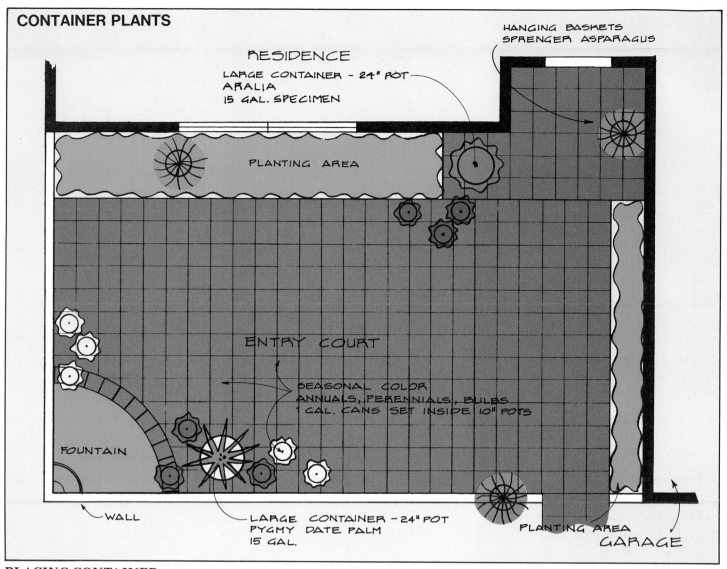

CONTAINER PLANTS

RESIDENCE
LARGE CONTAINER - 24" POT
ARALIA
15 GAL. SPECIMEN

HANGING BASKETS
SPRENGER ASPARAGUS

PLANTING AREA

ENTRY COURT

SEASONAL COLOR
ANNUALS, PERENNIALS, BULBS
1 GAL. CANS SET INSIDE 10" POTS

FOUNTAIN

WALL

LARGE CONTAINER - 24" POT
PYGMY DATE PALM
15 GAL.

PLANTING AREA
GARAGE

PLACING CONTAINER PLANTS

Selection and placement of container plants is tricky, but you don't have to do it perfectly the first time. Experiment a little. Containers can be moved, changed or even discarded easily.

The walled entry court of our corner lot from Chapter 2 is ideal for container plants and used here as an example. In this case, red clay pots are selected as appropriate for the Spanish-Mediterranean-style house and garden. Several 15-gallon specimens are placed at the front door and by the fountain as focal points. The cluster of flowering plants can be replaced when they are through blooming to provide continuous color. Hanging baskets at the entry, on top of the wall at the gate and in front of the bedroom windows add eye-level foliage.

Container plants can be replaced to take advantage of seasonal blooms, as with these poinsettias. Grouping is usually more effective than setting out single containers.

Grow Your Own 11

There are many reasons to include edible plants in your garden. Home-grown fruit and vegetables seem to taste better and are more nutritious. With food prices so high, you can more than recover the cash outlay for plants, seeds, fertilizer, sprays and water. Difficult-to-obtain and off-season items can often be grown if you give them a little extra attention. Increasingly precious fertilizer and water can be put to productive use, rather than only ornamental purposes.

Growing your own vegetables is a good way to introduce children to the wonders of gardening. They'll eat their "veggies" when they've had a hand in growing them. Nothing can beat the pleasure of picking a delicious morsel from your own yard.

When surplus crops become a problem, try setting up a trading arrangement with your food-growing friends and neighbors. If you have too many tomatoes and peaches while there are loads of plums and squash right next door, both parties will welcome a little variety. Cold storage, freezing and canning are ways to make best use of a bumper crop. With vegetables, spacing planting times can help avoid an oversupply. After a few seasons, you get to know how much of what kind to plant.

For properties with enough space, it is best to set aside a separate area for growing vegetables, preferably with a protective fence and beyond the view from outdoor living areas.

Some vegetables can be included in even the smallest lot and still not be an eyesore. Rhubarb, flowering kale, New Zealand spinach, rhubarb chard and Jerusalem artichoke look pre-

The vegetable gardens of Colonial Williamsburg represent an important part of our heritage.

A member of the sunflower family, Jerusalem artichoke puts on a nice display of flowers before dying back in the fall.

Some people cook the potato-like tubers. But a tastier use is raw as a crunchy substitute for water chestnuts.

Don't overlook flowers when you select *crops* to grow in your garden.

Beck didn't care much for vegetables until he started helping his grandpa in the garden.

Bright green- and red-leaved lettuce can be sown in a flower bed or between shrubs for a quick and delicious display.

New Zealand spinach thrives in hot climates where regular spinach is difficult to grow.

sentable for most of the growing season. Some nice short-term effects can be achieved by sowing red- and green-leaf lettuce, beets and onions between ornamental shrubs. Carrots look like small ferns when tucked into a shrub border. Look for compact varieties of squash, cucumber, cantaloupe, corn, okra, tomato and watermelon to make the most of a small plot.

GROWING VEGETABLES

Most vegetables are easy to grow. Meet the following requirements and success is practically assured.

Location—Select a location that gets sun most of the day. Obviously, a cool coastal or mountain garden will need more sun than one in a hot inland area. Corn, tomatoes, melons, okra, eggplant, cucumbers and other heat-lovers require lots of sun. Reasonably good crops of chard, beets, carrots, lettuce, radishes, turnips and other cool-season types can be grown if they receive at least half a day of sun. If disease is a problem in your area, good air movement and as much sun as possible is essential.

Soil—A well-drained, sandy loam soil is best. More than likely you'll need to incorporate plenty of organic material to improve what you have. Six cubic yards of organic material per 1,000 square feet dug in 12 inches deep is fine for average soils. You can achieve the same results with grass clippings, leaves and pine straw as

Organic material is dug deeply into this hill being prepared for summer squash.

A sheet of polyethylene extended the production of this tomato plant for more than a month into the fall.

long as you allow plenty of time for them to decompose before adding to the soil. A compost heap is an excellent source of organic material.

If you suspect your soil is overly acid, or infected with nematodes, get a soil test. Overacidity can be corrected with the proper amount of dolomitic lime. Nematodes are controlled by fumigation as described on page 129.

Alkaline soils are less common in the South. They can be made more acid by the addition of soil sulphur.

For average soils, incorporate 35 pounds of 8-8-8 complete fertilizer per 1,000 square feet at least a week before planting. Chapter 7 gives additional information on soil preparation.

Selection—Choose the right crop and variety for your specific climate and plant during the proper season. The back of the seed package will tell you a little. You can get more specific information from your cooperative extension agent or the HPBook, *Vegetables: How to Select, Grow and Enjoy.*

This small, pie-shaped corner contains plum, pear, apricot and peach trees. Annual pruning keeps them from overgrowing the limited space.

Tomato transplants are easy to grow from seed. I've had good results with plant cubes and plastic nursery containers.

Watering—Develop good watering practices tailored to the individual crop. Germinating seeds must not be allowed to dry out. Applying a *mulch,* a thin layer of organic material such as grass clippings over the new seeded crop helps keep the top layer of soil moist.

Many vegetables become bitter or go to seed if growth is slowed down by lack of water. Conversely, too much water can result in lots of foliage and fewer and smaller edible portions. It is helpful to have a hose-bibb nearby so you can apply water when rainfall is insufficient. Otherwise, concentrate on vegetables that can survive with a minimum of supplemental irrigation. Southern peas, okra, mustard, lima beans and corn tolerate dryness fairly well. Mulching will help conserve moisture and control weeds.

Mint makes an attractive ground cover in front of an apple espaliered on a fence.

Insects and Diseases—Watch carefully for insects and diseases. Many diseases can be avoided by planting resistant varieties. Pay a little more for high-quality seeds or transplants—it is worth it. Don't overlook the importance of good air circulation to minimize disease infections, especially in humid areas. The same insect control principles covered in Chapter 13 apply to vegetables as well as ornamentals. However, remember that you'll be eating the vegetables, so avoid materials with long residual effects.

Inspect the roots of tomatoes, okra, melons and other nematode-susceptible crops when you remove them in the fall to determine if fumigation is necessary. Try planting marigolds as a possible deterrent to nematodes and some insects. Tansy, nasturtiums, onions and garlic are other plants that offer some natural control. *Crop rotation* can also be of benefit. Don't plant the same vegetable year after year in the same location.

HERBS

Many herbs are valuable landscape subjects in addition to their culinary qualities. Rosemary, lavender, mint and thyme are especially useful. Gray-foliaged lavender is an interesting contrast to green shrubs. Prostrate rosemary and creeping thyme are excellent drought-tolerant ground covers. Give mint plenty of water and cut it back

once in a while. It will make an attractive filler. Strawberries also make a good ground cover.

FRUITS

Any garden can accommodate fruit trees of some kind. For maximum success, use the specific variety best suited to your climate zone. Your local nurseryman usually carries the types that have proven most reliable in your locality. If you're planning a small orchard, you might want to check with your local extension agent.

Citrus can be attractive landscape plants in a mild climate. This orange tree is placed at the top of a slope where it won't be drowned by normal garden watering.

You can eat the entire kumquat, skin and all. It is tart, but interesting. It makes an excellent container plant and has colorful fruit most of the year.

This 18-inch-tall container will be large enough for this dwarf peach for 3 to 5 years. Then it should be replanted.

Attractive and edible celtuce, rhubarb chard and tomato grow happily in 5-gallon containers. They need watering almost every day in hot weather.

Kale tastes good and has a fascinating texture. It grows well in a container.

In general, citrus, mango and other tender types are limited to relatively frost-free areas. Most deciduous fruits do best when they receive proper winter chilling. If you're in a mild area, look for special varieties with low-chilling requirements.

Where there is plenty of space, standard-size trees will produce larger crops and they can also serve for shade or background. Apple, pear, cherry, persimmon and plum fall into this category. In well-drained soils, they are all tolerant of normal garden watering. Pecans will tolerate lawn conditions and are excellent shade trees as well as nut producers.

Most other fruits fit well in smaller spaces—at least for many years. Peach, nectarine, fig and citrus can be grown in a 10x10' space with normal pruning. These trees are not recommended for lawns or frequent watering. They'll all do better with deep, infrequent irrigation.

Less common fruits that are sometimes grown include pomegranate, pineapple guava and loquat. The value of growing these is they are seldom sold in the market. The only way to get the fruit is from a friend or by growing it yourself.

If you live in Zone 10 or a favored spot in Zone 9, a whole world of

The loquat is a small tree that will fit into most gardens. Once you get used to the fruit, chances are you'll love it.

exotic fruit becomes possible. You can grow banana, mango, star fruit, cherimoya, lychee and even coconuts.

What if you don't have a 10x10' space? Figs, apples, persimmons, pears, citrus and loquats require only a narrow bed when espaliered on a wall or fence. Peaches, nectarines, apples, pears, avocados and citrus are readily available in dwarf form that bear full-size fruit. These can be grown in a space as small as 5x5'. If you have no open soil at all, almost any patio or balcony can accommodate a dwarf fruit tree in a large container such as a half-barrel. Surprisingly good vegetable crops can be raised entirely in containers.

If you inherit a mature fruit tree already growing on your property, try not to drastically change the watering schedule. Most orchard trees receive infrequent, deep watering rather than the typical several-times-a-week watering for home landscapes. Don't plant lawn or other moisture-requiring plants within the drip-line—the area covered by the tree's branches. Over-watering at the *crown* of an old fruit tree, where its trunk grows out of the soil, is usually fatal.

VINES AND BERRIES

Don't overlook food-bearing vines. You can have both grapes and summer shade by planting vines on an overhead structure. Muscadines are a great way to introduce some of the old South into your garden. The notorious kudzu is reportedly edible—I've never tasted it. Cook the tips like asparagus, the roots like potatoes and the leaves as vegetable greens. Caution: Avoid plants that may have been sprayed with a weed killer.

Chayote is an interesting perennial vine that produces large quantities of squash-like fruit. It dies back during winter in all but the mildest climates, and resumes growth as soon as the weather warms up in the spring.

Blackberries and raspberries can be trained against a fence or wall. Be sure to wear heavy gloves and long sleeves for protection from thorns.

Southern highbush blueberries, commonly called *rabbiteye,* are not only outstanding producers, but are

Boysen is a type of blackberry that produces well in warm climates. Raspberries grow better in cooler areas.

If you grow chayote, allow plenty of room and be prepared to give some away.

reasonably attractive landscape plants. Use them in Zones 8 and 9 where it is too warm for northern types. Their main requirements are sun, well-drained acid soil and adequate water. A thick mulch of pine needles, peat moss or ground bark will conserve water. An annual spring application of acid fertilizer along with iron will help produce superior plants.

Include more than one variety of plant to assure pollination. Don't expect fruit the first year or two. With proper care, good yields are possible the third year. Space blueberries 4 to 6 feet apart for a hedge, or 8 to 10 feet apart as individual specimen plants.

FOLIAGE

Some plants have such handsome leaves that they can be considered a type of ornamental crop. Smilax, loquat, various ferns, cast iron plant, aralia, cleyera and sweet viburnum are welcome additions to table arrangements. Hollies, Japanese aucuba

and pyracantha are great for the winter holidays for both foliage and berries.

Brilliant fall color is easy to come by in cold winter areas. In the deep South, displays are less predictable. Here are several ways to increase the chances of success no matter where you live. First, select plants that are known to give a good performance in your specific climate. If possible, buy in the fall, and choose plants with outstanding color in the nursery.

Look for varieties such as *'Burgundy'* and *'Palo Alto'* American sweet gum, *'Afterglow'* Chinese sweet gum, and *'Autumn Gold'* ginkgo grown for their consistent coloration. Place in a location with as much sun as possible for the type of plant. Reduce nitrogen fertilization and supplemental watering to a minimum in early fall. Hope for a little cooperation from the weather—a few crisp nights at the right time will produce a blaze of red, purple, orange and yellow.

Tupelo

Kousa Dogwood

Crape Myrtle

Sugar Maple

Cottonwood

Japanese Maple

PLANTS WITH COLORFUL FOLIAGE

The plants in this list are arranged according to hardiness. The most cold-tolerant are at the top, and the most sensitive at the bottom.

Gold coast juniper
Variegated plantain lily
Bronze ajuga
Purple-leaf plum
Redleaf barberry
Redleaf Japanese maple
Silverberry
Heavenly bamboo
Lily-of-the-valley shrub
Variegated liriope
Blue Atlas cedar
Lavender cotton
Blue China fir
Variegated osmanthus
Variegated Chinese privet
Variegated Japanese aucuba
Fraser photinia
Ternstroemia (Cleyera)
Pindo palm
Texas ranger
Variegated tobira
Silver buttonwood
Copper leaf
Variegated screw pine
Purple heart
Oyster plant
Croton

Many plants don't wait until fall to have colorful foliage. Some burst out with exciting new growth in spring. Others have colored leaves all year. These plants can add interest to a garden, especially when flowers are at low ebb. Use them with discretion—groupings are usually safer than spots of garish contrast. Don't overlook green as a color—it is not necessarily dull and monotonous. Subtle blends of various shades of green can impart a richness and dignity to the landscape that's easier to live with than brighter hues.

FLOWERS

With the price of cut flowers as high as it is, about the only way to have a fresh bouquet very often is to grow it yourself. The possibilities are limited only by climate and the amount of time you want to devote to the plants.

I've had good success with roses, calla lilies, gladiolas, snapdragons, stocks, tulips, daffodils, poinsettias, chrysanthemums, ranunculus and marigolds. Plant some of these and you can brighten up the house with blooms any season of the year. Care is similar to that described for vegetables. In fact, there's no reason why you can't combine them in the same plot.

Don't overlook flowering trees and shrubs as flower sources. Spirea, purple-leaf plum, dogwood, fringe tree, flowering cherry, Eastern redbud, Oriental and Southern magnolias, camellias and pampas grass can serve just as well as conventional flowers. In some cases, flowers from these trees are available in greater quantity and for a longer period than conventional cut flowers.

Gold Coast Juniper

Red-leaf Japanese Maple

Heavenly Bamboo

Barberry, Cotoneaster and Daylily

Fraser Photinia

Remodeling A Garden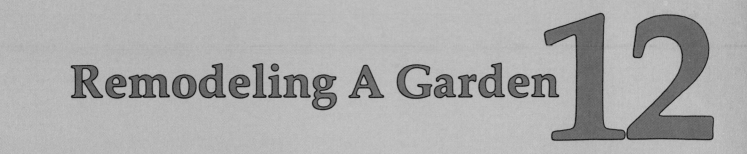

Ask any landscape architect about remodeling. It is much easier to start with a new house and bare land than to redo an existing garden. If you've just moved into an old property, it is better to wait a few months before doing anything drastic. If you've been living there all along, you probably have a much better feeling of what the good and bad features are.

Just as with new design, start with an overall assessment first. If the original garden was well-conceived and suits your requirements, only minor modifications may be involved. Otherwise, a master plan is called for, incorporating existing items into the overall scheme.

After you decide whether major or minor changes are in order, the difficult decisions begin. You need to decide what to save and what to tear out. Try to capitalize on any unique features that may exist.

An old stone wall, a stagnant fish pond, or even some scraggly bushes may be hidden treasures in disguise. The temptation is to raze everything in sight—but this is not always the best way to go. Take it easy. Don't be afraid to tear out hopeless items, but avoid wanton destruction. It is best to take it step by step. Let's consider paving and construction first.

UPGRADING PAVING

Wherever possible, it is sensible to save existing paving. Not only is it a big job to break up paving and haul it away, but you end up paying double—for removal *and* replacement.

Inspect existing paving to make sure it drains properly and to see if it has any structural cracks or is tilting and settling. By structural cracks I mean anything wider than 1/4 inch. If the paving appears sound, but doesn't look as good as it should, perhaps it can be *improved* rather than replaced. Where part of the paving is good, you can rent a concrete saw and cut out the bad portion.

A concrete stain was used to give the sidewalk a brownish rust color that ties in with the new wood landing. Stain reacts chemically with cement and, unlike paint, is permanent.

If a paved area is too small or a walk too narrow, add to it rather than starting over. Match it as closely as possible to avoid a patchy appearance. A safer way is to choose a contrasting material and make the addition a design feature.

A crack large enough for this quarter to fall into may mean the concrete isn't structurally sound and should be replaced.

A power saw slices right through concrete so undesirable sections can be removed.

Take an existing yard, add some paving and a shade trellis, furnish it with lush plants and then enjoy the results.

ADDING CONCRETE

After concrete is poured, 3/4-inch stones are sprinkled on the surface to give this walkway a texture.

Adding concrete follows the same procedure as shown in Chapter 3, "Laying Concrete." Here Billy Becher lends a hand while his father installs forms for an addition to a narrow front walk.

The stones are pressed into the wet concrete until barely covered.

As soon as the concrete starts to harden, it is swept lightly with a broom to expose the stone.

The crucial decision is when to start washing the surface with a light stream of water. This concrete is just about "ripe."

The exposed pebbles contrast subtly with the plain concrete of the old paving.

You can lay 1/2-inch-thick bricks in a mortar base over an existing concrete patio. Mortar joints are filled in later.

Tile is best laid on a concrete base, which makes it ideal for upgrading an old slab.

Acid stain can often transform dull, drab concrete into an attractive surface with a minimum of expense and effort. This method is especially effective in solving the problem of glare. For stain to take properly, it must soak in. The concrete must be clean and free of paint, wax, oil and grease. Trisodium phosphate or a dilution of one part muriatic acid to 20 parts water can be used to remove whatever you can't scrub off with a broom and hose. The cleaner the concrete, the better the results will be.

The stain is brushed on in two coats. Allow time for the first coat to dry before applying the second. In most cases the stain soaks in unevenly for a pleasing mottled effect. Don't expect it to be solid or to cover chips, cracks and other imperfections. Material cost is approximately 20 cents per square foot.

Another way to upgrade existing paving is to use it as a base for new paving such as tile. The trick here is to make sure that the extra thickness doesn't create a drainage problem or a dangerous small step. New concrete poured over the old should be at least 3 inches thick. Thinner layers tend to crack. Roughening the old surface and painting it with concrete glue will help form a bond. Usually the price will be similar to new work, but you still save the removal cost.

Here, 2x4 *sleepers* are glued to a concrete landing and redwood 2x4s nailed in place.

Common bricks or flagstone laid on a 1-inch-thick layer of sand or mortar bed on top of old paving will also raise the level approximately 3 inches. If this is too much, split-bricks or patio tiles can be set in mortar or mastic to keep the added thickness down to as little as 1 inch. Cost is often less than new work because there isn't any grading and excavating.

Pressure-treated or redwood planks are easily laid over existing concrete. They can be nailed to wood *sleepers* attached to the concrete using a

A 2x8 redwood trim board has been added and the wood bleached to blend with the house trim. Matching English hollies in wood barrels complement the lights. Design: Ken Smith, ASLA.

cartridge-fired stud gun or with counter-sunk carriage bolts set in expansion plugs.

Planks can also be laid directly in concrete glue. This works great on a small porch or landing where a single plank can be used without splicing. Figure approximately $1.50 per square foot for 2-inch planking. You'll probably have to do the work yourself. Finding a carpenter for a small job such as this is unlikely.

It is easy to seal-coat asphalt that looks shabby. Just sweep sand into the cracks and then broom on the emulsion. Material cost is about 10 cents per square foot. If the surface is really bad, you can sometimes have a paving company add a 1-inch layer of new asphalt on top of the old for much less than tearing it all out and starting over.

CONSTRUCTION

Consider the question of whether or not to keep walls, fences, shade trellises and other garden construction the same way as you approach paving. If it is structurally unsound or downright unsafe, remove it. Otherwise, look for ways to improve it. You can use the same acid stain on concrete block walls. Or you can use a cement-based paint or plaster. Wood fences can be stained or the frame salvaged and new paneling installed.

Shade trellises can be "beefed-up" by applying what are called *plant-ons*. A 4x4 post can be enhanced by nailing 1x2s on all four sides. Beams and rafters can be treated similarly. The key to success is a little ingenuity.

SWIMMING POOLS

A swimming pool represents a considerable amount of money. Undoubtedly you'll want to keep it unless it is not structurally sound or you can't stand water. Call in a qualified pool company to check out the filter and heater for maximum efficiency. If there's a nearby south-facing roof, maybe supplementary solar heating can be added.

Unsightly plaster can be acid-washed and painted or replastered if necessary. Consider a dark color for a mountain-lake effect, and updating the tile trim while you're at it. If there

Statuary, richly colored foliage and a central fountain turn this entrance into a real showplace. Landscape architect: Steve Coenen.

is concrete decking, follow the previous suggestions on page 167 to see if it is worth keeping or if it needs redoing. Old-style pre-cast concrete copings can be replaced with 12-inch-long bricks, or new concrete decking can be cantilevered over the edge for a clean look.

Add a sun-bathing area if it is needed. Perhaps the problem is lack of a shady spot. A shade trellis or gazebo is a good way to add comfort to an overly hot pool area. Screen coverings not only reduce heat, but provide protection from insects, and reduce pool cleaning.

Plantings around swimming pools often need refurbishing. Determine if there's too much paving. If so, saw-cut and remove some to introduce more foliage. Adding container plants and hanging baskets will help. Save, remove or transplant trees and shrubs as needed to balance and "refresh" the overall look. See the next page for helpful tips.

FRONT ENTRANCE

One place you might want to go a little overboard is at the front entrance to the house or property. Here is where you can add a personal touch

Screening can often make a pool more usable and easier to keep clean.

Inviting entry is highlighted by a well-designed trellis that seems to lead you into the house.

Wrought-iron doors and a pair of sago palms dramatize the entrance to this Houston home.

and get maximum return on your effort. This is an ideal opportunity to upgrade the paving by laying brick, tile, flagstone or wood over the typically uninspiring slab of concrete at the front door.

Where the roof overhang is lacking or minimal, a well-scaled wood trellis can turn a dull entry into an exciting, gracious one.

Don't be afraid of being dramatic. Bring in a few boulders, or cluster some sawed-off telephone poles or railroad ties as accents. Add a few choice plants in containers and include some low-voltage lighting to complete the picture.

This hillside gazebo was built to enjoy the view of the valley below.

VIEWS

Make the most of any particularly nice view. It doesn't have to be a panoramic sweep of a river, a deep canyon or an ocean shoreline. Sometimes a pleasant glimpse is enough to make it worthwhile. Add a path to a secluded bench or hammock where you can relax while you admire the wonders of nature or whatever. A gazebo makes a good destination point and offers shade in the absence of trees.

PLANTS

It is much more difficult to decide which plants to save. If you're remodeling your own garden, it becomes an emotional issue to cut down an undesirable plant, especially if you're the one who put it there in the first place. Try to remember that a plant is expendable once it no longer serves its purpose. Take out the obviously dead and dying plants first. Then determine which remaining ones are still doing a good job and which ones are ill-chosen.

Transplanting is always a risk and is often attempted with the erroneous belief that all plants are valuable. Moving a small plant is one thing; anything more than 4 feet high becomes a major task. In many cases it would be better to start with a new plant.

If you decide to go ahead, here are some general rules.

• Check with a nursery to see what a container plant of a comparable size would cost. Ask your nurseryman if the plant is easy to move.

• Determine if you have an actual need for the plant in your garden and if there is a place for it.

• Choose the best time of year for the specific plant. Camellias are dormant when in bloom, deciduous plants when leafless. Palms and bamboo can be moved most successfully in warm weather, pines in the fall. Most other plants have the best chance for survival if transplanted in the spring.

• Avoid clear, hot days. Cool, overcast weather is best. Provide temporary shade protection if it turns hot.

• Take as much of the root system as practical. Move it directly into the new position. Prune back to reduce leaf surface, apply a transplanting hormone such as Hormex or Super-thrive and keep moist until established.

Now is a good time to correct previous mistakes and to anticipate future problems. The most common example of this is overgrowth. Rather than hacking away at a large shrub next to a walk or under a window, it might be better to remove it.

If there is a reasonable space for a shrub to grow, don't be too hasty to take it out. When severely pruned back, many shrubs regrow to give many more years of service. An overgrown shrub can also be converted into a small tree by pruning the lower branches.

TREES

Where large trees are involved, it may be best to seek expert advice. It is truly sad to remove a beautiful old tree that might be rehabilitated by a good pruning. The cost of professional pruning may be less than total removal. Check on the estimated value of a tree before cutting it down—you may be destroying an extremely valuable specimen.

Most existing trees are very sensitive to changes in grade. Exceptions are palm trees, which are tolerant of fill. Soil should not be added more than a few inches deep within the area between the trunk to the outermost spread of the branches. If deeper fill is unavoidable, a wall several feet from the trunk will at least help to keep soil away from the trunk and save the tree from almost certain death. Likewise, lowering of grade within the drip-line area should be avoided.

Orchard trees such as peach and citrus are difficult garden subjects. Fruit and nut trees are normally grown with natural rainfall and a minimum of supplemental irrigation. Typical twice-weekly garden watering can lead to crown and root diseases, especially in poorly drained soil. A deep soaking during drought periods may be necessary, but it is best to avoid frequent sprinkling within the drip-line. This means that plantings requiring considerable moisture such as lawn, azaleas, ferns and pachysandra are incompatible with most orchard trees. If underplanting is considered essential, at least use material that requires infrequent watering. Or use plants in containers to keep excessive water from reaching the tree.

CASE HISTORY

The 15-year-old garden at right appeared overgrown and was just too shady for the hybrid bermudagrass to thrive. Rather than remove trees, they were severely thinned, and the lower branches removed. A new lawn shape was laid out on the ground with stakes and a hose. Permanent redwood edging was installed to emphasize the new flowing lines. Surface tree roots extending into the lawn area were removed and a trench was filled with gravel to discourage future growth.

To facilitate leaf raking, a ground cover of decomposed granite was used under the trees. Boulders with groupings of Southern Indian azaleas provided interest and presented beautiful color every spring. Sasanqua camellias were planted as a fall-blooming background against the concrete block wall.

There are complex formulas for estimating the value of a tree, but I'd call this magnificent old camphor tree priceless.

It is a good idea to lay out proposed changes on the ground to see how they look before doing anything drastic. Photo: Fred Kahn.

Remodeled garden is more spacious and airy, easier to maintain. Photo: Fred Kahn.

INSTALLING RAILROAD TIES

You can cut through a few ties with a hand saw if you have muscle and patience. A two-man cross-cut is better than a carpenter's saw.

Telephone pole sections set vertically in the ground are used at the corners for support and appearance.

A large circular saw is best to cut a lot of ties. A chain saw will also work if the blade has hardened tips.

Ties are combined with bricks for a stairway. A tie laid along the toe of the slope keeps soil in place.

These railroad-tie steps connect adjacent walks. Try to pick ties with smooth surfaces so people don't trip on rough spots.

RAILROAD TIES

Railroad ties aren't limited to remodeling projects by any means. However, they're so handy to add to an existing garden that it seems appropriate to include them here.

Prices have risen considerably since the days when they were available for a dollar apiece. You may still find a bargain, but $10 to $15 is what you can expect to pay now.

They're rather expensive when used as paving—the cost of the ties alone can be as much as two dollars per square foot. Best uses are for steps and low walls. They're heavy enough to hold themselves in place with only 30-penny nails to pin them together. Walls higher than two ties can be reinforced with 3/4-inch steel pipe driven through 1-inch-diameter holes. You'll need a heavy-duty drill for these.

The most obvious use of railroad ties is in the rustic or natural-style garden. Actually, they fit in well with all but the most sophisticated designs.

OTHER CONSIDERATIONS

Don't forget to adapt site drainage, sprinklers and lighting to any changes that are made. It would also be well to evaluate what kind of maintenance situation you've inherited. Maybe you don't have the time or interest to take care of a rose garden or a lot of annuals, or to do extensive hand watering. As long as the place is torn up, you might as well correct problems and make changes where desired.

Maintenance 13

I'd classify this well-tended garden in the medium-to-high maintenance category. Landscape architect: Roy Seifert.

The ideal garden is one that requires care only on cool, sunny weekends when you have nothing special planned, and when there's no important game on TV. Unfortunately, plants are like kids and pets. They always seem to need the most attention just when you have a million other things to do. However, you can have an enjoyable garden without being a slave. It takes careful planning and proper maintenance techniques along with a little ingenuity.

It appears that almost everyone wants a *low-maintenance* garden. The problem is that no one agrees as to just what that means. What we really need to determine is how many gardening hours are actually required to maintain the average-size garden. If you have a gardener, you may be less concerned than if you do all the work yourself. But good gardeners are hard to find and they do cost money. A good compromise is to hire a lawn-care service to mow, edge, fertilize and spray the lawn, and you do the rest.

It is important to reduce unnecessary consumption of fertilizer, chemicals and water. Whether you want a showplace or a "no care" garden, the following are sound ideas to get the most out of your maintenance effort and materials:

● Limit manicured lawn areas to visible and usable areas. Use ground covers and shrub covers for slopes and non-traffic areas.

● Install convenient hose-bibbs or a permanent sprinkler system.

● Space plants with ultimate size in mind. Don't overplant.

Maintenance Chart

Category	Description	Hours per Month
High Maintenance	Large lawn area, annual flowers and roses. Meticulous trimming. The showplace of the neighborhood.	24 and up
Medium Maintenance	Some lawn, a few annuals. Neat, but not perfect. Better than most.	16 to 20
Low Maintenance	No lawn or annuals. Paving and bark or stone mulches. Definite casual appearance. Can look run-down and shabby if not well-designed.	At least 8

Choose a level of maintenance appropriate to the style of your landscape and your available time. Landscape architects: Lang and Wood.

There's no denying the appeal of neatly clipped plants. For them to look their best, don't allow plants to get overgrown between shearings.

This "lawn" of green gravel requires little maintenance but is very artificial.

Landscape architect Roy Seifert placed these large junipers just the right distance from the driveway so they wouldn't be a problem. Likewise, he selected Japanese black pines rather than a larger species to avoid future overgrowth.

The large junipers in the photo at the left wouldn't work in this small bed. Compact 'Gold Coast' juniper is fine.

• Work with a plant's natural growth habit rather than fighting it.

• Select plants that are adapted to your specific climate and grow easily with little trouble from insects and diseases.

• Plant properly. Build watering basins for deep soaking. Mulch to retain moisture and limit weeds.

• Use generous areas of paving and semi-paving.

Let's get on to the various jobs and explore ways to reduce the time they take. This doesn't mean that you have to approach it like a professional who has to take care of ten places a day. The intent is to handle the tasks you least enjoy as efficiently as possible. If you want to spend half the day pruning your favorite tree or caring for your prize roses, or merely getting out in the sun and pulling weeds by hand, you'll have time to do it.

LAWN CARE

Lawns leave the most room for improvement. First, use an efficient mower and keep it sharp and in good repair. If exercise is desirable, a sturdy hand mower is fine for most grasses. However, toughies like bermudagrass, St. Augustine and zoysia require power equipment. Areas more than 2,000 square feet also justify the need for a power mower.

Reducing the size of your lawn will obviously shorten cutting time, but it may not help very much. Once you have the mower out, it is not much

Hybrid bermudagrass requires frequent, low mowing with a front-throw mower to look its best.

effort to cut a few more square feet. Eliminating narrow strips of grass and fancy edges that require lots of trimming *will* definitely save time. In some cases, you may be able to eliminate the lawn entirely. If so, be sure that what you replace it with will not be more of a chore.

To further reduce lawn care requirements, think of the lawn as a meadow rather than a putting green. You can select a less demanding type of grass, as discussed in Chapter 8. You can cut it less frequently and higher than normal. You will not only save mowing time, but most weeds will be shaded out or at least hidden.

In a casual garden, you can let the lawn grow where it may and eliminate some of the edging. It will still need some trimming next to paving,

though. Or you can use a spade, power edger or plastic-line trimmer to keep a definite edge. However, with no permanent line, the shape of the planting beds changes drastically through the years. Grass has a way of taking over ground covers and shrubs —especially creeping grasses such as bermuda and St. Augustine.

MOWING STRIPS

Mowing strips are essential if neat, permanent edges are desired. They relate directly to the finish grade of the lawn and are best installed in conjunction with that operation. The following are the most common types.

Wood edging is quite satisfactory except in constantly soggy soil. It is unobtrusive and relatively inexpensive. Use full, rough heartwood 2x4s of decay-resistant species such as redwood, cypress or cedar, or pressure-treated lumber. 1x4s or 1/2x4s should be laminated for curves because narrow strips break easily. Material cost is approximately 50 cents per lineal foot. Installed, it costs $1.50 and up.

Brick and concrete mowing strips are even more practical than redwood. Lay the bricks flat and side-by-side for an 8-inch-wide strip. Brick and concrete are strong design elements and should be carefully laid out lest they attract too much attention. Material cost is about 50 cents per lineal foot. Installed cost is $2.00 and up.

Steel edging is available with special splices and stakes at a cost of approximately $1.25 per lineal foot for 1/8-inch thick. The steel stakes are an

It takes twice as many bricks if you lay them side-by-side, but this strip of used brick is wide enough for the mower's wheel.

advantage in soil that resists having wooden stakes driven into it. Special plastic lawn edgings are extremely flexible, but are easily damaged by power edgers. Corrugated aluminum, bricks set jagged on end, large stones and similar designs are more trouble to trim around than a plain edge. Besides that, most of them are obtrusive in appearance, if not unsightly.

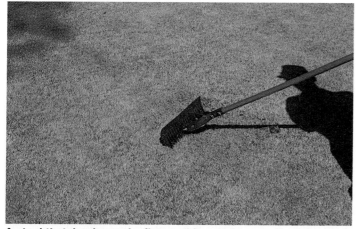
A steel thatch rake works fine on this zoysiagrass. It can be used on any lawn if you have the time and muscle.

Landscape architect Dick Harrington used a redwood 2x4 as edging between lawn and volcanic rock mulch to achieve a neat effect.

MOWING STRIPS

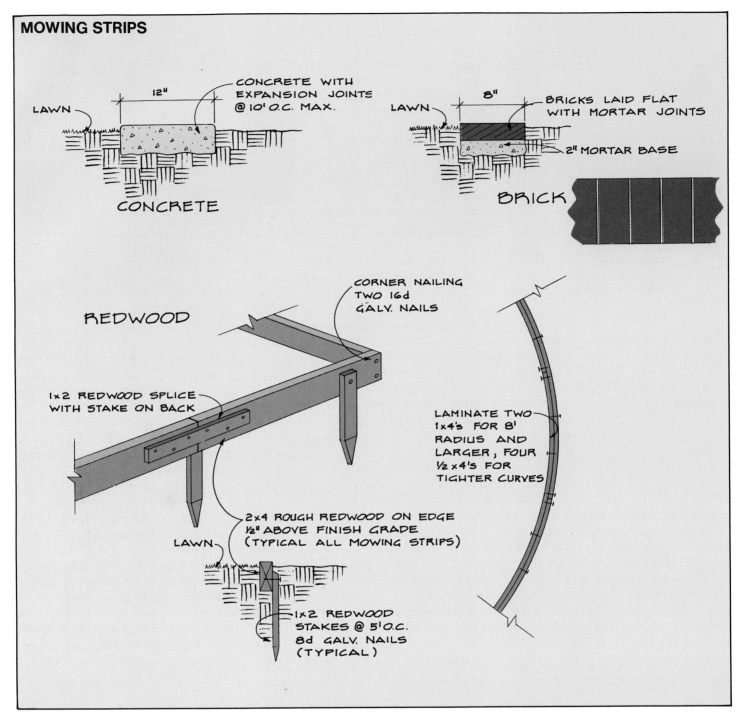

CONCRETE WITH EXPANSION JOINTES @ 10' O.C. MAX.

LAWN

12"

CONCRETE

LAWN

8"

BRICKS LAID FLAT WITH MORTAR JOINTS

2" MORTAR BASE

BRICK

REDWOOD

CORNER NAILING TWO 16d GALV. NAILS

1x2 REDWOOD SPLICE WITH STAKE ON BACK

LAMINATE TWO 1x4's FOR 8' RADIUS AND LARGER, FOUR ½ x 4's FOR TIGHTER CURVES

2x4 ROUGH REDWOOD ON EDGE ½" ABOVE FINISH GRADE (TYPICAL ALL MOWING STRIPS)

LAWN

1x2 REDWOOD STAKES @ 5' O.C. 8d GALV. NAILS (TYPICAL)

WATERING

Very few gardens can survive on rainfall alone. A little hand watering is unavoidable, and actually quite enjoyable. If it takes up the majority of your gardening time, a permanent sprinkler system may be advisable. It does not matter if the water is applied via rain, hose or sprinklers. The important thing for most plants is deep penetration. And this takes time.

I'm continually amazed when I dig down into a wet surface to find bone-dry soil just a few inches down. Be-cause proper watering and water conservation are so important, the subjects are covered at length in Chapters 5 and 14.

SWEEPING AND RAKING

Leaf and litter raking can be a time-consuming chore. Anyone who has had to contend with a row of cotton-woods or similar large-growing trees along his property line, a giant syca-more in the front lawn, or a mimosa in a paved area, knows just how big a job it can be.

Medium-size, relatively "clean" trees are best for paved areas, lawns and places where leaf accumulation is undesirable. Crape myrtle, ginkgo, Japanese black pine, yaupon holly, dogwood, Bradford pear and palms are in this category. Use "dirty" trees only if there is room for leaves to accumulate naturally, or if they can be raked at long intervals rather than daily. Along with cottonwood, syca-more and mimosa mentioned above, willow, Southern magnolia, pecan, Southern live oak, mulberry, most pines, Chinaberry, American elm and

Curved wood edging is made by laminating two strips of 1x4s for extra strength.

Gravel driveway is separated from lawn by a sturdy and unobtrusive steel edging.

Almost all large trees drop lots of leaves. This sycamore is in a natural setting where a pile of leaves doesn't matter.

Rather than constantly raking them up, pine needles are put to good use as a mulch.

fruit production for some plants, without excessive growth after reaching mature size. Light, frequent applications are more apt to achieve this goal, with less danger of burning than heavy applications once or twice a year. Generally, sandy soils have higher requirements than clay soils because leaching carries the nutrients through the root zone.

For most garden plants, a complete fertilizer supplying nitrogen, phosphorus and potassium is satisfactory when applied about 4 times a year. Other plants such as azaleas, camellias, citrus and roses will probably respond better to special formulations, which are worth the additional cost unless large quantities are involved.

When green foliage is the goal, such as lawns and leafy vegetables, a high-nitrogen formula will be more economical than a complete fertilizer. Lack of nitrogen shows on most plants as an overall pale green leaf color. Take care to apply the proper amount and water in immediately to avoid burning. Slow-release and time-release types are less apt to burn, and last longer. Lawn fertilizers that also contain insecticides and herbicides are okay for special situations, but there's no advantage in using them every time.

It really makes no difference to the plant if the fertilizer is applied in chemical or organic form, or in grains, pellets or liquid. Organic types are useful to enrich soil low in humus. Manures are good natural fertilizers, but are actually quite low in fertility content. They should be used with caution. Fresh manure can burn tender rootlets. Some sources contain weed seeds and many have considerable salt. They should be used in limited amounts, preferably composted and diluted with organic material.

When you fertilize is especially important for some plants. Camellias and azaleas should be fertilized after they bloom. Bamboo and palms should be fertilized only during the warm months. Tender plants, such as sub-tropicals and citrus, should be fertilized only in spring and summer. Fertilizing in fall promotes tender new growth that might be damaged by

very large trees fall into the "dirty" class.

Note that there are both evergreen and deciduous trees on the "clean" and "dirty" lists. Deciduous trees drop most of their leaves over a short period and seem to be "dirtier." Evergreen trees drop their leaves throughout the year so you may not notice it as much. Some trees shed fruit, flowers, small twigs and bark

that can be more objectionable than leaves. Large trees are more of a problem due to sheer volume.

FERTILIZING

Fertilization is a complex subject, confusing to most homeowners and many professionals. The general intent is to promote sturdy, rapid growth until the plant reaches ideal size, and then to maintain health and appearance. This includes flower and frost. Bluegrass and fescue need more feeding in spring and fall when they do most growing, while bermudagrass, St. Augustine and other warm-season grasses require most of their fertilization during the summer. Over-fertilizing lawns results in faster growth, which means more mowing and more water. Apply just enough to keep the grass green.

Liming is not fertilization, but makes certain elements more readily available to the plants by reducing acidity. If a soil test indicates the need for lime during the initial soil preparation, further applications will probably be needed every 3 or 4 years. Another soil test at that time will determine the amount required. While you're at it, have your soil tested for fertility to pinpoint the type and quantity of fertilizer the soil requires.

Iron chlorosis is a common problem and can be treated along with fertilization. Yellowing of leaves while the veins remain green is the identifying symptom. If left unchecked, the condition will often terminate with the entire plant turning yellow and dying. Sweet gum, camellia, azalea, gardenia, citrus, pyracantha, hollies, Mugo pine and ginkgo are frequently afflicted. Iron chelates are more successful than iron sulphate and should be applied when symptoms first appear.

When iron chlorosis is caused by high alkaline soil, soil sulphur will lower the pH and make iron more readily available to the plants. A shortage of magnesium or zinc will cause symptoms similar to iron chlorosis, but is less commonly encountered. Dolomitic lime and Epsom salts are effective in correcting magnesium problems.

INSECT AND DISEASE CONTROL

Insect and disease control is another complex subject. The main concern today is, "Are chemicals really necessary?" There are dangers involved in the use of most chemicals, but they are indispensible in many situations. Safety precautions should always be strictly observed and manufacturer's instructions carefully followed. Biological controls such as *Bacillus thuringiensis,* lacewings, praying mantis and ladybugs are worth trying if you want to avoid all chemicals.

Selecting plants that are relatively free from insects and disease has already been recommended. Some degree of prevention is possible by general good care because a healthy, vigorous plant is less susceptible to attack than a weak one. A clean garden also offers fewer breeding spots for insects and disease.

Hand picking and washing off with the hose will keep some insect populations at an acceptable level. Application of chemical control before a problem arises is possible in some instances. An example is applying a *systemic* to roses in early spring to control aphids. A systemic is absorbed into the plant and cannot be washed off.

Snail bait can be scattered before snails devour any plants. If you know fungus is going to strike certain plants in your garden, apply a fungicide at the onset of humid weather rather than wait until it gets out of hand. So many insects and diseases can affect lawns that periodic preventive spraying is practiced by most lawn care companies and appears to be justified.

Constant vigilance is the best answer to pest and disease problems. Indiscriminate spraying "whether it needs it or not" can create more problems than it solves by interfering with the balance of nature. Prompt and proper treatment will usually control the problem before serious damage is done. A weekly walk through the garden with potential problems in mind is a good way to avoid a nasty surprise. There's nothing that says you can't enjoy a little beauty while you stroll.

A knowledgeable nurseryman can really help in problem situations. Take in a sample of your problem—a leaf or twig—and he can usually recommend the latest and most effective means of control. Extension agents are usually available for advice as are tree companies and pest control firms. If you can't figure out what the problem is, don't be afraid to ask before it is too late.

Watch for new developments from time to time. A spray is being tested for lethal yellowing that affects many types of palms. A new nematocide will hopefully soon be available to control nematodes to replace the previous one taken off the market. A long-lasting systemic fungicide is being marketed that promises to eliminate the need for constant spraying.

WEED CONTROL

There are several keys to cutting down weeding time. These include eliminating the weeds before planting and removing new ones while they're still small—before they go to seed.

If your pyracantha or other plant has leaves that look like this, the plant may be suffering from lack of iron.

The tomato horn worm is really difficult to see. Hand picking is an effective control if you're not too squeamish. You can handle snails this way too.

Mulching around trees, shrubs and ground covers helps prevent weed growth. Use herbicides judiciously when hand methods fail or are impractical. Here are some typical weed situations and what you can do about them.

Broad-leaved weeds such as dandelion, oxalis and spotted spurge in a cool-season grass lawn can be sprayed with a mixture of 2,4-D, MCPP and dicamba, sold as *Trimec* and *Trex-San*. Most warm-season grasses are sensitive to 2,4-D in varying degrees. This chemical must be used very carefully according to specific directions to avoid damage to grass.

Grassy weeds such as bermudagrass, dallisgrass and Johnsongrass in broad-leaved ground cover, shrub beds or dichondra can be sprayed with a product containing dalapon, commercially sold as *Dowpon*. Bermudagrass roots can go down 3 feet or more. It is folly to pull them out by hand because they will come right back. Round-up or Kleen-up has been successfully used on bermudagrass and nutgrass growing in Asiatic jasmine and low junipers. Use it with caution for this purpose.

To control crabgrass and annual bluegrass in grass lawns or dichondra, apply bensulide, called *Betasan,* in early spring to prevent seed germination. Spray with disodium methyl arsenate (DSMA) *after* seeds have sprouted.

Nutgrass in a lawn is a toughie. *Basagran* (Bentazon), *DSMA* or *MSMA* applied to actively growing, emerged foliage will give some control. Heavy stands are almost impossible to control selectively. Have a professional applicator fumigate with methyl bromide and then replant.

Future weeds can be avoided by applying the following to bare earth: diphenamid, sold as *Enide;* trifluralin, sold as *Treflan;* EPTC, sold as *Eptam;* or a similar pre-emergent herbicide. A diphenamid and trifluralin mix is very effective. It kills germinating weed seeds without harming the established plants. Diphenamid can also be applied when planting dichondra seed or applied to an established dichondra lawn. EPTC inhibits newly emerging nutgrass and is worth a try.

Mixed weeds in a non-planted area such as semi-pavings and bare earth between shrubs and trees can be sprayed with fortified weed oil, amino triazole, cacodylic acid or a similar *knock-down* chemical. Glyphosate is non-residual and controls a wide range of weeds, including toughies such as bermudagrass, nutgrass and wild morning glory. It is sold as *Kleen-up* at approximately $15 per quart, or as higher strength *Round-up* at $80 per gallon for large areas. For non-planted areas and semi-pavings where there are no existing plants and you don't want to plant any, apply soil sterilants such as borate/chlorate, or simizine/amino triazole combinations. **CAUTION**—There's no good reason to use chemicals if simple hand weeding takes little or no more effort than spraying. If you do decide that a weedicide is advisable, take proper safety precautions and always follow all manufacturer's directions carefully. Spray when there is little or no wind to avoid drift onto desirable plants. Take care that spray or granules aren't washed off or dissolved where they can run off into plant basins and root areas.

PRUNING AND TRIMMING

There seem to be two extremes when it comes to pruning. Either the homeowner is afraid to snip off the smallest branch or he butchers the plant back to unsightly stubs. Some professionals are no better. They treat all plants either as a cube or sphere and entirely destroy the natural grace and form of the species.

When plants are selected with their natural growth habit and size in mind, you can throw away the hedge clippers. What pruning is necessary should be done regularly to guide the plant's growth, rather than waiting until the plant becomes unshapely and oversized.

There are a few general rules that are helpful. Dead wood is unsightly and a potential source of infection. It should always be removed. Traditionally, it has been accepted that deciduous plants should be pruned during the dormant period in winter. Latest research indicates that any time is okay for most species. Spring-

flowering types should be pruned during and after blooming or potential flowers will be cut off.

For most evergreen plants, light, frequent pruning is better than drastic measures at long intervals. Selective removal of stems and branches, sometimes called *feather* or *pick pruning,* is also better than shearing. If you want dense foliage, cut back the tips by clipping to induce growth. To feature a plant, clean out the inside to reveal the branch structure. This will also let air pass through a tree, lessening wind damage and weight from ice storms.

The HPBook, *Western Fruit, Berries & Nuts,* has excellent information on pruning fruit trees and vines in any part of the country. Choosing the wrong time and method can result in losing the crop.

Japanese privet is pruned out to reveal gray trunks. Foliage at top screens out neighbors' roofs. Landscape architect: Steve Coenen.

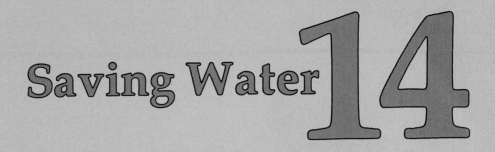
Water is no longer the cheap resource it used to be. The high cost of energy required for pumping has affected the price, and the rising population has affected the available supply. In areas of low rainfall this has a direct impact on the landscape and how much it will cost to maintain it. Even where rain is plentiful, water companies often have difficulty meeting peak demands during droughts and water shortages.

We must do some serious thinking about what kind of garden is really appropriate for present and future conditions. We have to manage our water use much better than in the past. An obvious answer is to concentrate on plants that will thrive on normal rainfall. With 50 inches or more of rain spread throughout the year, there is little problem for the average-size lot. Most plants will get by with a minimum of supplementary irrigation during dry spells. Larger properties with extensive lawns will require much more water.

One answer is to concentrate your landscaping efforts on the area adjacent to the house and let the fringes fend for themselves. With annual rainfall of less than 50 inches, and where there are normally several dry months, most plants and lawns will require considerable supplementary irrigation.

Careful thought should be given to plant selection in relation to water needs. Under extreme conditions, the *oasis concept* from desert regions can be adapted. This is where lush, cool, green plants are reserved for the entrance and outdoor living areas.

If you're planning a new garden or making extensive changes to an existing one, there are several things you can do to keep water requirements low. Use the tips on the following page, along with the plants listed on page 187. These ideas will help you save water and reduce maintenance.

This water-conscious neighborhood uses stone mulch instead of lawn. Young Jerusalem thorn and common mesquite trees get by with little irrigation and are already casting considerable shade.

By concentrating lush planting around a shaded patio, you can have a cool spot for relaxing and entertaining—without having to pour enormous quantities of water on the entire yard.

Well-adapted plants such as this native azalea can often survive on normal rainfall alone.

My neighbor Walt spreads crushed rock from the bed of the "Black Beauty." He wanted to reduce watering and maintenance and to have some extra parking space.

WATER-SAVING TIPS

- Limit lawn in size and to areas that will be both beautiful and usable.
- Install an efficient sprinkler system if supplementary irrigation is required throughout the year in your location.
- Select a type of lawn that gets by on less water and will survive drought periods.
- Avoid plants with high moisture requirements. A few azaleas, camellias and some ferns tucked into a shady corner won't affect total water usage very much. An entire garden comprised of plants that need constant watering will consume a great deal of water.
- Prepare the soil properly for new plantings. Include earth watering basins where excessive rain is not a problem.
- Mulch to retain moisture. Even plants with normal watering requirements do remarkably well during droughts when they have extensive root systems and are heavily mulched. Mulching also inhibits water-stealing weeds.
- Don't overplant. Space plants far enough apart so they have room to grow.
- Don't feel obligated to cover every square inch of your property with plants. There's nothing wrong with bare earth between shrubs and trees.
- Plant during the spring or fall so roots become established with a minimum of watering.

- Make extensive use of pavings and semi-pavings.
- Preserve existing woods and native plants rather than converting your entire property to lawn.
- Try to place shrubs where they will benefit from rainfall. Plantings under wide overhangs may require frequent watering.

WATERING

Get to know how plants signal for water. Grasses tend to lie flat after being stepped on if moisture is low, and the color is duller than normal. Many plants lose their gloss and start to droop before going into wilt. Some plants can recover without losing a leaf after sprawling flat on the ground. Others will defoliate, drop buds and flowers and may never be the same once they've dried out. Observation and experience are the best ways to learn which of your plants are sensitive and which are toughies.

Don't water on a rigid schedule. The time to water is when the plants need it. If in doubt, hold up on watering until you've made sure the soil is almost dry. The symptoms of waterlogged plants can sometimes be confused with dryness. Dig down below the surface rather than just guess. Use a soil sampler for a deeper look. Automatically controlled sprinkler systems should be constantly adjusted to varying weather conditions.

Try to water early in the morning to avoid excessive evaporation loss. Evening is not as good because fungus diseases have all night to attack moist foliage. Mornings are usually calmer and evaporation is less than when it is

windy, and less spray gets blown onto paving.

Some plants, such as azaleas, camellias, Japanese andromeda and ternstroemia (cleyera) have surface roots and benefit from frequent, light watering in addition to an occasional deep soaking. Most plants, including lawns, develop deeper root systems and tolerate drought better if watered deeply. Water penetrates easily in sandy soils. In clay soils, water must be applied slowly in order for it to soak in. Earth basins help confine water to within the drip-line of trees and shrubs and are helpful for new plantings.

DIFFICULT SITUATIONS

Compacted soil is subject to run-off. *Vertical mulching* is a procedure used at the drip-line of trees and shrubs to aid water penetration. Use your electric drill to make 1/2- to 1-inch-diameter holes about 12 inches apart and 12 inches deep all around the plant. You can also use the holes to apply fertilizer. Rent or buy extra-long bits and make sure the drill is properly grounded.

A root-feeder device attached to the hose is another way of getting water down into hard soil. Don't overlook a canvas or plastic soaker that can be coiled around a tree and allowed to run slowly for several hours.

Slopes are difficult to water without run-off and erosion. Earth basins can be used for individual trees and shrubs. Sprinklers should be turned on for short intervals and then repeated several times until penetration is achieved. Jute and plastic mesh,

Soil samplers give a good profile of underground conditions. They're available in 12- and 18-inch lengths.

Run-off from bare slopes can waste lots of water. Hall's honeysuckle covers rapidly and is drought tolerant. Warning: Use this and other rampant growers with caution.

No need to let the water run while you go back to shut it off when you use a spring-loaded hose spray.

Impact sprinklers are okay for large slopes if you don't leave them on too long at one time.

These Southern Indian azaleas are not drought tolerant, but they receive filtered shade all day long here and were properly planted. Supplemental irrigation is seldom needed.

organic mulches and straw help retard erosion and are essential on steep slopes.

LAWNS

As discussed in Chapter 8, choosing a grass that is reasonably drought tolerant will reduce watering needs considerably. A well-designed, permanent sprinkler system is more efficient than hand or portable sprinkler watering. If you need to water often, the water and labor savings will eventually pay for the system.

Thatch, the layer of dead plant parts that accumulates at the soil level, is an enemy of good water penetration. Periodic verti-cutting will reduce run-off and encourage healthier growth and deeper rooting.

Aeration also improves water pene- tration. Hollow tines remove cores of soil and reduce the effects of compaction. For small areas, it can be done by hand. Large lawns call for a motorized aerator. Chemical soil penetrants can also help water soak in better, but results are relatively short-lived.

Raise mowing height during hot weather. Roots are kept cooler by taller grass and less water is required.

A hand aerator is great for opening up those packed down spots in a lawn where water won't penetrate.

The business end of a verti-cutter. It slices through lawn thatch to allow water filtration.

This formidable-looking machine aerator is a necessity for large lawns.

Lawns don't have to be gigantic. This intimate terrace benefits from generous background plantings. Landscape architect: C.C. Pat Fleming.

WATER-SAVING PLANTS

Here are some plants that withstand heat and do especially well with little water. Once established, they can often survive on natural rainfall alone—no need to drag out the hose during dry spells. See the plant lists in Chapter 6 for additional information.

The plants in these lists are arranged according to hardiness. The most cold-tolerant are at the top, and the most sensitive at the bottom.

Drought-Tolerant Plants

Goldmoss sedum/Stonecrop
Hall's honeysuckle
Silverberry
Pampas grass
Lavender cotton
Curveleaf yucca
Texas ranger
Chinaberry tree
Prostrate rosemary
Century plant
Sotol
Mediterranean fan palm
Pindo palm
Oleander
Jerusalem thorn
Lantana

Some Drought Tolerance

Dwarf red-leaf barberry
Fruitless mulberry
Purple-leaf winter creeper
Vinca major
Silk tree/Mimosa
Chinese flame tree
Italian cypress
Australian pine/River she-oak
Texas mountain laurel
Glossy privet
Pineapple guava
Cat's claw
Mexican fan palm
Sprenger asparagus

Pampas Grass

Oleander

Curveleaf Yucca

Lantana

Sources Of Information

Although I've tried to include as much information as possible in this book, additional questions will undoubtedly arise as you work on your landscape. A surprising number of them will answer themselves with a little thought and common sense. Where do you get the answers to the more technical ones?

As mentioned earlier, a good way to learn how to do something is to watch a craftsman do it. Second best is to look at the finished results. I built an entire house this way, from the ground up.

The people who sell a product generally know a great deal about it. An experienced person at a building supply company, lumber yard or nursery is a potential goldmine of information. Contractors are the ones who really know how to do their specialty, but they're not in the business of dispensing free or paid advice. You have to hire them to do the work in order to benefit from their knowledge.

Now we come to the "experts." Landscape architects and designers were discussed in Chapter 2, along with landscape contractors, gardeners and nurserymen. You can get some help from the local county or state building department—but mostly on the application and interpretation of the rules and regulations. Building inspectors and clerks are often courteous and helpful. Generally, the approach is from the negative side: They tell you what you can't do.

State agricultural extension offices usually have agents or specialists available to answer questions concerning plants, soil, insecticides and similar subjects. State universities will often offer advice. My experience has been that extension agents and university personnel are well qualified and their publications are excellent. Check under County Government in the phone book and look for Farm Advisor or Cooperative Extension Service. Also check with the agricultural department of the nearest state university.

COOPERATIVE EXTENSION SERVICES

Alabama
Auburn University
Auburn, Alabama 36830

Arkansas
University of Arkansas
Little Rock, Arkansas 72203

Florida
University of Florida
Institute of Food and Agricultural
 Sciences
Gainesville, Florida 32601

Georgia
University of Georgia
College of Agriculture
Athens, Georgia 30601

Kentucky
University of Kentucky
College of Agriculture
Lexington, Kentucky 40506

Louisiana
State University A&M College
University Station
Baton Rouge, Louisiana 70803

Maryland
University of Maryland
College Park, Maryland 20742

Mississippi
Mississippi State University
State College, Mississippi 39762

North Carolina
North Carolina State University
Raleigh, North Carolina 27607

Oklahoma
Oklahoma State University
Stillwater, Oklahoma 74074

South Carolina
Clemson University
Clemson, South Carolina 29631

Tennessee
University of Tennessee
Knoxville, Tennessee 37901

Texas
Texas A&M University
College Station, Texas 77843

Virginia
Virginia Polytechnic Institute
Blacksburg, Virginia 24061

West Virginia
West Virginia University
Morgantown, West Virginia 26506

INDUSTRIAL INFORMATION

Industry publications are often helpful. Describe what information you need and the publishers will send it to you free or let you know what the charges are.

Brick Institute of America
1750 Old Meadow Road
McLean, Virginia 22101

California Redwood Association
617 Montgomery Street
San Francisco, California 94411

Portland Cement Association
Old Orchard Road
Skokie, Illinois 60076

Georgia-Pacific Corporation
900 S.W. Fifth Avenue
Portland, Oregon 97204

You should also be able to get free or low-cost commercially prepared publications such as: nursery and garden catalogs; spa, hot tub and pool booklets; sprinkler and lighting pamphlets; decking and patio materials brochures; and fertilizer, weed killer, insecticide and similar product description sheets.

GOVERNMENT AND LIBRARY SOURCES

Don't overlook the Federal Government. Write to the Superintendent of Documents, Government Printing Office, Washington, D.C. 20402 and ask for *List of Available Publications of the U.S.D.A.*—Bulletin No. 11. It costs 45 cents.

The library and book store are not intended to be last resorts. You may find what you're looking for faster and more easily there than through the other sources. When plants are involved, some books ignore or only superficially recognize the tremendous differences in growing conditions in different climates. Look through the racks carefully to see whether or not a book is written for your specific region and if it offers information that applies to your needs.

PUBLIC GARDENS AND ARBORETUMS

The best way to find out what kind of garden you want and what plants you like is to look at as many good examples as possible. There are numerous beautiful public gardens and institutions with outstanding landscaping throughout the South. Make it a point to visit one or two whenever you're on a trip. Check with local garden clubs for others, and for special tours of private homes and gardens.

Arboretum of the University of Alabama
Tuscaloosa, Alabama

Ashville Botanical Garden
Ashville, North Carolina

Bellingrath Gardens
Theodore, Alabama

Boone Hall Plantation
Mt. Pleasant, South Carolina

Brookgreen Gardens
Murrells Inlet, South Carolina

Callaway Gardens
Pine Mountain, Georgia

Cheekwood
Nashville, Tennessee

Colonial Williamsburg
Williamsburg, Virginia

Cypress Gardens
Winter Haven, Florida

Disneyworld
Orlando, Florida

Fairchild Tropical Gardens
Miami, Florida

Forsyth Park
Savannah, Georgia

Fort Worth Botanical Garden
Ft. Worth, Texas

General Electric Appliance Park
Lousiville, Kentucky

Hodges Gardens
Many, Louisiana

Leu Gardens
Orlando, Florida

Longue Vue Gardens
New Orleans, Louisiana

Magnolia Gardens
Charleston, South Carolina

Memphis Botanical Garden
Memphis, Tennessee

Middleton Gardens
Charleston, South Carolina

Mynella Gardens
Jackson, Mississippi

Norfolk Botanical Garden
Norfolk, Virginia

Orland E. White Research Arboretum
Boyce, Virginia

Rosedown Plantation
St. Francisville, Louisiana

Sarah P. Duke Gardens
Durham, North Carolina

Sunken Gardens
San Antonio, Texas

U.S. National Arboretum
Washington, D.C.

University of Southwestern Louisiana
Lafayette, Louisiana

University of Tennessee Arboretum
Oak Ridge, Tennessee

Valley Botanical Gardens
McAllen, Texas

Virginia Polytechnic Institute Arboretum
Blacksburg, Virginia

West Virginia University Arboretum
Morgantown, West Virginia

Zilker Park
San Antonio, Texas

Sunken Gardens—San Antonio, Texas.

Callaway Gardens—Pine Mountain, Georgia.

Norfolk Botanical Garden—Norfolk, Virginia.

Index

Acknowledgements

Regional Consultants

Robert S. Bateman
Landscape Architect, ASLA
Robert S. Bateman & Associates,
   Inc.
Mobile, Alabama

Stephen F. Coenen
Landscape Architect
Chervet's Garden Center, Inc.
Metairie, Louisiana

Fred C. Galle
Director of Horticulture
Callaway Gardens
Pine Mountain, Georgia

Edith Henderson
Landscape Architect, FASLA
Atlanta, Georgia

Richard A. Kesselring, Sr.
Landscape Architect, ASLA
Green Tree Nursery & Landscape
Ocala, Florida

Donna Pittman Kinnaird
Landscape Architect
Pittman Nurseries Company
Magnolia, Arkansas

Henry C. Martin
Landscape Architect, ASLA
Martin's Nursery
Tallahassee, Florida

Eldon G. Russell
Landscape Architect, ASLA
Eldon Russell Landscape
   Consultants
Houston, Texas

Gene Schrickel, Jr.
Kent Besley
Landscape Architects, ASLA
Schrickel, Rollins & Associates,
   Inc.
Arlington, Texas

**Horticultural and Photographic
Advisor**

William Aplin